LOCKOUT

LOCKOUT

The Story of the Homestead Strike of 1892:

A Study of Violence, Unionism, and

the Carnegie Steel Empire

LEON WOLFF

HARPER & ROW, PUBLISHERS

New York, Evanston, and London

Contents

Illustrations follow page 114. Maps of the Pittsburgh and Homestead-Munhall areas follow page 108.

Acknowledgments

I wish to thank Professor John R. Coleman of the Carnegie Institute of Technology for his assistance in the initial stages of my research. Mr. Edward Lucas, vice-president of Homestead Local Union 1397, kindly escorted me on a long, fascinating tour of both boroughs on the south bank of the Monongahela, in the course of which he helped me eliminate dozens of blunders from my manuscript. He later sent me vital maps, photographs and further data by mail. This book depends a good deal upon his cooperation. Mrs. Susan Cohn of Pittsburgh unearthed much material for me in the various archives of that city. The Pittsburgh Chamber of Commerce was cooperative, as were the facilities of the Carnegie Library, also in Pittsburgh. I am grateful to Mr. M. E. Moran, Public Relations Department, United Steelworkers of America, for considerable information.

I would have been helpless without the vast combined

facilities of the University of California library at Los Angeles and the Los Angeles Public Library. At the latter, Mrs. Francine Freedman was exceptionally diligent in my behalf. My wife, as usual, typed the second draft of the entire manuscript and made numerous suggestions of value. I also thank my publishers for their comments and corrections. I accept the blame for errors which remain. In self-defense it may be suggested that matters of inviolate fact are not too easy to ascertain three generations after an event involving such violence, prevarication, hatreds, passions, and blind prejudice.

L.W.

Foreword

In the history of American labor there is no more savage or significant chapter than the events which took place at Homestead, Pennsylvania, in the summer of 1892. A proud and (for the United States at the time) well-entrenched craft union collided head on with the rising profit potential of large-scale mass production. The results included catastrophe for the union, the blacklisting and dispersal of all its officers and active members, dozens of dead and hundreds of wounded, public scorn for the management of the Carnegie Steel Company, and a briefly popular song— "Father Was Killed by the Pinkerton Men."

Historians have usually hastened by the Homestead strike and lockout with a "plague on both your houses" attitude. Mr. Wolff's vivid and powerful book is the first to explore fully the human passions and suffering involved. It is interesting to discover here how much the union leaders relied on the public statements of Andrew Carnegie—and how completely they misjudged him. For years Carnegie had been preaching "brotherhood" be-

tween invested capital and labor, defending the workers'
right to organize, and denouncing strikebreakers in
Biblical terms. At the same time, in his daily business
activities he was known as an utterly ruthless competitor
and the severest of taskmasters.

When the showdown came at Homestead, Carnegie
holed up in his Scottish castle, avoiding all contact with
the union and saying nothing whatever in public. His
hard-boiled partner and manager, Henry Clay Frick, attended to the dirty business of hiring "scab" workmen and
Pinkerton guards. The hatred which grew later between
Carnegie and Frick ostensibly had nothing to do with the
Homestead strike. (Or did it?) For years the two men did
not speak to each other. Eventually, Mr. Wolff tells us,
Carnegie sent word to Frick that he would like to shake
hands and let bygones be bygones.

"Tell your friend Carnegie," was the ungracious response, "that I will see him in hell, where we are both
going."

The defeat of union labor at Homestead was total, in-
flicting social and psychological scars that are traced by
Mr. Wolff in this book down to the present day. He also
shows us, with facts and figures, how profitable the battle
was to the men who won it. After the strike Frick cut wages
by almost one-half, reinstated the twelve-hour working
day, and manned Homestead and other mills with eager,
newly arrived immigrants. A tremendous upward surge of
steel profits followed, which carried other industries with
it and culminated in the formation, in 1901, of the United
States Steel Corporation. Not long before the bloody
doings at Homestead, Carnegie had considered selling out
for a few tens of millions of dollars. Less than a decade
later he collected $250 million in five-per-cent gold bonds

for his share of the steel industry. All of this and much more he gave away to good causes before he died; today he is thought of primarily as one of the world's most lavish philanthropists.

Frick, who amassed a large fortune too, built a marble home on New York's Fifth Avenue and installed a pipe organ on which were given daily performances of his favorite tune—"Dearie, my dearie—Nothing's worth while but dreams of you . . ." He left his house, a famous collection of paintings, and an important research library to the public, along with a $15 million endowment. He was generous also to Princeton University, and he gave the city of Pittsburgh a park and $2 million.

Perhaps both of these men had read Walt Whitman, who wrote: "I perceive clearly that the extreme business energy, and this almost maniacal appetite for wealth prevalent in the United States, are parts of amelioration and progress, indispensably needed to prepare the very results I demand. My theory includes riches, and the getting of riches . . ." Such words would have been no comfort to the steelworkers and Pinkerton mercenaries who met in mortal combat at Homestead. But they help to explain Messrs. Carnegie and Frick.

ROGER BUTTERFIELD

LOCKOUT

*The rights and interests of the laboring man
will be protected and cared for—not by the
labor agitators, but by the Christian men to
whom God in His infinite wisdom has given
control of the property interests of this
country.*

—George F. Baer

I *The Famed Decade*

The administration may have been most unworthy, but
President Benjamin Harrison stood haughtily above the
squalor. Small, gray-haired, intelligent, dignified in manner, thoroughly honest, conservative to the core, for three
years he had been unable or unwilling to resist pressure
groups, to curb the spoilsmen, to loosen the grip of business upon government. No longer was the voting public
enchanted with him. To the dismay of Republican party
leaders he had already indicated an aloof desire to be re-
nominated. There was nothing they could do. They would
have to choose him and lose. It was early 1892.

There is irony in the fact that he, who under more
felicitous circumstances might have been an excellent executive, should have presided over a Congress that epito-
mized Jim Fisk's classic summation: "Nothing is lost, save
honor." It was the culmination of a generation of political
shabbiness and vacuity unmatched before or since—the
administrations of Hayes, Arthur, Cleveland, and now
Harrison. "During the whole of this period," notes one
historian, "the electorate played a game of blind man's
buff. Never before had American politics been so intellec-
tually bankrupt." Virtually no meaningful legislation was
passed. With few exceptions, the machine politicians

sought only re-election, patronage, and graft. Duty and morality played little part in their legislative antics. There was a grave farm issue, a money problem, a tariff conundrum, a civil service calamity that cried to high heaven for reform, and a labor question which had already led to something resembling class warfare and threatened even social revolution if not at least partly resolved.

Bereft of understanding and interest, the politicians merely filled their pockets, rewarded their friends, and avoided deviating from party lines. "One might search the whole list of Congress, judiciary, and executive during the twenty-five years 1870–1895," wrote Henry Adams, "and find little but damaged reputation. The period was poor in purpose and barren in results."

Both parties were conservative and, for all practical purposes except the tariff, identical. In the words of Charles Beard: "If a Martian visitor had examined the statutes . . . he could not have discovered from their volume and nature that the people were divided into two major parties which were in turn possessed of the power of governing, for the oscillations in the fortunes of parties in presidential elections bore little or no relation to the course of legislative action." Unless the newborn Populist Party enlivened matters, the coming November elections promised to be, as usual, full of sound and fury, signifying nothing for the man in the street.

Never was a decade so ineptly christened. The Gay '90s were far from gay; during its early stages, in fact, portents of the 1893–1897 economic collapse were already at hand. More strikes had erupted in 1890 than during any other year in history. Within this era about twelve hundred strikes took place each and every year, on the average. Soil erosion, rising costs, debt, falling market prices, and dwindling profits had brought most farmers to the end of their ropes. "There are three great crops raised in Nebraska," a farm journalist wrote. "One is a crop of corn, one a crop of freight rates, and one a crop of interest." Cotton had plunged to six cents per pound, corn and wheat to ten and forty-nine cents per bushel respectively. In some farm counties, 90 percent of all farm acreage was taken over by bankers between 1889 and 1893. There was one mortgage for every two adults in Kansas—an extreme example. And much of what man doggedly grew God destroyed—for reasons of His own—through dust storms, timber destruction, floods, drought, and the terrible ravages of insect pests against which there was then absolutely no defense.

If the farmer was in desperate trouble, the industrial worker was no better off. Technology was remorselessly depreciating the only commodity that skilled laborers could sell at a premium: their skills. The average workday was between ten and eleven hours. Insecure because of several recessions and even full-fledged panics since the Civil War, laborers were in a morose and dangerous mood. They, the first American proletariat, dared not take advantage of alleged opportunities outside their job; for they lacked the cutthroat cleverness, the experience, the ruthlessness, the capital, the feeling for entrepreneurship.

So the workers smoldered, frequently living in slums that beggar description even by comparison with Chicago's South Side Black Belt today. Never could their wages keep pace with living costs. When they struck they were met with the injunction, the lockout, the blacklist, Pinkerton thugs, the National Guard, and hordes of strikebreakers. They almost never won. Floods of immigrants were avid for their jobs—any jobs. The unskilled were paid an average of ten dollars weekly, the skilled less than twenty dollars.[1] In all the republic, the highest average women's pay existed in San Francisco: $6.91 per week. One Christmas day at Chicago's Hull House several youngsters refused their candy presents. It was learned that they worked in a candy factory from seven in the morning until nine at night; they were fatigued and sick of sweets. New York City bakers worked 84 to 120 hours weekly. Jane Addams tells of women in a sewing shop "assisted by incredibly small children. I remember a little girl of four who pulled out basting threads hour after hour, sitting on a stool at the feet of her Bohemian mother, a little bunch of human misery." The Minnesota legislature had to enjoin state railroads from working their firemen and engineers more than eighteen hours daily.

And there were two sets of ethics: "Combination of capital was regarded as in accordance with natural laws; combination of labor as a conspiracy. Monopoly was good business . . . but the closed shop was un-American. It was the duty of government to aid business . . . aid to labor was socialistic. That business should go into politics was common sense, but that labor should go into politics was contrary to the American tradition. Property had a natural right to a fair return on its value, but the return which labor might enjoy was to be regulated strictly by the law of supply and demand. . . . Brokers who organized business combines were respectable public servants, but labor organizers were agitators. The use of Pinkerton detectives to protect business property was preserving law and order, but the use of force to protect the job was violence. To curtail production in the face of an oversupply of con-

---

[1] The 1892 dollar was worth $4.20 by 1964 standards; for example, a $20 weekly wage was the equivalent in purchasing power to $84 today.

sumers' goods was sound business practice, but to strike for shorter hours in the face of an oversupply of labor was unsound."

So wrote historians Morison and Commager.

In 1892 (the year upon which this narrative pivots) the Negro found the decade even less gay than usual. More were lynched than in any other year in the history of the republic; the tabulated figure was 231 and the actual number may have exceeded half a thousand. The industrial revolution was gathering steam; the machine age had already arrived. Primitive shop and mining methods were ending. In basic industries such as coal, clothing, and metals, the old-time employer who used to work alongside his men had given way to impersonal corporations and great combinations.

The frontier, once a beckoning image of opportunity, no longer beckoned. Idaho, Wyoming, North and South Dakota, Montana, and Washington were admitted to the Union in 1889 or 1890, thus creating an unbroken belt of states from east to west. Oklahoma had been dramatically settled in 1889 (starting at noon, April 22) under provisions of the Homestead Act. Only the interior territories of Utah, Arizona, and New Mexico remained outside the Union. True, in all western states and territories Uncle Sam was selling land cheaply or even giving it away; but the best acreage had been snapped up long ago. Thousands upon thousands of eastern factory hands, miners, sweatshop workers, and day laborers longed to go west; but they knew nothing of farming, and they lacked the cash to move a family, to build and finance a farm. "I never saw over a $20 bill," one Fall River worker harshly told a Senate committee. "If someone would give me $1,500 I will go."

A few tried it, but most of them returned east in wagons bearing scrawled messages such as "In God we trusted, in Kansas we busted."

Such were the gaieties of the '90s.

"The good Lord gave me my money," said John D. Rockefeller cryptically. Thundered the Baptist minister, Reverend Russell Conwell, "To secure wealth is an honorable ambition . . . Money is power. Every good man and woman ought to strive for power, to do good with it when attained." Six thousand times he delivered verbatim his lecture "Acres of Diamonds" throughout the East and Middle West (thereby acquiring acres of dollars for himself). "I say, Get rich, get rich! But get money honestly, or it will be a withering curse." His listeners would have been delighted to oblige; but how? By 1892 a whiff of middle-class cynicism was in the air. Horatio Alger's rags-to-riches, luck-and-pluck stories were a joke to all but children and the simple-minded. The white-collar man wanted to believe, tried hard to believe, but his faith was faltering. Marshall Field's people earned twelve dollars per week (maximum) for fifty-nine hours of work, while their master drew six hundred dollars each hour of every day, twenty-four hours around the clock. Dry-goods clerks no longer expected to marry the boss's daughter. Typically Andrew Carnegie had written, "Now the poorest laborer in America . . . who can handle a pick and shovel, stands upon equal terms with the purchaser of his labor"; and still there were pathetically earnest souls who swallowed this fable whole. But that was a few years ago, and times were changing fast.

Industrialists applauded when a college textbook of ethics stated, "By the proper use of wealth man may greatly elevate and extend his moral work. It is therefore his duty to secure wealth . . . The Moral Governor has placed the power of acquisitiveness in man for a good and noble purpose." It was Mr. Carnegie's *Gospel of Wealth* rephrased, a perfect formula for reconciling Protestantism with profits; and it led, of course, to the concept of the divinity of property. In 1892 Princeton ex-President James McCosh wrote that property and power were gifts of God, and he termed it "theft . . . to deprive us of the right to earn property or to use it as we see fit." The idea dated back to seventeenth-century Puritanism—Cotton Mather, among others, had spoken of it often—but by the '90s it further implied laissez faire, antiunionism, antitaxation, and antagonism to centralized government.

What, in return, was the duty of the wealthy? One suspects that Professor McCosh might simply have replied "none," but Mr. Carnegie was more elaborate: "First, to set an example of modest, unostentatious living, shunning display or extravagance . . ." Next, to become a "trustee for his poorer brethren, bringing to their service his superior wisdom . . . doing for them better than they would or could do for themselves." To intellectuals of the '90s the words (especially "would") undoubtedly seemed patronizing and annoying. The great steel master, however, believed what he said, and at the drop of a hat could dictate such improbable homilies by the ream.

"Avenues greater in number, wider in extent, easier of access than ever before existed," he intoned, "stand open to the frugal, energetic and able mechanic, to the scientifically educated youth, to the office boy and the clerk—avenues through which they can reap greater successes than ever before within the reach of these classes in the history of the world . . . The millionaires who are in active control started as poor boys—and were trained in that sternest of all schools—poverty." Most of his readers, unhappily training in the school Carnegie recommended, desiring just a little wealth, not very much, could not understand wherein they had failed. Others, more sophisticated, may have recognized such platitudes as only a propaganda device (perhaps subconscious) to safeguard a lopsided economic and social system from mass assault.

Later they called it the Gilded Age, those years spanning the end of Reconstruction to the end of the century. Certainly they were pleasant enough for the privileged—the upper middle class, the newly rich, the few still-solvent remnants of southern aristocracy.

The plutocracy overplayed its hand and was either neurotically envied or murderously hated by all. Confounded by the problem of evaluating a collection of art, one copper millionaire simplified matters by purchasing the entire museum. Cigarettes wrapped in hundred-dollar bills were a feature of the season. Front teeth were filled with diamonds. A young lady was given a necklace costing $600,-000 (duly publicized) by her fond parents. The dukes and duchesses of lucre, the postwar monarchs of soap and armor plate, the field marshals of real estate, coal, and beef came mostly to New York, where for years they ran the theory of conspicuous consumption into the ground. A little dog received a $15,000 diamond collar and a social banquet. Chorus girls emerged from pies; at another party the swimming pool was laced with human goldfish. Mrs. Astor and her Four Hundred reigned fatuously but dynamically supreme. And scores of opulent young ladies were married off into British and French nobility—a crowning blow to ultrawealthy climbers who could not follow suit.

For the less triumphant there were other pleasures and milder excesses. "All the worst of Tennyson's poems were known by heart," commented Beer; and Stevenson was also being diligently read. The circus was a national passion, and vaudeville, and Barnum's "Greatest Show on Earth," and Buffalo Bill Cody's fraudulent melodramas. With bated breath a million blanched at the perils and indignities to which Nellie the Beautiful Cloak Model was subjected, while lesser multitudes turned to Mark Twain, Joel Chandler Harris and Henry James. Free of life-and-death tensions, the period was in many respects pleasant. No nation possessed the power of annihilating our citizenry; neither warplanes nor nuclear-tipped rockets existed; the issues at hand were relatively minor; the military was everywhere quiescent; and at least from this point of view we are entitled to classify the early '90s as placid, although not entirely idyllic.

The clop-clop of horses gently disturbed the peace of pleasant residential streets. At dusk boys on bicycles lighted each gas street lamp with a flaming stick. Many a farm was rich and lushly groomed; John L. Sullivan was king, his mustache was copied by all corpulent policemen and bartenders; and beyond swinging doors men tossed down beer and straight whiskey and spat into the sawdust. "Father, dear father, come home with me now," chorused the prohibitionists, "the clock in the steeple strikes one!" To which father responded, "Pat, order me up another shot of that booze."

Anthony Comstock had become a nuisance. People were at last bored by his prurient strictures against innumerable books he considered lewd, dealers in athletic goods who showed elastic football breechcloths in their store windows, and photographs in saloons of seminude ladies. The fight to enfranchise women was in full swing. Frederic

Remington's superb sketches of the west, and the first of Owen Wister's stories, were becoming famous. In sundry periodicals Prof. (*sic*) Harley Parker, F.R.A.S. (*sic*), was advertising "THE HUMAN HAIR: Why It Falls Off, Turns Grey, and the Remedy"; and the W. L. Douglas Co. stated that its three-dollar shoe was "the Best Shoe in the World for the Money."

Architecture and interior decoration were ghastly: "flamboyant lines and meaningless details. . . . A stuffy and fussy riot of fancy." And another writer noted, "Even the human figure seemed to take on the prevailing grossness. People overate and overdressed. Men affected longskirted coats of black broadcloth, wore polished, heavy top boots, permitted their faces to become covered with hair. The women were encased in a series of enfolding garments that concealed the natural contours of their bodies and left no parts revealed but face and hands."

Aesthetically, culturally, and politically the United States was a wasteland. Morally it was otiose and feebly sanctimonious; it spoke of freedom and the egalitarian ethos, but delivered precious little of either to its peasant-farmers, lower urban classes, Negroes, immigrants, and Indians. It had even to some degree perverted Darwin's theories into a rationale for predatory business behavior. The poor deserved to be poor. The small manufacturer deserved to be gobbled up. Competition, wrote Mr. Carnegie in his most complacent vein (while he crushed competition and moved toward a subsidized semimonopoly), "is here; we cannot evade it; no substitutes for it have been found; and while the law may sometimes be hard on the individual, it is best for the race, because it ensures the survival of the fittest. . . . We accept and welcome, therefore, great inequality of environment; the concentration of business

. . . in the hands of the few." Plainly big business was in the saddle; Congress was industry's lackey; and the wage earner who did the physical work of supplying the nation's needs had nearly abandoned all earthly hopes.

The first trust (Standard Oil) had reared its head in 1879, and soon there arrived dozens of combinations (petroleum, whiskey, lead, railroads, sugar, cordage, linseed oil, and so on) designed to eliminate wasteful competition and to place not only the consumer at their price-mercy but basic producers and freight-haulers as well. Trusts were legal until 1890. There was no technical reason why individual corporations (who did not surrender their identity) could not assign stock shares to a board of trustees, which assumed the power of voting them, issuing trust certificates, and then issuing dividends on a proportional basis. In the course of this process, over five thousand small industrial establishments were absorbed or crushed during one generation. Not one of these combines was capitalized for less than fifty million dollars, and each was driving toward total monopoly. National ire against them was strong. Senator Sherman warned that "there will soon be a trust for every production and a master to fix the price for every necessity of life." But his famous antitrust act was watered down and phrased obscurely; it accomplished next to nothing. Illegally the trusts continued to flourish. The act was mainly used later against trade unions.[2]

By 1892 winds of protest were sweeping across cities and farmlands—protest against a quarter-century of injustice, graft, gross inequalities, supercorporations, contempt for the farmer, hostility toward the industrial worker, resent-

2 Between 1890 and 1946 antitrust suits brought convictions against 198 defendants. All sentences imposed on businessmen were suspended, while 108 labor union officials were imprisoned.

ment against the wretched urban rookeries in which millions lived, the ostentation of parvenus, the strangling of
small-scale industry.

Foremost among the dissidents were the Populists. Starting in the West, originally an agrarian movement, almost
immediately the party galvanized the nation from the
Rockies to Maine. It demanded an end to the trusts; public possession of railroads, telegraph, and telephone; abol-
ishment of the tariff; land ownership by United States citizens only; unlimited coinage of silver at sixteen to one; a
graduated income tax; the seizure of excess railroad lands
and their subsequent sale to the people. Capitalists blasted
the program as pure socialism. Others uneasily agreed, and
how it would fare at the polls next fall remained to be
seen.

Progress and Poverty, the telling title of an acridly accurate book published in 1879, was still the bible of the
disillusioned, the liberal, the underdog. A pale misan-
thrope of thirty-eight when he wrote it, Henry George's
description and analysis of the prevailing economic chaos
constitutes a classic to this day. His theory (unsound) of a
single tax on land was for some years considered a panacea,
both here and abroad.

Looking Backward from the year 2000, Edward Bellamy
envisioned a cooperative utopian society of ease and cul-
ture in which machines did practically all the work. There
were no profits, nor did money exist. In his novel, which
had sold over a million copies by 1892, the citizens of a
heavenly land explain how socialism had captured monopoly and set men free; and they look back in wonder at the
people of the late nineteenth century, who tolerated "the
imbecility of the system of private enterprise as a method
of enriching a nation . . . in an age of such general pov-

erty and want of everything." Over a hundred Bellamy clubs sprang up. Sourly Henry George called the book "a castle in the air with clouds for its foundation"; and soon Populism, a more practical program for confronting an unbalanced economy, destroyed Bellamy's dream world.

An unusually devout country, the United States also produced more than its share of religious cranks, chiliasts, and self-appointed messiahs who claimed they possessed supernatural nostrums with which to cure the nation's ills. And there were various types of Marxian agitators and journalists. A different breed of protestant cat, these had sharper claws. They were more or less rational; they did not dream or petulantly meow; and some had unpleasant ideas concerning Direct Action, as they termed it. Altogether they were relatively few, but enough to comprise a scapegoat. "The Red Scare, already old, had been elevated into an institution," writes a labor historian. "What it lacked in exactitude it made up for in violence. To the newspapers every striker was a foreigner, and every foreigner a Communist, Anarchist, or Socialist or Nihilist." And he quotes another observer concerning the Chicago press: "The unemployed, if they bore foreign names, were 'European scum.' If Americans, they were tramps, bummers and loafers. Discontented workingmen had no real grievances but were always dupes of foreign agitators. . . . A 'Communist' was always a 'German communist.' Strikes and labor demonstrations were always mobs composed of foreign scum, beer-smelling Germans, ignorant Bohemians, uncouth Poles, wild-eyed Russians."

Deep in his heart, however, the double-dyed capitalist of the decade probably did not fear the Marxists or the theories of Messrs. George and Bellamy. No doubt the Populists did mildly trouble his sleep. But to him the most alarming threat of all was labor unions, for they literally meant business. In 1892 only two mattered: Powderly's Knights of Labor and Gompers's American Federation of Labor. The Knights of Labor envisioned inevitable class conflict and saw nothing in common between employer and employed. They were dangerous, theoretically.

Organized in 1870 with a membership of nine, by 1884 they were up to 728,000; by 1892 down to about 95,000; by 1901 zero. There were two major reasons why the organization had soared like a rocket: (1) any worker could join—man or woman, white or Negro, skilled or unskilled; (2) it had recently achieved the most sensational victory thus far in the annals of American labor by defeating the puissant Jay Gould in two Wabash railroad strikes. But there were reasons why it had fallen like the stick. One was the Haymarket massacre of 1886; indirectly and illogically it led to national revulsion against semisecret labor brotherhoods like the Knights, with their rigamarole of passwords, mystic oaths, childish nomenclature, odd handclasps, and the like. Another was the dead weight of masses of unskilled during times of crisis. Trained craftsmen "tired of pulling the chestnuts out of the fire for the unskilled," although one now perceives that perhaps they should have continued patiently to do so.

And, among other problems, there was Terence V. Powderly, its Grand Master Workman since 1879. Trim, slim, foppishly dressed, psychopathically vain, he hated his office and wished to resign. Whenever it came time to do so, however, he invariably changed his mind.[3] The union had made him (formerly an impoverished machinist) impor-

---

[3] Year after year, through viselike control of the union's voting machinery, he continued, unhappily, to be re-elected.

tant and well-to-do. Twice he had been elected mayor of Scranton, Pennsylvania. He opposed all strikes—even the Wabash strikes, which the rank and file had won without his blessing—and advocated arbitration and conciliation instead.

"Mr. Powderly," he was asked, "do you concede the right of an employer to employ and discharge whom he pleases?"

"I do. . . . If I was an employer I can see how I would strive to make the most money out of the work done by my employees."

At the apex of Knights of Labor power, Powderly complained that he was ill almost unto death, unable or unwilling to cope with his responsibilities, almost hysterically opposed to the unanimous demand of his membership for an eight-hour day. While thousands clamored for admission, he announced that the Knights would accept no more members. It never occurred to him to increase the membership, to add more union officials, to delegate authority.

He refused to address one gathering because, he stated, "I will talk at no picnics where the girls as well as the boys will swill beer." All through the violent '80s hundreds of thousands of his men struck, and belligerently struck again and again. Not once—there are no exceptions—did Powderly approve. With despairing irony he wrote a friend, "Just think of it! Opposing strikes and always striking!" He commenced refusing to advance funds to any striking local from the national treasury. Recently he had throttled a strike at Mr. Carnegie's Edgar Thomson steel mill by denouncing it, calling it officially off, and thus causing the plant to become non-union forevermore. Appreciatively that lord of creation stated to a Pittsburgh *Dispatch* reporter, "Mr. Powderly seems to me to be one of the wisest counsellors that labor ever had." The union leader seems to have been rather antilabor.

Far more worrisome to management was the American Federation of Labor. The A.F. of L. was willing to live with capitalism; but its numbers and powers were mushrooming, and unlike the Knights it was not led by a collection of nebulous windbags. Wealthy, confident, bulwarked by the strongest individual craft unions in the hemisphere, efficiently organized, it was a menace to profits because of its insistence on shorter hours, higher pay, and (mainly in steel and railroads) a small but irritating amount of featherbedding. Worst of all, the A.F. of L. executive board was ready, if not anxious, to strike when necessary.

Samuel Gompers, its English-born half-Jewish president, adhered to a policy of keeping the federation out of politics, as a rule, although at times it stepped into the fray to reward friends and punish enemies. He was dedicated to a simple wage-and-hours rubric. When a congressman asked him what labor wanted, he replied, "More!" One of his deputies, Adolph Strasser, told a Senate committee, "We have no ultimate ends. We are going on from day to day. We are fighting only for immediate objects . . ." Women, Negroes, and the unskilled seldom gained admission to the A.F. of L. Gompers saw no reason to protect them. He was parochially concerned only with the craftsmen who made up his organization, and as to them his fundamental principle—"a fair day's wage for a fair day's work"—never varied.

Squat, stubborn, aggressive, dictatorial, strictly pragmatic, a former cigar maker, Gompers was a labor leader who got results and who has been unduly maligned by others more progressive. It is true that his prime objectives were to maintain personal power and to collect dues. He had toyed with Marxism in his youth, but during and after the Mauve Decade was a pillar of conservatism. "At no time in my life," he admitted, "have I worked out a definitely articulated economic theory." Organized in 1881, the A.F. of L. numbered a quarter million by 1892. (It was to reach four million before Gompers' death.) Its pride and joy, the most potent single craft union in the world, with twenty-four thousand dues-paying members, was the Amalgamated Association of Iron and Steel Workers. Its nearly three hundred sublodges were widely scattered, but western Pennsylvania was its central area. Within this region the focus was an obscure Pittsburgh suburb a few miles up the Monongahela River.

Immigration was a serious threat to the federation; and it was largely the A.F. of L.'s own fault, for it refused to admit the flood of foreigners (eleven million since the Civil War) into membership. Aside from being short-sighted morally and strategically, the policy worked against the A.F. of L. tactically. True, these unskilled European workers and farmers were usually illiterate by our standard and ignorant by any standard. But they accepted any kind of work at substandard wages; they crammed themselves into mining, meat-packing, needlework and steel, and created chaos in the labor market.

Poor as church mice, one and all, came the Magyars and Italians, still a few Irish and Hungarians, and Poles, Croats, Czechs, Slavs, some English and Welsh, a smattering of North Europe blonds, a swarm of Jews from Russia and other nations, and Germans almost genetically sullen and socialistic. During those years immigration regulations were mild, to put it mildly, a fact evidenced by the inability of many newcomers admitted to our shores to speak a single word of English. One woman was routinely asked by an Ellis Island official if she approved the overthrow of the United States government by subversion or violence. After a long silence she replied helplessly, "Violence."

For reasons not entirely clear, the Slavs, Hungarians, and Rumanians tended to gravitate toward coal and steel jobs available near Chicago and west Pennsylvania. Great numbers of them first encountered the American dream in the role of strikebreakers: ". . . frequently herded from steerage to a scene of nightmare violence where they passed between lines of struggling men . . . The vicious snap of rifle fire was almost the first sound heard in America by many a bewildered immigrant."

Jobs and bloodshed were especially abundant in the unique industrial complex that surrounded Pittsburgh. From a steel manufacturing standpoint the area was unsurpassed. It was a mecca for railroads. Swift-flowing rivers connected it without a single break to all supply sources east of the Mississippi. The Connellsville region, forty miles up the Monongahela, contained coal of uncommon purity which small ovens could convert into coke, an ideal fuel for smelting pig iron. In the nearby hills lay limestone deposits, also crucial to the manufacture of steel, and even beds of iron ore itself. But the latter were hardly needed, because of the discovery of unlimited iron resources just west of Lake Superior. While these ranges were a thousand miles away, a complete water route enabled ore ships to reach lower Lake Erie, on Pittsburgh's front door, with ease and relative speed except during occasional periods of extreme icing.

Iron was still being made, but compared to steel it had been declining since the Civil War. It could not cope with the industrial revolution. Iron rails wore out with maddening speed; and they sometimes cracked without warning, causing train wrecks. With deadly regularity cast-iron bridges collapsed. Iron tools and plows dulled quickly. Wrought iron was more versatile than cast iron, but its manufacture was too slow to keep pace with the feverishly increasing demand for armor plate, rails, pipes, nails, structural material, rods, sheets, and bars. The trouble was that wrought iron was almost impervious to mechanization; even by the 1890s the basic puddling, squeezing, and rolling operations were still completely manual. During this decade most iron furnaces were dismantled. In 1892, for the first time, United States steel tonnage exceeded that of iron.

Steel was stronger, tougher, and more elastic. With different alloys and varying production techniques it could be compounded in scores of ways to accommodate great buildings, or steak knives, or rifle barrels. Rails in 1892 accounted for half the total production. An experiment had demonstrated that one Bessemer-steel rail could outlast eighteen wrought-iron rails. Best of all, steel—whether by the old Bessemer or the new open-hearth process—was susceptible to extreme mechanization, could be manufactured cheaply, in enormous quantity, and at relatively low labor cost. With pardonable pride might Carnegie write: "Two pounds of iron stone mined upon Lake Superior and transported nine hundred miles to Pittsburgh; one pound and one-half of coal mined and manufactured into coke, and transported to Pittsburgh; a small amount of manganese ore mined in Virginia and brought to Pittsburgh—and these four pounds of materials manufactured into one pound of steel, for which the consumer pays one cent."

Truly stated; and the Age of Steel would have emerged even sooner, had it not been for a dilemma in connection with Sir Henry Bessemer's marvelous invention: it was quite worthless unless the phosphorus content of the ore was under one-half of 1 percent. Little iron ore met that standard. Sir Henry's method of converting molten pig iron into steel was therefore of limited value until about 1870, when various northern lake country ranges, which were fairly free of phosphorus, began delivering in earnest. It was the death blow to iron's three-thousand-year reign.

Uncle Sam (to go back some years) had been financing surveying and prospecting expeditions since the 1840s, when iron deposits of respectable quality were discovered in the upper Michigan peninsula. At the same time the Mesabi range (the word for "giant" in Chippewa) in Minnesota was casually noted and ignored. In 1890 seven related men named Merritt stumbled upon the fact that it was the largest bed of soft hematite ore in the world. Its phosphorus content was practically nil. The ore lay on the surface. It was not necessary to dig pits; one merely scooped it up like sand with steam shovels. A wild rush of prospectors and claims ensued, but soon enough the Mesabi range was almost exclusively in the hands of John D. Rockefeller and Andrew Carnegie. The first shipment reached Pittsburgh in 1892.

But, oddly, the unparalleled purity of the product had become of diminishing importance, due to the slow replacement of Bessemer converters by open-hearth furnaces starting twenty years earlier. The new process was somewhat costlier but it had great advantages. It utilized cheap ore of high phosphorus content just as efficiently as unadulterated ores. It was foolproof, whereas a split-second error in judgment on the part of a blower could ruin ten tons of Bessemer steel. It was ideal for reconverting scrap. It turned out steel uniformly at any desired quality level. And it could outproduce the average Bessemer furnace by six to one per "heat." America's largest, most modern steel plant, at Homestead, in 1892 manufactured steel in sixteen open-hearth furnaces and only one Bessemer converter. (This mill was exceptional, of course. Total United States open-hearth production did not exceed Bessemer figures until 1908.)

The man who at first had ridiculed the Mesabi range as inconsequential, and who had then suddenly changed his mind, with results of the first magnitude, was a gelid individual named Henry Clay Frick.

His youth had been dull, lonely and unpleasant, largely owing to poor health. Until the day he died he was plagued by rheumatism, chronic indigestion, and a weak heart. He possessed a few acquaintances, a violent temper held in check, a forbidding personality, and (by 1892) several million dollars. He was then forty-two years old—a pale, vindictive, silent, withdrawn man, brown-eyed, medium in height, smartly attired each day in a dark blue pinstriped suit. Occasionally he permitted himself a small smile. His sense of humor was practically nil. In normal conversation, his voice was soft and melodious. Cigars were his only vice. He neither drank nor swore, and he loved children. In all the world he had not one friend.

Frick was born in Westmoreland County, Pennsylvania, of German-Swiss ancestry. His parents had little money, but his grandfather, Abraham Overholt, was a wealthy rye whiskey distiller and pious Mennonite who gave him a job as bookkeeper at a salary of a thousand dollars per year. He had no time for books, music or idle conversation. Sixteen years old, he had already determined that business was to be his life, the pursuit of money his prime passion. He went to bed at ten, slept precisely nine hours, walked to the distillery, and worked until dinner, after which he went to business college, where he studied accounting and banking. His only hobby (significantly) was solitaire; he sometimes indulged in an exciting game before bedtime.

In 1870 his attention had been drawn to the bituminous coal region around Connellsville. The product was ideal for "coking," which in turn was essential for Bessemer conversion. (Coke is almost pure carbon, derived by heating coal and forcing out its volatile constituents. When burned in furnaces delivering a strong draught, coke—once contemptuously called "cinders"—produces heat sufficiently intense to liquefy pig iron.) Next year, through loans, he acquired over one hundred acres. The panic of 1873 was helpful. It enabled him to purchase much additional acreage—always on credit—at depressed prices. Within a few years he possessed practically all the Connellsville coal lands, and was selling most of his coke to the Edgar Thomson iron and steel mill owned by the Carnegie brothers.

Ruthlessly he forced out or bought out his competitors and erstwhile partners. He then turned the screws on the metal workers, of whom the Carnegie company was by far his largest customer. They could buy coke only from Mr. Frick, and the Coke King set the price. First he almost doubled it to $3.60 per ton, then raised it again to five dollars. Precociously mature in more ways than one, by the age of thirty Frick was a millionaire, was mining five thousand acres of coal land, and was producing mountains of coke each day from countless ovens which splattered the black, evil-looking terrain.

In the past, the Carnegies had purchased fuel cheaply

from a congeries of small plants who were constantly and stupidly trying to underprice each other. Competitive anarchy reigned. The 1873 economic collapse (during which coke dropped to as low as ninety cents per ton) delivered most of these firms into the tender hands of Mr. Frick, who weathered the storm through ceaseless credit techniques, as usual, and emerged as the only man who could adequately supply Carnegie. The great steelmaker was mortified; it was costly and humiliating to be at the mercy of this youngster. "We found," he wrote plaintively, "that we could not get on without a supply of the fuel essential to the smelting of pig iron; and a very thorough investigation of the question led us to the conclusion that the Frick Coke Company had not only the best coal and coke property, but that it had in Mr. Frick himself a man with a positive genius for its management."

And he remarked to a friend, "We must attach this young man Frick to our concern. He has great ability and energy. Moreover, he has the coke—and we need it." The two companies complemented each other. In 1882 Frick allowed Carnegie Brothers & Co. to purchase half his firm's stock for $1,500,000. The deal was kept secret for a short time, until Carnegie and his mother entertained Frick, honeymooning with his bride, Adelaide, at the Windsor Hotel in New York. When lunch was over, Carnegie announced exuberantly that he and Frick had become partners. After a pause, the old woman asked, "Surely, Andrew, that will be a fine thing for Mr. Frick, but what will be the gain to us?"

The gain to all concerned turned out enormous. In the words of one historian: "Carnegie and Frick made an extraordinary team. The former was the imaginative master of industry. . . . Frick was the hard-headed man of affairs who filled Pittsburgh with tens of thousands of imported laborers from every obscure hamlet of Eastern and Southern Europe. . . . Between them they created a great vertical trust of coal fields, coke ovens, limestone deposits, iron mines, ore ships, and railroads. . . . These men had the touch of Midas."

After buying out stockholders other than Frick, the Carnegie company soon possessed a majority interest in the former's coal fields and coke business. As the sad '90s approached, it owned thirty-five thousand acres of coal land and was operating about ten thousand ovens. From a fuel standpoint, Carnegie's position was consolidated. Frick was no longer a menace but an asset; his interest in his own company, in fact, had been reduced to a minority.

The next step was to bring Frick into the Carnegie operation. The Coke King knew nothing about steel, cared less, and wished to continue operating the company which was his first love. Finally, however, in 1888 he accepted a personal (and unnecessary) loan from Andrew Carnegie to acquire a token interest in the steel company. In time he was made chairman and general manager of the entire organization, his interest having reached 11 percent, second only to Andrew Carnegie's 55.

With the arrival of this genius, order and efficiency were brought into the chaos which had previously marred the vast, helter-skelter Carnegie empire. Output and profits began to soar. When Frick entered the firm, profits and steel tonnage that year had been $1,941,555 and 332,111 respectively. When he left it years later the corresponding figures were $40,000,000 and 3,000,000. His peers—even Mr. Carnegie—regarded him with awe, admiration and guarded respect.

Other gentlemen in coke and steel, however, were somewhat less than thrilled with Henry Clay Frick. The Connellsville laborers (Frick usually called them "hands") hated his every ounce. They worked hard, these muscular Slavs and Hungarians, bare to the waist, sweating over their lurid coke ovens twelve hours daily, every day, for about a dime an hour. The lot of the coal miners was similar. Since the 1870s they had struck many times—always unsuccessfully, for they had a weak, unrecognized union, no money, poor leadership. "The fields of Connellsville might literally run red with blood, as they sometimes did," wrote Matthew Josephson in *The Robber Barons,* "but in the end the miners must yield to the law of Frick."

His method of dealing with a strike was not unique, but it was as swiftly efficient as everything else he did. He crushed it with force and made no concessions. As soon as trouble began, he usually called upon the governor for the state militia, brought in as many Pinkerton "detectives" as he thought necessary, and employed an independent but legal-sounding organization called the Coal and Iron Police. As to labor unions, he never equivocated; he was no pseudo philosopher like other magnates of his time. Flatly and frequently he stated that unions should not exist. They interfered with profits, with plant management, and with the concept of competition (not only between business rivals but between employer and employee) which he considered the keystone of American industry. It follows that he detested union leaders and organizers like a plague, especially Powderly and Gompers, with both of whom he refused to communicate even in writing.

For some reason, his dislike for the swarthy Hungarians and Slavs at Connellsville was exceptional. He seemed to consider them subhuman. Strong-arm methods were intensified when he encountered them during a dispute. The coal strike of 1890 was an extreme example of Frick's harshness and rigidity. Carnegie, in Scotland, had cabled him a free hand to handle it as he saw fit. Frick declined to negotiate with a workmen's committee, and when the miners and ovenmen walked out on strike he flattened them with Pinkertons, several hundred sheriff's deputies, strikebreakers, and arrest warrants. Dynamite also was used both by his hirelings and the strikers. So easily were the miners beaten that one wonders why he thought it necessary to ask the governor to send portions of the Pennsylvania Guard. They arrived anyway, stayed for two months, and, as the state executive remarked, had "a very salutary effect on turbulent strikers." In the predictable words of Frick's official biographer: "The Frick Company was fully prepared for a siege and, accepting the issue forced upon it, calmly proceeded to fetch non-union workers into service. The enraged strikers and their sympathizers adopted a policy of terrorism and 'the whole region was given over to rioting, arson and murder'—but to no avail . . . the County authorities intervened sternly on behalf of law and order, shooting to kill and actually killing, until at the end of three months the rioters had been driven out of the region, and mining was resumed peaceably, without recognition of the union, upon the company's own terms, which incidentally proved to be eminently satisfactory to the miners."

One may question a word or phrase of the above, but it can scarcely be doubted that the effect of this strike upon all steelworkers in and around Pittsburgh was of apprehensiveness; for Frick had become chairman and general manager of the Carnegie domain in January, 1889. He had proved that he could beat down his ignorant foreign miners and coke workers without difficulty. But the iron and steel men—especially union members—at Duquesne, the Upper and Lower Union mills, the Edgar Thomson plant at Braddock, Homestead, and Beaver Falls constituted a different story. How would he cope with them? To what degree would Mr. Carnegie restrain him? Also, Frick had fought the Connellsville strike with a blatant ferocity unusual even for him. Impervious to public scrutiny, he seemed to care nothing for the opinions or morale of the minions who worked under him; and increasingly he demonstrated more than willingness to have a showdown, once and for all, with the Amalgamated.

This union was concentrated in the gem of the world's steel plants—Homestead—and its contract with the company was due to expire June 30, 1892. Fortunately, Mr. Carnegie had never wavered (in print) from his support of labor generally and labor unions in particular; and it was he, in his famous *Forum* article, who had added an amendment to the Decalogue: *Thou shalt not take thy neighbor's job.*

I would have the public give due con-
sideration to the terrible temptation to
which the workingman on a strike is some-
times subjected. To expect that one depend-
ent on his daily wage for the necessaries of
life will stand by peaceably, and see a new
man employed in his stead is to expect much.
The poor man may have a wife and children
dependent on his labor. Whether medicine
for a sick child, or even nourishing food for
a delicate wife, is procurable, depends upon
his steady employment. . . . No wise em-
ployer will lightly lose his old employés.
Length of service counts for much in many
ways. Calling upon strange men should be
the last resort.

—Andrew Carnegie

II *Homestead*

Years ago it had been a land of bloodshed. Twice the
French had warded off savage British attacks against Fort
Duquesne. In 1755 General Braddock ("cursing feebly")
and his troops were slaughtered here in tangled thickets.
The date was July 9, and one notes how history later almost repeated itself. It was the rendezvous of the "Whiskey
Insurgents" army. All along the Monongahela river Alexander Hamilton had upheld "strong government" through
terrorism, using armed marauders who emerged at night to
raid peaceful farmsteads. And Indian attacks were commonplace until the middle of that century.

Then peace came to Pittsburgh. Early next century a
gentleman farmer named John McClure built a home and
a great farm at a sharp bend a few miles upstream. He
called the place Amity Homestead. In 1872 his grandson

sold much land to an insurance and banking firm which laid out a little town and named it Homestead. Nearly six hundred people lived there in 1879, that fateful year during which a combination of iron- and steel-makers began to erect an unprecedently modern plant over sixty acres of barren waterfront land within the town limits. In time, as we shall see, the Carnegie company acquired this mill, drastically enlarged it, increased its output, and diversified its products. The population of Homestead was roughly eleven thousand by 1892. Virtually every able-bodied man and youth in the borough worked at the steel mill, which had thirty-eight hundred on its payroll. Even the burgess, or mayor, of the town—John McLuckie—was a mere assistant roller earning sixty-five dollars monthly (at most) in one of the plate mills.

A tributary of the Ohio River, the brownish Monongahela was eight hundred feet wide at Homestead, swift-running and deep. Its banks were lined with cinders and other refuse, metal scrap, and sickly ground upon which little grew but scattered weeds and dry, scrubby bushes. Contaminated by the sewage of many small and middle-sized towns and cities upstream, the water was saturated with chemicals (notably sulphuric acid) used in making metals and coke. "No respectable microbe would live in it," remarked one Homestead resident; and typhoid was indeed rare in the town compared to Pittsburgh. Otherwise the water was unhealthy and ill-tasting, but other than poor well water there was nothing else to use or drink.

The mill curved for a mile along the sharp waterfront bend; and the Homestead operation was only one of several similar in the immediate vicinity, all exhaling dust, dirt, and smoke against which housewives fought helplessly. Rarely could the sun penetrate the yellowish arti-

ficial clouds and haze, the product of dense black smoke
from hundreds of stacks, which hung over the borough.

Where the works ended the town immediately began,
sloping south up from First and Eighth Avenues to the top
of a hill, where it dwindled off at the apex of a triangle.
There were no paved streets and no sewage system. Outdoor privies were standard even for the better homes.
Every tenement, rooming house, home, shack, shanty, and
business structure was of frame construction, and all were
of identical hue: dirt-gray. The hill, being irregular and
cut up by dips and small ravines, had given the building
contractors a problem which they had solved by erecting
each structure in conformity with the grade at that point.
The result was incredible. Houses faced in any and all
directions, rarely conforming to the geometric pattern of
the streets. This densely packed maze of dwellings (each lot
only about twenty feet in frontage) was further complicated by alleys which wandered aimlessly throughout the
town. They were, of course, calamities of filth, sagging
sheds, privies, debris, and garbage.

So-called "squares" were formed in the back yards, enclosed by the buildings; they were social centers for the
families around them. Here deplorably dirty children
romped and shot marbles, women gossiped, men played
cards and smoked their pipes. "The streets were horrible,"
wrote journalist Hamlin Garland; "the buildings were
poor; the sidewalks were sunken and full of holes; and the
crossings were formed of sharp-edged stones like rocks in a
river bed. Everywhere the yellow mud of streets lay
kneaded into sticky masses, through which groups of pale,
lean men slouched in faded garments, grimy with the soot
and dirt of the mills. The town was as squalid as could well
be imagined, and the people were mainly of the discour-

aged and sullen type to be found everywhere where labor passes into the brutalizing stage of severity."

The better residences were located further up the hill. Most of them had four rooms, two per floor, with perhaps a patch of grass or even a garden facing the street. Perfectly uniform in construction, they pressed against each other, separated by narrow passageways. The sun seldom touched the front and dining rooms on the ground floor. Relatively luxurious houses boasted a single cold-water faucet in the kitchen.

Most tenements and rooming houses were clustered west of the plant near the river. Unmarried men and poorer families occupied one room at a weekly rental of about two dollars. The low flatland eastward, leading up to the borough of Munhall, had not yet been plotted and was without streets. Yet swarms lived here in shacks and improvised lean-tos. These rock-bottom humans, usually Slavs, had at least the consolation of paying little or no rent.

Except after heavy rain, even the trees were gray with dust. At night the lurid grandeur of belching fire spectrally illuminated the entire town, pulsing and throbbing to the never-ending clamor of machinery; and periodically the uproar was accentuated by train traffic on rail lines which traversed Homestead and Munhall from east to west in the vicinity of Fifth Avenue.

All was not ugliness and gloom. The men earned fairly good wages for that era; they were, by and large, satisfied; and even the most tightly budgeted families were able to indulge in a little luxury spending. Employees had $140,-000 on deposit with the Carnegie company, earning 6 percent interest. Scores of them had borrowed an average of over six hundred dollars from the firm, also at 6 percent, with which to buy homes. Several were already paid for in full. Socially and recreationally, however, the picture was not bright. The men worked every day of the year, except Christmas and July 4, the majority twelve hours daily; and they had little time or energy for outside activities. Iron puddlers reported in at 2 A.M. or P.M., and most other shifts were worked from 6 to 6. Such schedules made socializing difficult.

"Tell me, how can a man get any pleasure out of life working that way?" one inquired. "I'm at work most of the day, and I'm so tired at night that I just go to bed as soon as I've eaten supper. I have ideas of what a home ought to be, all right, but the way things are now I just eat and sleep here." The peculiar work hours made family life quite erratic, what with the women making breakfasts, dinners and suppers at odd hours of the day and night, especially when two or more men of the household worked different shifts. It was not uncommon for father and son to see each other momentarily or not at all for extended periods.

The "turn" every two weeks was a mixed blessing. After working a double shift (the twelve-hour men had to put in twenty-four straight hours), employees were given the following day off. Usually they were too weary to take much advantage of it. Fathers and mothers, both overburdened, had problems with their daughters. As a result of irregular and unnatural living conditions, many teen-age girls ran wild and developed a distressing tendency to escape to Pittsburgh whenever they could, for fun and excitement.

The borough possessed a handful of elementary schools, one skating rink, and a theater where traveling performers occasionally appeared. Those were great occasions. The women formed clubs, the younger men found time for baseball, the old-timers played a little poker and drank.

All visitors to Homestead were struck by the abnormal number of saloons along Eighth Avenue. At work the men drank so much water that it left them bloated and nauseous. Upon leaving they usually stopped for a beer or a shot. The general belief was that they needed alcohol as a stimulant, to settle their stomachs, and to keep themselves from breaking down. Under their murderous working conditions, chronic drunkenness was impossible. They were not dedicated drinkers, except for some blast-furnace men whose long hours and particularly grim work had led them to the brink of despair. Others lined up at the bars after work, drank silently, paid only for their own liquor, and then trudged homeward up the hill or to their rooms near the railroad.

Saturday night was more convivial, as was payday every second Friday. The saloons became social centers during the early evening hours. Drinking was heavier, there was much treating, and sometimes the bartender served a free round. Pittsburgh offered more diversions, but it was an hour away; there was no time for traveling to and fro; and the little trip cost extra pennies. The East Europeans brought their liquor home and drank with friends in one-room hovels, for although many of them were intelligent and sensitive, they had no relationships with other Europeans or native Americans; the language barrier was formidable.

Aristocrats of the working force, the Amalgamated men were clannish and seldom mingled with any but the members of their lodges. Homestead's seven churches brought families together for services and social functions, but they were attended mainly by women and children. The men were tired, indifferent toward formal religion, and held the preachers in low esteem. Constant sermons concerning intemperate drinking bored them. "Let the preachers go into the mills," a worker recommended, "and see the men at work in the heat, and outside the mills let them notice the men with crushed hands or broken arms or with a leg missing. If they would stop their preaching long enough to look around a little they could do something for us, if they wanted to try." Perhaps America was a "Christian nation," as Supreme Court Justice Brewer had just proclaimed in *Holy Trinity Church* v. *United States* (1892); but, if so, Homestead was atypical.

And aside from working conditions the accident rate was appalling. No over-all death and injury figures exist for 1892, but one may extrapolate backward from certain statistics and contemporary writings to recreate the nightmare. In a single later year 195 men were killed in Pittsburgh's iron and steel mills: twenty-two from hot metal explosions, five from asphyxiation, ten from rolling accidents, seventy-three during the operation of cars and cranes, twenty-four from falling from heights or into pits, seven from electric shocks, eight while loading and piling, forty-six through miscellaneous causes. Total deaths in 1891 were probably around three hundred, because there was more handwork and less safety equipment. Accidents that year surely exceeded two thousand.[1] Mechanization was still in its infancy and (especially in Bessemer processing) the men worked only inches away from brimming ladles of molten metal.

The little dinkeys had no automatic couplers and were joined manually. An engineer said that he had lost count of the men whose hands were smashed during hook-ons. Foreigners were especially vulnerable. "Unacquainted

[1] These estimates apply to all iron and steel mills in and near Pittsburgh owned by the Carnegie company and its competitors.

with the machinery, and with an exasperated boss shouting unintelligible orders, the Slav workman is as likely to run into danger as out of it," a social worker wrote. Near the end of their shift the men were in more peril, due to carelessness and exhaustion and slower reactions.

A "slip" meant disaster. When liquid stock hung at the top of a furnace it might suddenly fall, bursting the bottom and killing the crew. Often metal streaming into a converter struck the edge of the mold, throwing a shower in all directions and burning nearby workers. Every "hot-job" man experienced this one time or another, and the clothes of men on the pouring platforms were full of small holes. Even in the safer open-hearth department, fluid steel might break out sooner than expected. Or a crane lifting several tons out of the pit might fail, dropping the load from a height, whereupon it would lethally explode.

In hot departments water hissed on the floor plates as on a stove. Everyone wore shoes with thick wooden soles. Blast furnaces were worked by three men alternately, a third of the time each; each furnace was ninety feet high and accompanied by several superheating stoves of the same height. The puddlers, most picturesque and independent of all workers, stirred the molten pig iron with an iron rod through a hole in the furnace door. Gradually, under increasing heat, they worked the pig into iron balls weighing about five hundred pounds. The process was fairly inhuman. At Homestead not one furnace was shielded by water-cooled plates, an innovation recently adopted by other plants.

A member of the British Iron and Steel Institute, when visiting Pennsylvania, noted the speed of operations and the high pressure placed upon the workers. "The men, I dare say, are paid well, but it was hot weather when I was

there, and they were certainly selling their lives." A steelworker referred to charging an open-hearth furnace by
hand as "working aside of hell ahead of time." Dante's
Inferno comes to mind when one reads of steel work in
those days, with its heat, its furnaces fantastically glaring,
the long black darting shadows of the men. An employee
admitted to Garland that the work had coarsened him.
"You can't help it . . . you become more and more a
machine, and pleasures are few and far between. It's like
any severe labor; it drags you down mentally and morally
just as it does physically. I wouldn't mind it so much but
for the long hours. Twelve hours is too long."

Even Carnegie's official and sympathetic biographer,
Bernard Alderson, says this of Garland's trip to the Homestead plant: "Everywhere in the enormous sheds were pits
gaping like the mouth of hell, and ovens emitting a terrible degree of heat, with grimy men filling and lining
them. One man jumps down, works desperately for a few
minutes, and is then pulled up, exhausted. Another immediately takes his place; there is no hesitation. When he
spoke to the men they laughed. It was winter when he
made his visit. They told him to come in the summer. . . ." Those who dumped iron ore into blast furnaces were called top fillers and were not envied. They
worked in temperatures near 128 degrees and were envel-
oped in noxious fumes when the wind turned. "Gorilla
men are what we need," said one official.

In raggedy trousers, shirt sleeves cut off at the shoulder,
sweat pouring, muscles bunched into knots, the heater's
helper pulled out billet after billet and tossed them to the
rougher. Feverishly he shoved them into the roller. When
he turned around another billet was waiting. All was
handwork, with hardly a break. Agility was necessary.

Since a false step could mean death, this job was never given to older men. The craneman worked twelve hot, lonely hours. Nobody could relieve him, nor could he get down from his cab for any reason—not even the call of nature. He was careful to take advance precautions.

Pressure work in the rolling, blooming, and plate mills (as contrasted to hot jobs) was cooler but equally nerve-racking, due to incessant vibration of the machinery and the maddening screech of cold saws ripping through steel. In time the men became hard of hearing. The din within the huge sheds forced them to yell to each other all day long. They and their clothes were covered with minuscule, shiny grains of steel. They complained about respiratory ailments and drank liquor after work, as one man said, to "take the dust out of my throat." Chronic irritation of the mucous membranes, it was thought, induced catarrh and tuberculosis.

There was no meal period. Dirty-handed, the men ate fruits and leftovers from their lunch pails whenever they had a chance. Before leaving work, for lack of bathing facilities they washed their arms and shoulders in a "bosh," a trough of water in which tools were placed to cool off.

By modern standards, the danger of working in the pressure divisions is hard to believe. A brief period of about a month at Homestead (soon after this narrative) entailed sixty-five accidents, seven of which were fatal. About half the remainder were sprained ankles, smashed feet, and lacerated hands. The other half added up thus: ten head wounds, three broken arms or legs, two amputated arms, four eye injuries, eight internal injuries, and one case of paralysis. Obviously few of these injuries could have occurred in the smelting and converting departments.

The Carnegie company awarded not a cent in recom-

pense for bodily damage or death, except for a few isolated
acts of generosity. Sometimes the men or their survivors
sued in court. Since the legal definition of employer re-
sponsibility was so narrow, the management (backed by a
powerful liability insurance firm) hardly ever lost. Discouraged, the men took out their own tiny policies. Food
might run low, rent and clothing expenditures could be in
arrears, but the insurance premium of about a dollar
weekly was paid, and paid first. Friends and relatives often
contributed to the stricken family. The local Amalgamated lodges in Homestead maintained a meager death
and disability account, but its members numbered only
about a tenth of the work force. In any event, the benefits
were temporary. As for the Amalgamated national, its
$25,000 treasury was purely a strike fund.

So the fear of an accident which might take a wage
earner off the payroll more than briefly hung over each
household like Damocles' sword. The cost of living had
been irregularly on the rise for a generation, while (except
for a small minority of tonnage men, whose pay was tied to
output) wages had remained constant. No increases had
ever been sought or granted in the Carnegie works, and if
hundreds of men had bank accounts the average balance
was pathetically small.

How could the Slavs with wives and children exist? One
and all were unskilled day laborers (called "dinkey men"
or "bohunks") at fourteen cents per hour, ten hours per
day, $9.80 weekly. They were excluded from the Amal-
gamated as a matter of course. At the other end of the
curve was a coterie of technicians (rollers, screwdowns,
heaters, heaters' helpers, tablemen, and shearmen) who
worked the eight-hour day, earning a weekly maximum at
peak production ranging from $34.80 to $71.04. Years

later a historian wrote that such employees were driven to work in private carriages, and another recites an old story about rollers and heaters coming to the plant "in Prince Albert coats wearing top hats to collect their wages." While these pleasant anecdotes can no longer be proved or disproved, the extraordinary wages paid by Carnegie to such men is a matter of record.

The earnings of hundreds of semiskilled men are harder to compute. Some were on a tonnage basis, others were not. Some worked eight hours, some ten, some twelve; and their week varied between six and seven days. Production vacillated wildly. For long periods the protean works would roar and pulsate to the tune of highest possible output, only to be followed by many days (sometimes a full week) when practically every employee was laid off. A congressional report later stated flatly that workers in the 119-inch plate mill, Homestead's largest department, averaged $120 monthly. Perhaps it is safe to estimate the grand average at a hundred dollars, since the plate mill was a mechanized operation employing few unskilled men.

A showdown between the Amalgamated and Frick was due as soon as the three-year union-management contract approached its expiration—there was no doubt about it— and as early as spring, 1892, the Homestead lodges of the Amalgamated Iron and Steel Workers were in difficulties for which they themselves were to blame. It was all very well to chant, "Whether you work by the piece or work by the day, decreasing the hours increases the pay," but what was gained by excluding from membership not only common day laborers but the semiskilled as well? Nearly two thousand of the latter were employed at Homestead. Members of the local Amalgamated, as previously noted, numbered under four hundred. When it dawned upon them that a collision with Mr. Frick was imminent they conducted a last-minute membership drive which brought the figure to 752 by June. This comparative failure was due in part to the fact that men of the Amalgamated (as a body) were resented by the other workers. Few cared to join them on the eve of battle. They were supercilious, practiced social apartheid, were arrogant in their demands; nor did their high wages further their popularity. The central committee dictated labor policy and made flunkeys out of the so-called foremen. Their arbitrary spirit was more extreme at Homestead than at any other steel plant in the country, and never did they accomplish, or attempt to accomplish, anything for the non-unionists.

Within this privileged circle there circled inner circles. The Irish ran the Bessemer converter, the Welsh the rolling mill, and so on. The Irish were at odds with the English, the lodges quarreled with each other, specialists were jealous of other specialists; but en masse the Amalgamated men considered themselves unbeatable in any labor conflict. They had no inkling that their union was already archaic—nothing more, really, than an old, oversized puddlers' clan. It had been organized at Pittsburgh in 1876, the combination of three former steelworker groups. A few Negroes were granted segregated-lodge membership, but (in accordance with written rules) not one foreman. Dues were a dollar yearly, and might have been tripled. The lodges were kept small, always well under a hundred men, so as not to dare challenge the authority of the central committee. Each lodge was rigidly restricted to a single branch of the trade, such as finishers, heaters, and boilers.

President of this coast-to-coast anachronism was "the Giant Puddler," William Weihe, a huge, deliberate, ad-

mired man of forty-seven who was no iron puddler but a
former boiler by occupation. The Amalgamated had always elected conservative leaders and Weihe was no exception. He had served a term in the Pennsylvania state
legislature, abhorred strikes, espoused conciliation, and
tried (usually with success) to restrain his belligerent
thousands. Placidly he had held office for a decade, living
with his family on Pittsburgh's South Side. He was resigned to technological advances and the resultant loss of
jobs. "The Association never objects to improvements," he
said. "They believe in the American idea that the genius
of the country should not be retarded." When better
machinery at the Edgar Thomson plant displaced hundreds of men in 1885, he and the union offered no re-
sistance, although two lodges there at once evaporated.
When automation (it was called "labor-saving" at the
time) led to increased output and abnormally high tonnage wages, reduced rates were usually, if reluctantly,
accepted. To take one example, this had happened at
Homestead in 1889, when the Amalgamated agreed to
decreases on a new scale 50 percent lower than that at
Jones and Laughlin's competitive plant, where similar machines had not yet been installed.

Yet, in the old narrow sense, matters remained much the
same as ever. Each Homestead department had a committee led by a chairman who felt that he had to bluff or fold.
Almost daily some foreman was presented with another
demand or complaint, preposterous or otherwise. No vacant job could be filled without Amalgamated approval;
and testily a historian observed, "The method of appor-
tioning the work, of regulating the turns, of altering the
machinery, in short, every detail of working the great
plant, was subject to the interference of some busybody

representing the Amalgamated Association . . . The
heats of a turn were designated, as were the weights of the
various charges constituting a heat. The product per
worker was limited; the proportion of scrap that might be
used in running a furnace was fixed; the quality of pig-
iron was stated; the puddlers' use of brick and fire clay was
forbidden . . . the teaching of other workmen was pro-
hibited; nor might one man lend his tools to another . . ."

Because steel companies feared the mighty Amalgamated, and because union officers were moderate in policy,
strikes were rare. Those that did occur had to be authorized by an executive committee and were kept strictly lo-
calized. Paid benefits were four dollars weekly per man,
starting a month after a strike had been approved.

The Amalgamated had eight lodges in Homestead.
Their combined offices consisted of two desolate rooms located in an Eighth Avenue building above a grocery store.
Except for files and a few roll-top desks, tables, and chairs,
the premises were bare. Clerical work was done sporadically and without pay by volunteer union members. At
times during the day the offices were left deserted. There
was no telephone and, as yet, no telegraph connection.
Occasionally Mr. Weihe dropped in from Pittsburgh. Most
of the work and planning was done by heater Hugh
O'Donnell, William Roberts of the armor plate division,
and shearman Hugh Ross, three sagacious young men soon
to become better known.

In our age of anxiety almost everyone—whether he
works for the local board of education or a missile plant—is
considered a potential security risk. Nearly all industrial
establishments (producing, say, aluminum tubing or service shoes) are "sensitive" operations protected like the

Fort Knox mint. Consider, with alarm, the Homestead plant in 1892. It was not enclosed. Strangers could wander in and out of it. A few unarmed guards chased away children trying to steal bits of coke or metal scrap. There was supposed to be a high wooden fence around the works, and it did exist near the main entrance on Eighth Avenue for a few hundred feet on both sides. Then suddenly it stopped. Here and there desultorily over the years attempts had been made to extend it; and when Mr. Frick had assumed command he is said to have issued orders to that effect. They had not yet been carried out. Without bothering to use the main gate, most workers casually came in and went out from near McClure Street in Homestead or from the Munhall flats to the southeast. So it was hard to tell where the works ended and the boroughs of Homestead and Munhall began. Legally the plant occupied a specific area of six hundred acres, thirty-seven of them under roof. Not a blade of grass grew within the arid confines of the wondrous mill. Railroad tracks crisscrossed the yards. The offices of Superintendent Potter, containing his corps of clerks, engineers, and draftsmen, were situated near the Munhall side, and farther back were substantial residences occupied by assistant managers. Near these homes a clubhouse had been built for the use of guests and company officials. To exist in these homes and facilities was like living next door to a madhouse.

There was another so-called entrance on the Monongahela waterfront, but it had no dock and was useless except for landing personnel in small boats. A bridge crossing the river touched just east of this point. It was used for traffic to and from Pittsburgh by people on foot, on horseback, or in carriages. The primary purpose of the "hot metal" bridge a few blocks west was to carry molten pig iron by rail cars from the Carrie furnaces southward toward the great converters. (It could be kept liquid for fully an hour by covering it with iron dust and shavings.) Little iron ore was smelted in Homestead. Like all other Carnegie steel plants it was rather specialized, and its *raison d'être* was to manufacture structural iron and steel (mostly girders and beams) for fireproof buildings and for bridges, and armor plate for the United States Navy. Previously the firm of Carnegie, Phipps & Co., which had been organized to run the Homestead works, had won government contracts for two warships, the *Monterey* and the second-class battleship *Maine*. A pacifist, Mr. Carnegie had twice refused the military contract; he had, however, signed on the dotted line the third time around. By now, in fact, Homestead was the top manufacturer of armor plate in the country, exceeding even the rival plate mill at Bethlehem, Pennsylvania.

The plant also produced boiler plate and a small tonnage of rough billets, but no rails. It boasted the nation's most gigantic hydraulic press in the 119-inch plate mill, a vast machine shop, its own waterworks and natural gas producers. Its value was estimated conservatively by Mr. Frick at about six million dollars—an enormous sum for a single mill in those days. The superintendent at Homestead, thirty-two-year-old John A. Potter, connoisseur of guns and gunfire, was no friend of the workers.

It is now pertinent to examine briefly Carnegie's other fragments which, like a jigsaw puzzle, fitted together and formed a meticulous, almost aesthetic, metallic entity.

The Duquesne plant lay five miles up the river. Captured in 1890 by Mr. Carnegie (largely through fraud and without the outlay of a dollar bill), its ultramodern facilities had been converted mainly into the production of variously sized billets. Carnegie workers everywhere looked upon it as a phony billet-mill designed to flood the market, to lower prices, and thereby to reduce the sliding-scale of wages based upon the tonnage of 4 by 4 billets. Some rails were also finished here. Duquesne was non-union.

At Braddock, directly across the river from Homestead, the J. Edgar Thomson works produced steel rails in unheard-of quantity, as well as a little pig iron. Following a lost strike in 1888, it too was non-union.

Forty miles down the Ohio River, far beyond Pittsburgh, we encounter an aberration in the Carnegie-Frick profit structure: the unqualified failure at Beaver Falls called the Hartman Steel Works. Largely experimental, its function was intended to work into many forms the billets and sheets roughed at other Carnegie plants, but although its equipment was good and its operation efficient it was a loser and a headache from the start. By 1892 this white elephant was specializing half-heartedly in nails and steel rods while company officials tried to solve its future. It was partially unionized in the manner of Homestead.

The Union Iron Mills were composed of the Upper Union Mill on 29th Street and the Lower Union Mill on 33rd Street, both near the heart of Pittsburgh. Grudgingly the company recognized the Amalgamated in these adjacent plants, which were extremely prosperous—in Carnegie's words "the leading mills in the United States for all sorts of structural shapes."

And finally there were the Lucy and Isabella blast furnaces (named after wives of certain company partners) at 51st Street in Pittsburgh. Starting as gigantic, recordbreaking, rival blast furnaces years ago, they now numbered several more; and their single purpose in the scheme of things was to smelt pig iron which was then rushed to the eager, ever-waiting converters at Braddock, Homestead, and Duquesne. Many Amalgamated men worked at Lucy and Isabella, but the union did not officially exist here. The Carrie furnaces lay directly north of Homestead.

All these colonies comprised the Carnegie empire of iron and steel. Productively (with the regrettable exception of Beaver Falls) they operated independently but with clockwork interdependence to create profits and products of astonishing scope, under the brilliant—almost inhuman and singlehanded—organizational leadership of Henry Clay Frick. Only two factors disturbed him. One was the unbearable panache of the Amalgamated Association which, he felt, hampered progress and diluted dividends. The other was accounting procedure. Since each unit of the commonwealth kept its own books and functioned fiscally apart from the others, it was impossible for his auditors to determine composite costs, overhead, capitalization, net returns on investment, and interest charges. Also, the splintered structure of the company had led inevitably to cumbersome and even dissident management relations. For some years, he had suggested to Carnegie that all components should be combined monolithically. The idea had been agreed to and a new company formed— the Carnegie Steel Company, Limited, a noncorporate partnership, capitalization $25 million—which was to exist formally July 1, 1892. By a coincidence, that was the date of the expiration of the company's contract with the Amalgamated.

Carnegie personally continued to possess a few modest extraneous assets. His control of Frick's former coke business, a gold mine in itself, has been noted. Also in his steel grip were the Keystone Bridge Works of Pittsburgh, the Carnegie Natural Gas Company, the Scotia ore mines in

Pennsylvania's Centre County, the American Manganese operation, a small mill at Lawrenceville, heavy interests in several Lake Superior iron-ore companies, as well as a few minor railways and steamship lines. What manner of man was he, now only in his fifties, whose youthful dream had been for his entire family to earn a total of "twenty-five dollars monthly, which I figured was the sum required to keep us without being dependent upon others"?

*The urban workmen are denied the right
to organize for self-protection, imported
pauperized labor beats down their wages,
a hireling standing army, unrecognized by
our laws, is established to shoot them down,
and they are rapidly degenerating into
European conditions. The fruits of the toil
of millions are boldly stolen to build up
colossal fortunes for a few, unprecedented
in the history of mankind. . . . From the
same prolific womb of governmental in-
justices we breed two great classes—tramps
and millionaires.*

—*From the Populist preamble, 1892*

III *Mr. Carnegie*

Rich in history and tradition for a millennium, the pleasant town of Dunfermline rests on high ground near the
mouth of the Firth of Forth. When Andrew Carnegie was
born there in a tile-roofed cottage, 1835, it was Scotland's
center for the manufacture of table linen. His father, William, wove fine damask in his own home, employed helpers at several looms, and was moderately prosperous until
steam-loom factory weaving replaced handwork and put
him out of business. For some years he and his wife, Margaret—a shrewd and strong-minded person—struggled
against hopeless odds. They sold their house, sold all the
looms, opened and closed a tiny shop, and finally gave up
the good fight when even the proceeds from these sales
approached the vanishing point. Their younger son, Tom,
a handsome blond lad, was five years old when the family
sailed for the United States in 1848, so reduced in circumstances that Mrs. Carnegie had to borrow twenty pounds
from a friend before booking passage on the schooner *Wiscasset.*

Andrew was cheerful and intelligent, he was teacher's pet, he was high-spirited and industrious; he saved his money, washed his face, loved his parents, dressed neatly, read widely and usefully; and always he kept his piercing blue eyes fixed upon the main chance. He was all the copybook maxims wrapped up into one small package of dynamite.

In Dunfermline, the most radical town in Scotland, he had scented the prevailing winds of change. His own father was a local leader in denouncing monarchism, the stifling privileges of the rich and bureaucratic, and of war. Republicanism was the ideal; America—land of liberty and individualism—was the dream; the American Revolution was still on everyone's lips. He learned Scottish history and came to hate England, she who had crushed the clans and demolished the Highland society a century ago. Haphazardly he read scraps and volumes of many sorts, especially Shakespeare and Burns. His memory was phenomenal. Decades later he could still recite long passages from these two, his most beloved authors. As for religion, he was raised by his parents as a moderate skeptic, and became practically an agnostic in time. (In subsequent years he studied the world's major faiths and sects, and judged them all equally implausible. As a youth, however, he had toyed with the Swedenborgian Society; subsequently he even donated an organ to their church in Allegheny.)

Seven weeks out of Glasgow the *Wiscasset* dropped anchor in New York harbor. The Carnegies proceeded to Allegheny City and moved in with friends from the old country, while Andrew "fairly panted to get to work . . . The prospect of want had become to me a frightful nightmare." His first job paid $1.20 per week. As a bobbin boy, he worked in a cellar from sunup to dark, hating every minute of it. The family was barely hanging on. His next

job paid two dollars. Since it involved—in addition to some
clerical duties—the nauseous chore of bathing spools in vats
of oil, the thirteen-year-old boy frequently vomited his
breakfast or lunch. Desperate, he began to attend an
evening class in double-entry bookkeeping. Two bad
years passed, while his father drove himself in a cotton
factory toward an early grave (he died in five years) and
his mother took in washing and sewing. Then a relative,
Uncle Hogan, helped Andrew to become a messenger boy
for the Ohio Telegraph Company. It was the tiniest of
openings, but the bird slipped through and flew the coop,
never to return.

He was called a "Mercury." In a green uniform, he soon
became a familiar sight all over downtown Pittsburgh.
Precociously he learned the name and face of every leading
merchant. Always on the run, he delivered telegrams to
them in their carriages, on sidewalks, at lunch counters.
He became a telegraph operator for the company when he
was fifteen. Soon he was one of only three persons in the
nation able to transcribe Morse by ear. Up the ladder he
went. He joined the Pennsylvania Railroad as secretary
and clerk in 1853, became a division superintendent, and
commenced earning the incredible salary of thirty-five dollars monthly. He promised his mother he would not marry
until after her death, a curious vow which he kept. His
height was five feet, four inches. It is difficult for an ama-
teur psychologist not to draw apparent deductions.

Like Napoleon (five feet, two inches) he perhaps com-
pensated for his stature by aggressiveness other than sexual
or physical. His demand for money and power and acclaim
was insatiable until the declining years set in; and seldom
was there limit to his optimism. Quite early he sensed the
nation's remorseless drive. "Our public lands for almost

unlimited extent are becoming settled with an enterprising people," he wrote to a friend in Scotland. "Our dense forests are falling under the ax of the hardy woodsman. The Wolf and the Buffalo are startled by the shrill scream of the Iron Horse where a few years ago they roamed undisturbed. Towns and cities spring up as if by magic. . . . Our railroads extend 13,000 miles. You cannot supply iron fast enough to keep us going. This country is completely cut up with Railroad Tracks, Telegraphs, and Canals. . . . Pauperism is unknown. . . . Everything around us is in motion."

By age twenty, Andy, too, was in motion, and with a vengeance. He purchased stock in the Adams Express Company by mortgaging his mother's house. Upon receiving his first dividend check for ten dollars, he remarked, "Here's the goose that lays the golden eggs." He borrowed slightly over two hundred dollars to finance his entry into Woodruff's Palace Car company, forerunner of the Pullman company. Two years later the venture was paying him five thousand yearly. He snapped up some speculative oil land in western Pennsylvania; immediately oil began gushing from it. While the Civil War raged his fingers were in at least a dozen commercial pies. "Oh, I'm rich! I'm rich!" he joyously told a friend.

In 1863 his earnings listed for war-tax purposes were $47,860.67. His speculations and investments accelerated at a dizzy pace. In his thirtieth year he resigned from a promising future in the Pennsylvania road, entered the Kloman iron works, and organized the Upper and Lower Union Mills with his brother and others on a capitalization of half a million dollars.

The end of the war and subsequent drying-up of government contracts almost ruined them all. Bitterly Andrew reproached himself for getting involved in such a "most hazardous enterprise." But the tide soon turned— mainly because of the renewed demand for rails—and again he saw that his future was to be linked with iron. "Whatever I engage in I must push inordinately," he told his diary. Earlier he had bought into the Piper and Schiffler bridge firm; he increased his holding steadily, changed the name to the Keystone Bridge Company, and began selling himself a good deal of metal from his Union Mills. Similarly (1866) he organized the Pittsburgh Loco- motive Works, to which he sold his own iron.

Next year, after dolefully deprecating to his partners the value and future of the Union Mills, and even talking about selling his stock, he indirectly purchased over two thousand additional shares, a transaction which brought his interest to 39 percent and made him the largest indi- vidual shareholder. Business was booming febrilely when he jotted down this personal memorandum: "Thirty three and an income of $50,000 per annum! [equivalent now to over a quarter of a million tax-free]. . . . Beyond this never earn—make no effort to increase fortune, but spend the surplus each year for benevolent purposes. . . . Settle in Oxford and get a thorough education, making the ac- quaintance of literary men—this will take three years' ac- tive work—pay special attention to speaking in public. Settle then in London and purchase a controlling interest in some newspaper . . . connected with education and improvement of the poorer classes. . . . Amassing of wealth is one of the worst species of idolatry. . . . I will resign business at thirty-five."

Much water was to flow under Keystone bridges before these plans became a reality. "To continue much longer," he scribbled on, "with most of my thoughts wholly upon the way to make more money in the shortest time, must degrade me beyond hope of permanent recovery." He continued and recovered. The details are not without interest, but only the highlights follow.

The peerless Edgar Thomson Steel Company (tactfully named after the railroad magnate, a top customer) was built at Braddock out of $700,000 issued capital. Carnegie bought a minority interest of $250,000. By 1878 he was in control, by possession of 58 percent of the outstanding shares. Inordinately he pushed onward, ever upward, vain as a peacock, genial, the incarnation of progress and financial lust, the salesman par excellence. With convertible bonds or on credit he acquired rail and steamship lines, not at random, but to cut costs and protect his flanks. To his interests in Pennsylvania ore lands he added the sensational Mesabi range on the shores of Lake Superior, through a leasing deal with John D. Rockefeller which eventually resulted in his outright control. It gave him, according to *Iron Age,* "a position unequalled by any producer in the world."

His aim was a vertical trust, a semimonopoly, and in time he almost achieved it. To most pleas for trade agreements and price-fixing arrangements between him and his rivals he turned a deaf ear. In Wall Street they called him "the little Scotch pirate." He ignored the Street and owned no stocks or bonds outside his own companies. Combinations he eschewed; he preferred the competition of the jungle. He priced the shares of his firm at a thousand dollars each, to keep them from circulating, and threatened his partners with hellfire to keep them from speculating.

Occasionally, during good years when demand outstripped supply, he joined a price-fixing pool in rails or

plate. When the market softened, Carnegie bolted. Down
went prices and costs; up (if possible) went production.
His competitors might cry treason and double cross when
he told his board of directors to step out of the rail pool,
but Carnegie remained placid: "I get no sweet dividend
out of second fiddle business, and I do know that the way
to make even money *is to lead.* . . . we needn't hesitate,
take orders and run full, there's a margin."

He gathered unto himself a redoubtable congeries of
technical experts, paid them superb salaries, and often allowed them to buy into the operation via notes to be retired through future dividends. The percentages may have
been one-twelfth or one-sixth of 1 percent, but in later
years these minuscule holdings made millionaires of over
forty gifted foremen and minor office officials. One exception was the formidable Captain William R. Jones—an in-
dividualistic superintendent who furiously resigned a
dozen times and always came back for more—the greatest
mechanical genius ever employed by Carnegie. Jones refused to purchase shares. "I have enough trouble looking
after these works," he told the boss. "Just give me a hell of
a salary if you think I'm worth it." Carnegie replied, "All
right, Captain, the salary of the President of the United
States is yours." When shortly thereafter the grim little
Welshman died horribly in an accident involving the explosion of a cauldron of molten steel, young Charles
Schwab took his place at Braddock—another of Carnegie's
uncanny choices.

Carnegie, as noted, acquired dominance of Frick's coke
works in the 1880s. At that time his yearly income was
almost two million dollars; his total fortune was nearing
fifteen millions. Organized in 1881, the Carnegie Brothers
and Company, Limited, encompassed the Edgar Thom-

son plant, the Union Iron Mills, and the Lucy Furnaces. Of the five million capitalization Carnegie possessed slightly over half. He personally sold what he manufactured. "Bubbling with enthusiasm," writes Matthew Josephson, "and full of brass, he intruded himself everywhere, buttonholed everyone, listened to everything. He cajoled and flattered the influential men he knew, Scott and Thomson and other railroad chiefs, with telling effects." He subdued his partners and dominated his quiet, capable brother. Orders flowed in with the violence of a burst dam. As early as 1879 the Edgar Thomson mill was producing 107,877 tons of ingots, 76,043 of which were rolled into rails. Profits here alone that year were $1,625,-000; and orders had been booked for 80,000 tons in 1880.

True, he had hesitated about the Bessemer process, which refined iron into steel within ten minutes. "Pioneering don't pay," he remarked sourly; but Carnegie did his share, frequently with the obsession of a gambler who senses a winning streak coming up. During a trip to London he met the "crazy Frenchman," Bessemer (who was an Englishman of French extraction), watched in awe the fiery converter in action, and was in turn converted. He jumped the first steamer home and arrived in Pittsburgh proclaiming, *"The day of Iron has passed—Steel is King!"* A madness hit Braddock. "We must start the manufacture of steel rails and start at once," he ordered his partners. The switch from iron to steel was performed with desperate rapidity.

He knew little about the mechanics of steel conversion, and cared less. It was up to his subordinates to deliver. From his New York office on Broad Street, from his Pittsburgh mansion, from Europe (where he traveled many months each year) he goaded them with threats, promises, and barbed humor: "Puppy dog number three, you have

been beaten by puppy dog number two on fuel. Puppy
dog number two, you are higher on labor than puppy dog
number one."

When a manager cabled, "We broke all records for making steel last week," he responded, "Congratulations! *Why
not do it every week?*"

When an official reported an enormous order delivered
on time, he answered, "Good boy. Next!"

"Lucy Furnace No. 8 broke all records today." The reply: "What were the other ten furnaces doing?"

He cut prices, raised prices, broke contracts—all on a
moment's notice, without warning—obtained surreptitious
rebates from the biggest carriers, bribed rail purchasing
agents with undercover payouts as high as two dollars per
ton ("simply stealing," observed the president of the Santa
Fe). No stockholder existed to bother him if he wished to
pass a dividend to wreck part of a plant and erect new
facilities upon the ruins.

"When was there ever such a business!" exclaimed Carnegie. He was, in the words of one biographer, the cruelest
taskmaster in American industrial history. He hounded his
workers, managers, and partners, set one official against the
other, worked upon their jealousies and rivalries until one
would hardly speak to another, while he himself "drove
the whole bandwagon." Production and profits relentlessly
climbed. He seldom visited his plants. (A month in Pittsburgh, said a visiting English friend, would justify anybody to commit suicide.) When he did, it was to speed up
operations, to dispense cheer and encouragement, and to
enjoy democratically being called Andy by his workmen.
Once a government inspector stopped him. "Mr. Carnegie,
they tell me at the office they cannot guarantee more than

20,000 modulus of elasticity for the bridge. I must have at least 25,000."

"That sounds reasonable," said Carnegie. When the inspector voiced doubts, he added, "Yes, yes, I know all about that. I'll see that you get your full 25,000." After the man left, Carnegie called for an associate. "Dod, what on earth is a modulus of elasticity?" But Uncle Sam got his full 25,000, whatever it was.

In 1883 he gobbled up the Homestead mill.

For some time Carnegie and his associates had been uneasily watching the development of their powerful new rival on the Monongahela. Originally designed to manufacture a variety of products for its owning syndicate of six firms, it had been stampeded into the exclusive production of rails. The temptation to cash in on this single item is understandable, even though the mill was not built for it and had to be remodeled recklessly. The first rail was made in August, 1881. A month later Homestead was rolling two hundred tons of rails daily and had booked orders for fifteen thousand more. Prices were high, profits were strong, and the future looked rosy. In charge of the works was William Clark, implacable foe of labor unions and a skilled strikebreaker. Strike after bloody strike took place. Sabotage was rampant. Clark resigned. A scab who had shot one of the workers "in self-defense" was employed on a regular basis, while the man he had wounded was discharged. A decisive walkout followed.

The six member-firms were now in hopeless difficulties; a year of violence had disorganized the mill and slashed its output. The stockholders began quarreling. It was, in the slang expression of the day, a hell of a way to run a railroad—or a steel mill. Operating capital dwindled. Suddenly, somehow, Mr. Frick's coke was hard to buy. To make matters worse, business was poor and steel prices were tumbling. At this stage Carnegie, whose merry blue eyes had been watching the debacle, offered $350,000, giving the owners their option of accepting notes or an equivalent amount in Carnegie shares. All snatched the notes except William Singer, of Singer, Nimick & Company, who thought things over for a day and then decided to take shares. Carnegie extended his hand and said, "Wise man. Shake, pard." Singer's fifty-thousand-dollar allotment was later sold for about $8 million.

Soon Homestead had been enlarged, modernized, and reconverted almost completely to the manufacture of structural steel and armor plate. (There was no need for it to make rails; Braddock sufficed.) Purchased for a few scraps of paper, easily redeemed out of dividends within two years, it paid for itself a hundredfold by 1892.

During the mid-1880s Carnegie established the Hartman Steel Works at Beaver Falls—a minor accretion but a rather costly one which suffered a loss almost every year until it was sold, with relief, to the Wire Trust.

And finally (1890) the Carnegie firm consummated what was to be the last major industrial purchase of his life, although it was in fact Frick who captured Duquesne. That massive plant had gone into action early in 1889, using a new method of rolling to reduce the cost of rails and billets. Duquesne was underselling Braddock! Carnegie's response was to mail secretly a circular to all railroad purchasing agents throughout the country; it stated falsely that such rails were defective and it warned these gentlemen not to buy them. For months Carnegie exerted mighty pressures against the rail pool, which, at length, reluctantly excluded Duquesne from all desirable contracts. One Carnegie partner admitted that he ordinarily "would not have thought it legitimate; but the competition set up by the Duquesne people was also not legitimate, because of their use of this direct rolling process. They were a thorn in our flesh and they reduced the price of rails. If they had made rails by our method, we would have recognized them as legitimate competitors. . . ." The diagnosis was childlike, but the medicine worked. After a year of parleying with Frick, the Duquesne owners (beset further by the usual labor afflictions and a cash squeeze) accepted $1 million in bonds for the property and stepped aside. No cash had changed hands, and the works paid for themselves within a year.

Since direct rolling made better rails for less, it was continued at Duquesne and adopted at once in all other Carnegie steel mills.

The battle for supremacy in United States iron and steel was over. It had raged from 1865 to 1890 and had established Carnegie as its master and one of the most affluent men in the nation. Competition from Jones and Laughlin, the eastern Bethlehem firm, the Gary and Chicago group, Cambria, and others was minor and could be underpriced at will. Only the cry for steel, more and more steel, kept them all in business and estopped Carnegie from winning a majority of the total market. The twelve steel and coke works near Pittsburgh, employing thirteen thousand men, poured into his private pockets net untaxed profits between $2 million and $20 million per year, before and after his semiretirement in the eighties. His brother Tom[1] had been a marvel of efficiency and support.

[1] He died in November, 1886, a few days before the death of Mrs. Carnegie. Released from his vow, Andrew married Louise Whitfield of New York some months later. Their ages were fifty-two and twenty-eight.

Frick was a vital factor, of course. So were luck, able and energetic partners, the cream of the land's skilled metal-workers, plus outstanding plant superintendents. But in the final analysis one must return to Andrew Carnegie as the creator of his own destiny.

In tactical brilliance, audacity, charm, doggedness, and broadness of vision not even the methodical, calculating Mr. Frick could match him; and when it came time for battle Carnegie was ready for that, too. "Presently," wrote David Graham Phillips, "he would descend from his rail-perch, catch up a great club, and lay frantically about him. Bruised skulls here; broken skulls there; corpses yonder; fellows with raw heads and aching bones, crawling rapidly into the cover of the tall grass; imprecations filling the air. A scene of peaceful industry transformed into a shambles. Grinning grimly at his club, Carnegie would stroll back to his rail-perch. . . ." He was unbeatable. No firm could match his prices, his volume in rails, and his impregnable position as a supplier of crude steel, such as billets, to men like John Gates (American Steel and Wire) and William Moore (National Steel) who worked it into finished products.

As the nineties approached, his was by far the largest steel unit in America, accounting for over a fourth of the national output. Bad times only forced out marginal producers and helped strengthen Carnegie's grip. For example, between 1880 and 1885 rails plummeted from eighty-five to twenty-seven dollars per ton and still delivered him an adequate profit, to put it delicately. From his subsidiary Carnegie purchased coke at cost or below, while the Frick company sold it to outsiders at high figures. The differential here alone may have been decisive.

The tariff wall, as regards metals, played a diminishing

role, and its continuance after the high Tariff Act of 1883 was automatic and meaningless. Years before the Homestead affair the average United States steelworker was making 555 tons of steel yearly, compared to 420 tons in England's best plants at Sheffield and Birmingham. Add shipping charges, and it is plain that European suppliers could no longer compete successfully with Carnegie, even given free-trade conditions. Protection had continued long enough after the Civil War to permit survival of the embryonic American industry. Around 1880 the enormous duty of twenty-eight dollars per ton was levied on English and German rails, to keep them out of this country. The subsidy should not be underestimated. Yet at the same time Carnegie was rolling rails per ton at $37.77 and selling them for as high as eighty-five dollars. And still the demand for all types of iron and steel increased beyond the capacity of Americans to produce. As late as 1882 we were still importing foreign steel to the tune of $68 million. The profits, if any, realized by its makers overseas must have been meager indeed.

Passage of the McKinley Tariff Act of 1890 was like shooting a corpse. Except for a curious reduction in the rate on steel billets, it raised the duty on almost everything, especially the two major items—woolens and steel rails—but by then little steel (except billets) was entering the United States anyway. Since international trade is a double-edged sword, McKinley's bill left us with surpluses of pork, beef, wheat, and bitterness on the part of western farm interests. In a year when the Carnegie company was earning $40 million net, Mr. Carnegie at last suggested that the duties on foreign steel be dropped.

A selective tariff on British workers might have been more to his liking. The English, Scots, Welsh, and Irish

had always been troublemakers. Largely due to their independence and belligerence (and skills), his road to riches
was paved with poor labor relations. He won an initial
victory in 1867 by locking out his iron puddlers, who had
protested a wage reduction, and hiring large numbers of
foreign replacements. In 1875 he forestalled a strike at
Edgar Thomson by shutting down the works completely,
whereupon the men signed Carnegie's original agreement.
The 1884 strike at Beaver Falls was an outright test between the company and the Amalgamated. Carnegie entered the fray with some reluctance, remarking to a partner that nobody could whip that union "within the smoke
of Pittsburgh." It was done by importing workers from
adjacent areas. Riot and violence ensued, and were put
down, following which the ringleaders were tried and convicted on sundry counts. The union was forever barred
from the plant. Next year, again at the Edgar Thomson
works in Braddock, Captain Bill Jones fired practically the
entire working force and then forced them to return on his
terms: a severe wage cut and a return to the twelve-hour
day. By now the fog of hatred at Braddock could be cut
with a knife. And in 1877, at the same unhappy plant,
seven hundred men were fired outright and replaced by
non-unionists.

Such disputes were all too normal in the seething '70s.
The puzzle lies in Mr. Carnegie, whose left hand seemed
not to know what the right was doing. His didactic views
were well known; they had appeared in a series of *Forum*
articles during 1876. "The right of the workingmen to
combine," he wrote, "and to form trades-unions is no less
sacred than the right of the manufacturer to enter into
associations and conferences with his fellows, and it must
be sooner or later conceded." But less than a year later he

flatly declared Braddock non-union; henceforth no person
would be employed unless he signed an open-shop pledge.
The result was the 1877 incident noted above, and another
walkout.

It was the next to last strike at the Edgar Thomson
works in Braddock, and it lasted five gloomy months. Captain Jones kept the mill creaking along by calling in domestic and foreign strikebreakers, protected by a small
army of Pinkerton guards. The customary skirmishes and
murders took place before the company triumphed. Simultaneously, Carnegie's articles and book, *Triumphant Democracy,* were preaching the glories of labor and the evil
of strikebreaking. As for unions: ". . . it gives one a poor
opinion of the American workman if he permits himself to
be deprived of a right which his fellow in England has
conquered for himself long since. My experience has been
that trades-unions upon the whole are beneficial both to
labor and to capital."

He talked about arbitration, wrote of conciliation, and
was bold enough to condemn the twelve-hour day when it
was operational in each of his steel plants and the Frick
Coke Company. "Calling upon strange men should be the
last resort," he had written, referring to scabs. It was a "last
resort" incessantly with Mr. Carnegie. He retreated only
once. In 1887 the coke workers struck when he badly
needed fuel to keep his seven furnaces banked. The sequel
was unusually gory. Strikebreakers were beaten up and
shot, machinery wrecked, mines blown up by dynamite,
and not even the ubiquitous Pinkertons could stop thousands of tons of coke from spoiling in their ovens. Carnegie, honeymooning at his ten-thousand-acre Cluny
Castle estate in Scotland's Grampian Hills and doubtless in
a mellow mood, cabled Frick to capitulate. In a rage the

latter did so, and then momentarily resigned the presidency of his former company.

Carnegie had been caught napping. When another dispute arose in 1890 he was ready, with a substantial quantity of coke in inventory. He gave Frick a free hand. The results were the worst yet; they involved three months of slaughter and destruction, military formations on both sides, night raids by mobs of armed men, guerrilla warfare in the countryside, arson on a large scale, other acts of systematic sabotage, and, in the bitter end, total victory for management. The nearby iron and metal workers noted these remarkable events with surprise, for Carnegie's control of the coke firm was common knowledge. Was this the man, lovable little Andy, who had told America to improve the lot of the workers, who had reiterated the copartnership between labor and management? Was he the same Carnegie who so often had insisted (in writing) on collective bargaining, who hoped "that the ties of brotherhood may still bind together the rich and poor in harmonious relationship"?

No industrialist of his era had made a more favorable impression upon the nation. His writings and speeches were pro-union, liberal, humane, philanthropic, enlightened. The policies of his company were in stark contrast. Abominable working conditions were the rule, and hardly a year passed without a walkout or lockout of varying magnitude in one plant or another. The cleavage between theory and practice was bewildering. Did he believe what he wrote? When the chips were down and vital interests at stake, did his memory fail him? His later statement that he had never hired a strikebreaker is palpably untrue, except that he personally did no hiring or firing; but this is quibbling. Since we cannot read his mind, may we assume on the basis of the evidence that he was hypocritical? A clue is to be found in his observation "that upon the sacredness of property civilization itself depends—the right of the laborer to his hundred dollars in the saving bank, and equally the legal right of the millionaire to his millions." So both had their rights, but one side had enormously more than the other.

Presumably he meant well toward his workmen. Possibly he favored unions, provided they were nothing more than company unions, toys of management, without striking power. He seemed to enjoy talking personally to his men about their grievances, provided they deferred to him, cap in hand, accepted his benign decisions, and did not talk back. It may be that the role of a kindly dictator suited him. Certainly his *Autobiography* abounds with soggy condescensions and an almost ethnic distinction between rich and poor, employer and employee: "If I returned to work tomorrow, fear of labor troubles would not enter my mind, but tenderness for poor and sometimes misguided though well-meaning laborers would fill my heart and soften it. . . ."

What union official sent this cable during the biggest strike of all? "Kind master, tell us what you wish us to do and we shall do it for you." The phrasing sounds more like Carnegie, writing his memoirs in 1916, than an Amalgamated man imploring him a generation earlier; nor does the cable appear to exist today.

He quotes himself in conference with a mill committee: " 'There spoke the true American workman,' I said. 'I am proud of you.' "

After a small joke by Carnegie before another labor committee: "There was loud laughter, followed by applause, and then more laughter. I laughed with them."

After the smashing of a strike: "Although their labor union is dissolved another and better one has taken its place—a cordial union between the employers and their men, the best union of all for both parties." Here, perhaps, is the most revealing statement of all. In the last analysis, each observer will judge the man as he sees fit.

Mr. Carnegie was planning to be in Scotland for the grouse season of early 1889. William L. Abbott had just taken over as general manager and chairman of the board. At this juncture a problem arose at Homestead.

"Carnegie never wanted to know the profits," observed one partner. "He always wanted to know the cost." He was the first steelmaker to introduce a primitive cost-accounting system. The search for economy led him into constant collisions with his labor force; thus, in 1889 his proposed wage scale amounted to a 25 percent cut across the board. In addition, each man was asked to sign an individual agreement, which meant the end of collective bargaining. They were to be protected, on the other hand, by Mr. Carnegie's famous sliding scale (already in effect at Braddock and Duquesne), which tied wages to the selling price, month by month, of 4-inch by 4-inch Bessemer steel billets: a basic, rough, unfinished product. When billets went up or down in the market, their pay would do the same and in the identical proportion, except that during the three-year duration of the contract the wage scale would not be affected if billets fell below twenty-five dollars per ton. There was to be no maximum.

The men turned the proposition down. Mr. Carnegie brought in detectives disguised as laborers. They listened to the talk in saloons and stores, took rooms in Homestead, and conversed with the employees' mothers and wives. Reports of the gossip were sent to the steel master, who perused them in his New York library, the walls of which were splattered with heraldic Scottish devices and framed quotations praising the virtues of the workingman. Exhorting his partners to stand fast, he left for Scotland in April. The virtuous workingmen then walked out en masse. When the sheriff deputized about a hundred idlers from the streets and saloons of Pittsburgh and brought them to Homestead, they were given a rude reception. Women threw scalding water at them. Mobs of strikers divested them of their caps, coats, and "billies." Not one deputy or strikebreaker, whom the former was to protect, got into the plant. Those who tried to land at the waterfront entrance were also turned away. Mass picketing set in, as the two sides finally sat down to negotiate.

Mr. Abbott had always been a production man, pure and simple. Even with Mr. Frick at his elbow, he was evidently not equipped to handle labor relations on a scale this large; for the agreement signed in July was a clear-cut victory in principle for the Amalgamated as well as the non-unionists—despite Abbott's assertion that "both sides are victors, and both sides are probably vanquished in minute details." Each contestant was satisfied with the sliding scale. The company knew where it stood from a labor-cost view, and had no fear of sudden, irrational strikes for three years. The workers saw no flaw in it and appreciated the $25-per-ton base. Having been recognized, and negotiated with, the Amalgamated was jubilant. The proposed wage reductions were compromised, and some annoying procedural demands of the workers were surprisingly accepted. Mr. Carnegie was stunned when he heard the news; from Europe he wrote his partners that it had been wrong to settle with "law breakers." But the deed was writ, nor could it be erased until after June 30, 1892. Since 4 by 4's were selling for $26.50 in July, 1889, the tonnage men immediately received a wage "plus" for that month of 6 percent over the minimum.

Only Mr. Frick had soured the milk of victory. Over and over during the conversations, in his quiet way he had suggested that the Amalgamated Association at Homestead should dissolve, that the lodges should in effect commit suicide. He had been overruled, but his rising power in the Carnegie domain was understood; clearly he boded no good for the future. For the present, in the words of a labor journal, the Amalgamated stood "head and shoulders higher than ever before, for it comes out of one of the most difficult crises in its history intact, with honor and with the renewed confidence of the public."

Then, too, there had been a rumor concerning the Pinkertons. It is true that 120 of them had been engaged (sources vary as to who exactly had hired them); however, Mr. Abbott had come to terms before their arrival, for fear that widespread destruction of company property was imminent.

So for three uneasy years both sides had something to think about. Carnegie and Frick balefully contemplated the Amalgamated, a bone in their throats. The employees considered Mr. Frick, watched his methods in the Connellsville coke strike of 1890, and pondered his ominous words. They also noted his continuing affinity toward the use of Pinkerton guards in large numbers, to intimidate strikers and to escort strikebreakers. But July, 1892, was still quite a distance away, and meanwhile the price of billets held steady between $25.25 and $26.50, after an exhilarating jump to $36.00 in December, 1889.

Like a time bomb, the months ticked by in the half-day, half-night, smoke-laden gloom of Pittsburgh and its gaunt, clamorous suburbs, all of which were now infiltrated by

Pinkerton labor spies. Generally these men were recruited by advertisements such as this:

WANTED—A bright, experienced salesman to handle a good line. Salary and commission. Excellent opportunity for right man to connect with first-class house. State age, experience and references. W–276–Post.

A large majority of applicants rejected the Pinkerton offer upon ascertaining the nature of their duties. Each selected "operative" was sent (say) to Homestead, where he took a single room, secured a job in the plant instantly (*mirabile dictu*), and began reporting names, facts, and fantasies—always in writing—to a fictitious name in care of a post-office box. He was paid about eighteen dollars weekly, plus expenses; peculiarly, his wages at the plant were remitted to the Pinkerton office and credited to Carnegie. The spy lived in constant fear of detection; if exposed he was likely to be badly beaten, run out of town, and never again employed by Pinkerton.

The Pinkerton National Detective Agency and its operatives were pathologically detested by the American working class. Since its founding under Allan Pinkerton at mid-century it had participated, always on the side of management, in seventy major labor disputes. Its two thousand trained active men and thirty thousand reserves totaled more than the standing army of the nation. An unpleasant number of them were trigger-happy. Their latest exploit had just taken place (1890) during a strike at Mr. Vanderbilt's New York Central Railway, in the course of which they had killed five people, including a woman. Ex-soldiers and ex-policemen were given preference by agency interviewers. Once a radical, Allan Pinkerton had written frankly in 1878 that "since the strikes of '77, my agencies

have been busily employed by great railway, manufacturing and other corporations, for the purpose of bringing the
leaders and instigators [of strikes] to the punishment they
so richly deserve. Hundreds have been punished. Hundreds more will be punished." Upon his death in 1884, the
agency passed under the thumbs of his sons, Robert and
William, who continued to do business as usual. Their
men were invariably armed—the undercover operatives as
well as uniformed guards—and almost never were deputized. Having no legality, they amounted to a private army
available for hire. Little had been done to curb them, although a few states (such as New York) had passed anti-
Pinkerton statutes of varying degrees of severity; and it
had been established in court that the carrying of arms
across state borders by groups of associated men was a criminal offense.

From their main offices in Chicago and New York City,
Pinkerton commanders continued to evade these rather
mild restrictions by subterfuge or smooth technicalities.
The motto of the agency was "We Never Sleep." Its trade-
mark was an open left eye ("eye sinister"), which led to
the colloquial term "private eye"—later simply "eye."

Peacefully the famous decade dawned. Business was
firm. At Homestead between 1889 and 1892 the 32-inch
slabbing mill had raised its output 20 percent, the 119-
inch mill 52 percent, the open-hearth furnaces about 17
percent. March and December were designated "record"
months, when at Carnegie's personal insistence the men
and the mills were pushed to the limit. The labor force
worked overtime at extra pay, and not even for an hour
did the works come to a halt. When a record was broken,
Superintendent John Potter passed out cigars. Country-

wide the average yearly wage paid to iron and steel workers climbed slowly to over $550. In early 1892, however,
the price of billets sagged to $23.75; and, while tonnage
men continued to be paid relative to the minimum base of
$25.00, it was generally felt that the situation was not alto-
gether healthy.

Mr. Carnegie, now somewhat paunchy and quite gray,
continued to spend half of each year in Europe, endowing
libraries and hobnobbing with royalty, writers, statesmen,
artists, and assorted celebrities. His new possession, Skibo
Castle in the Highlands near Dornoch Firth, made the old
Cluny Castle estate appear a hovel by comparison. Here,
gaily imperious, he held court. Some visitors were known
furtively to leave the premises because of his mode of life.
Everyone was awakened early in the morning to the skirl-
ing of bagpipes. Organ music escorted them to breakfast.
They had to golf, ride, sail, and eat upon command, and
listen to his endless discourses. Carnegie abhorred smoking
and would not allow it in his home. He drank wine lightly
at meals and (the crowning blow) even insisted upon regulating the alcoholic intake of his visitors.

Back at home, baseball was the national sport, and even
in toil-ridden towns like Homestead the fortunes of the
Pittsburgh Pirates were followed with intensity. "Ta-ra-ra-
boom-de-ay" was the hit song, followed by "The Picture
That Is Turned to the Wall" and "My Sweetheart's the
Man in the Moon." That man, William Jennings Bryan of
Illinois, soon to become an ogre in the eyes of conservatives, sat in Congress, having converted the large Republican majority of his district into a handy Democratic majority in November, 1890.

The Democratic governor of Pennsylvania, Robert E.
Pattison, was presiding for his second term at the state

capital in Harrisburg. He was a handsome man in his early forties, a former attorney, a strong and liberal executive. Committed to economy and reform, his administration had taken a courageous stand against certain abuses of the railroads and holding companies. He had appointed one William H. McCleary as sheriff of Allegheny County, which encompassed all the Carnegie iron and steel works. McCleary's prime qualification for the job was a drooping handle-bar mustache, without which no law officer of those days would be caught dead. Otherwise he was a tall, gangly, ineffective man held in low esteem by the citizenry.

Early in 1892 two young immigrants were living together in sin (one regrets to report) and operating a small restaurant in Worcester, Massachusetts. Considering their ideology, it was doing disturbingly well. In time it might have made them capitalists. The girl was twenty-two, somewhat plump but not unattractive. Her lover was a year older: thin, dark, muscular, morose. These Russian Jews had fled to America in 1885 and 1888 respectively, and both Emma Goldman and Alexander Berkman were extreme anarchists of the direct-action school. Perhaps they had never heard of Henry Clay Frick.

SEN. JACOB H. GALLINGER (*Rep., N.H.*): *Then you did not find these men whom the Pinkertons employed a very high grade of men, did you?*

ROBERT BRUCE (*private detective*): *They were the scum of the earth. I have known him to employ ex-convicts. He has a man, manager of his agency now, that was run out of Cincinnati for blackmail—Charles Wappenstein.*

GALLINGER: *They were irresponsible men, of little account, as a class?*

BRUCE: *There is not one out of ten that would not commit murder.*

GALLINGER: *Would you, from your knowledge of these men, be inclined to accept without verification the reports they would make?*

BRUCE: *I would not believe any detective under oath without his evidence was corroborated.*

GALLINGER: *Does that apply to yourself?*

BRUCE: *Yes, sir; it will apply to myself.*

—*Senate testimony*

IV *The Issue Joined*

In January the company asked the Amalgamated to prepare a new wage scale. Presented to Superintendent Potter next month at the company's Fifth Street offices in Pittsburgh, it was similar to the prevailing agreement except that—evidently for bargaining purposes—some small increases were requested in various departments. Potter merely glanced at it, and in return handed Mr. Frick's prepared counteroffer to William T. Roberts of the union. The committee crowded around and read it with some dismay.

Three fundamental demands leaped from the typewritten pages: First, the minimum would be reduced to a market price of twenty-two dollars per ton of steel billets. Second, the expiration date would be changed from June 30 to December 31, 1893, the worst possible time of year for a strike or layoff. Third, a reduction in tonnage rates would take effect in the 32-inch slabbing mill, the 119-inch plate mill, and the open-hearth furnaces—those very departments which employed practically all 325 Amalgamated men. The document admitted that they would be reduced 18 percent in take-home pay. On the other hand, a few men working elsewhere in the plant would be raised. Roberts noted that his own rate would drop from $3.11 per hundred tons to $2.13. Almost apologetically Potter said, "Billy, you haven't any idea of the large amount of money our heaters are drawing here, and the firm has come to the conclusion that somebody must take a reduction."

Roberts (himself a thirty-six-year-old heater who drew about one hundred dollars monthly) replied, "If that is the case, why have you made the reductions on the men who have made nothing for so long? These men you propose to reduce have not averaged over one dollar a day for the past eight weeks."

Otis Childs, Frick's chief assistant and a prominent shareholder, interposed, "There must be some mistake there. There is no one in our mill working for so little money." Potter explained to him that the department in question had been frequently idle since the year began. (Since heaters were tonnage men protected by the twenty-five dollar minimum, their pay had not yet been adjusted.) After an embarrassed pause, Mr. Childs announced an adjournment for two weeks.

Meetings held March 1, May 29, and June 23 clarified

and hardened the issues; and except for a slight compromise by both sides in the last session, to be noted later, and a willingness on the part of the union to abandon its increased wage demands, they involved no changes in the positions taken. Basically the differences were minor, and might have been easily resolved. But the arguments were clouded by semantic confusion; arithmetic was pulled, pushed, and strained to the breaking point; statistics were twisted out of shape to prove a point or to disprove the same point. The Amalgamated Association was scarcely discussed at all, whereas the great unspoken fear of that organization was that any concessions permitted at Homestead would ruin its bargaining power coast to coast, and perhaps the union itself. Was it the intention of Frick and Carnegie to liquidate the Amalgamated at Homestead, or dilute its powers? If even today it is difficult to reach clear-cut opinions on the issues at stake, it was impossible in the overheated atmosphere of 1892. Step by step, the logic on both sides was contradictory and yet correct; for each party was opposed to the other's interests and could only fathom its own. Any discussion, however rational, between a Christian and a Mohammedan is not likely to convert either to the other's faith, especially if one secretly intends to slay the other in order to teach him respect for the true faith. The dispute over the three-dollar base reduction illustrates the dichotomy of interest between the company and the union, and therefore the dichotomy of reasoning.

Carnegie officials said it was unfair to have a minimum base at all. There was no maximum. Why should the scale not slide freely in both directions? Suppose billets went sky-high, while other products remained stable in price; should wages soar only in relation to the former? Suppose billets plunged to twenty, or fifteen, or heaven knows what low price, at which the company would suffer losses; why should the workers not suffer accordingly? Indeed, by spring the market price of billets had dropped to twenty-two dollars. The company claimed it was being generous by reducing the minimum to that figure, instead of eliminating the bottom base altogether.

But why, inquired the Amalgamated, had billets declined almost 40 percent in slightly over two years? For one thing, the Duquesne mill was capable of breakneck production. Carnegie could, and did, swamp the land with cheap billets, sell them near cost, and thereby depress those wages at Homestead which were pegged to them. They claimed that his leverage at Duquesne was a never-ending menace. It was the Homestead craftsmen who paid, in truth, whenever Carnegie wished to undercut his competitors in the billet market. They also asserted that he had secretly helped bring about that singular lowering of duties on foreign billets in the McKinley Tariff, which brought more 4 by 4's into the United States market and even further downward pressures. Finally, they alluded to the possibility of Carnegie conniving with his buyers and competitors to suppress billet prices. For these reasons they insisted upon the protection of the current minimum.

As to terminating the contract in December rather than June, management pointed out that its contracts for materials and sales were usually signed soon after the first of each year. Thus, if labor costs were to be fixed just prior to that time, the company could accurately compute how much to pay for raw materials and what to charge for finished products.

The workmen derided this viewpoint, which implied that Carnegie scrupulously reflected conditions within the market rather than vice versa. Also, they were willing to have the wage contract run for any number of years, and the company could determine its wage costs in advance whenever it pleased. Anyway, they said, the whole argument was nonsense because of the fact that wages were adjusted every six months to correlate with average billet prices during the previous six months. They made no secret of the fact that previous midwinter strikes, with their attendant hardships, rendered them helpless to resist. Company officials, in rebuttal, produced evidence that in the South Chicago steel rail mill (a competitor of Carnegie) the Amalgamated allowed its scale to end on December 31. Why not at Homestead? The union replied that the Chicago contract was unique, in order to compete with non-union Braddock.

When it came to the scale itself, management was adamant. Millions had been spent on new equipment—by whom? When output rocketed as a result, the workers paid on tonnage received spiraling wages without expending more time or energy. Why should they benefit from the company's enormous capital expenditures? Consider the 119-inch mill. In 1889 plates had been rolled directly from ingots, and the average tonnage was 2,500 monthly. Now they passed through a new million-dollar 32-inch slabbing machine before entering the 119-inch mill. Consequently tonnage had risen over 50 percent without the men lifting a finger or investing a cent. A similar development had occurred in the open-hearth department. Only 325 men out of 3,800, furthermore, would be affected by pay cuts; and these cuts would average a mere 18 percent. To cap the climax, all non-union men in eight of the twelve departments had just signed a new three-year contract with the company. Obviously they were satisfied. And what if they later joined the Amalgamated? Impossible; they were ineligible under union rules.

The organized men showed figures which proved that their pay would drop over 25 percent, not 18. They said the reductions amounted to 18 percent on tonnage alone, plus 7 percent on the scale. They claimed that all 3,800 workers would be harmed by at least one of the three proposals. They said that the skilled employees had suggested, or actually designed, many of the improvements. Why should they not get part of the credit in hard cash? And what of the layoffs due to increased efficiency? The savings in wages were absorbed by the company, not the remaining men. They disputed the claim that their work was easier than before, insisted that more mental concentration, physical strength, and danger were involved in handling the massive, complex new machinery. True, 3,500 men were not affected by the new scale; but what if Mr. Frick decided to put everybody (except day laborers) on tonnage rates? Nobody could stop him from throwing all the semiskilled mechanics into the same boat as the Amalgamated members, and, in fact, the former were known to be worried about precisely that. They and the day men had signed up mainly because they felt that the company was bluffing, as it apparently did in 1889. Good old Andy, "the little boss," would not fight his own laborers nor disturb their organization, his affection for unions being surpassed only by his love for the American workingman. In any event, without his ultraskilled Amalgamated specialists he simply could not make steel at Homestead. So ran their arguments and reasoning.

As to which side had the better case, history provides no clear answer. A curiosity of the imbroglio is the appalling moral and statistical difficulty in appraising the respective arguments generations later, when all the evidence is at hand. What, for example, could be more demonstrably correct than the union's stand concerning the minimum billet base? But *was* it correct? Mr. Frick insisted that its basic premise was not.

These are his words (uttered in July, but apropos here): "Mr. McLuckie stated that we had purchased the Duquesne steel plant for the purpose of making billets in order to reduce the price of billets and thus affect the wages at the Homestead works . . . to show how absurd this is, our pay roll at Homestead for the month of May was over $200,000. Only about 40 percent of the pay roll is affected by the sliding scale . . . say it is $80,000. We manufacture at Duquesne about 20,000 tons of billets monthly. Say we reduce the price of billets $1 per ton in order that it might have an effect upon the wages at Homestead. A reduction of $1 would mean a loss of $20,-000 at these works to us. We will succeed by that, we will say, in reducing the wages of our Homestead men, which amounts to $80,000 a month, 3.78 percent—we will call it 4 percent; 4 percent of $80,000 is $3,200. So, according to the reasoning of Mr. McLuckie, by losing $20,000 at Duquesne we would save $3,200 at Homestead. I think that will be plain to anybody . . . eventually we would have to go into bankruptcy."

What is plain to anybody is that confusion, bias, and what is now called double-talk reigned in all areas of the argument; there are no exceptions, including the above quotation, which can as easily be torn apart as any other.

The meeting held March 1 was brief and accomplished nothing. Potter told Roberts to come back with power to act and to sign. Roberts visited Amalgamated headquarters and returned next day carrying a written authorization. "You can tell your people," he said, "we are willing to make any reductions where they can show any reductions are necessary. We want to settle it without trouble; don't want a strike." Potter was evasive and the matter rested for three entire months. During this time the Homestead lodges hurriedly recruited new members and brought their strength up to almost seven hundred, with more to join during June. Nationally the Amalgamated Association had also made big gains since the 1889 event. Its membership had increased by half, its treasury from $25,000 to $146,-000. In steel plants throughout America its members grew more pugnacious, aggressive, self-confident. Manufacturers began talking gloomily about forming an employers' association, but did nothing. They merely prayed for Mr. Carnegie, their St. George, to battle and destroy the dragon which menaced them all.

Early in May the great man sailed for Europe, after drafting a "notice" to Homestead employees stating in part: "These Works having been consolidated with the Edgar Thomson and Duquesne, and other mills, there has been forced upon this Firm the question whether its Works are to be run 'Union' or 'Non-Union.' As the vast majority of our employees are Non-Union, the Firm has decided that the minority must give place to the majority. These works, therefore, will be necessarily Non-Union after the expiration of the present agreement. . . . This action is not taken in any spirit of hostility to labor organizations, but every man will see that the firm cannot run Union and Non-Union. It must be one or the other."

The notice was sent from New York to Frick in Pittsburgh. Frick regarded it as premature and refused to publish it. He did, however, pay heed to a marginal note added by Carnegie: "Should this be determined upon, Mr. Potter *should roll a large lot of plates ahead,* which can be finished, should the works be stopped for a time."[1] In consequence, production was pushed to an abnormal peak in May. While tonnage men benefited accordingly, it was questionable for management to refer to these wages as though they were typical.

For the time all was superficially quiet. Mr. Frick still could not decide whether the fight should be fought, and wrote Carnegie that "the magnitude of our business is such that there are plenty of important matters to take up without being troubled with strikes." His moment of doubt was brief. On May 29 the union committee was called in once more, and Mr. Frick's paper was read to them. After a review of the company position, and a passage complaining about intolerable wages being paid that month, Frick announced that the union men would have to accept his scale by June 24. If not, they would be dealt with individually. The challenge to the Amalagmated could not have been more blunt; it could surrender, it could disband, or it could strike.

Grim with anger, Roberts faced Potter. "Do you think this is fair; do you think this is giving us a chance to talk the matter over? You people, when I was here last, told me if I would come back with power to make a scale, that you were willing to enter into negotiations and try and arrange things in an amicable manner."

"I cannot help it. It is Mr. Frick's ultimatum."

"John, I don't think that is a square deal." There was little more to say. The company and union officials on

---

1 Similarly, prior to the steel walkout of July, 1959, the industry produced enough steel in six months to keep the economy supplied almost to the end of the year.

hand knew that the ultimatum would be spurned; they knew that Frick knew it; and probably all would have agreed with Roberts "that they did it with the intention of forcing this trouble." For the record, Frick wrote Potter a day after the blow had fallen, "The scales have had most careful consideration, with a desire to act toward our employés in the most liberal manner. A number of rates have been advanced upon your recommendation, and the wages which will be earned thereunder are considerably in advance of those received by the employés of any of our competitors in the same lines. You can say to the committee that these scales are in all respects the most liberal that can be offered. We do not care whether a man belongs to a union or not, nor do we wish to interfere . . . but we think our employés at Homestead Steel Works would fare much better working under the system [non-union] in vogue at Edgar Thomson and Duquesne."

The anti-union sentiments of Carnegie's officials became increasingly clear. One partner stated that "the Amalgamated placed a tax on improvements" and therefore had to go. It was the crux of the matter. Correspondence from Mr. Carnegie, then in England, swelled in volume and fervor. On June 10: "As I understand matters at Homestead, it is not only the wages paid, but the number of men required by Amalgamated rules which makes our labor rates so much higher than those in the East. . . . I know you will decline all conferences, as you have taken your stand and have nothing more to say. It is fortunate that only a part of the Works are concerned. Provided you have plenty of plates rolled, I suppose you can keep on with armor. Potter will, no doubt, intimate to the men that refusal of scale means running only as Non-Union. This may cause acceptance, but I do not think so."

He counterpointed the theme on June 17: "Perhaps if Homestead men understand that *non-acceptance means Non-Union forever*, they will accept." Again, on June 28: "Cables do not seem favorable to a settlement at Homestead. If these be correct, this is your chance to reorganize the whole affair, and someone over Potter should exact good reasons for *employing every man*. Far too many men required by Amalgamated rules."[2] And in a later communication from Frick to Carnegie: "The mills have never been able to turn out the product they should, owing to being held back by the Amalgamated men." There were too many workers, in other words, and one union too many.

The annual Amalgamated convention was held in Pittsburgh starting June 7. In a packed meeting at the Opera House, brawny John McLuckie shouted, "We were persuaded to vote the Republican ticket four years ago . . . voted for high tariff and you get high fences, Pinkerton detectives, thugs and militia!" What inspired this wild prediction? Other speakers advised the Homestead men to stand firm, but to act moderately.

Cleveland was chosen by the Democrats in Chicago. One of the strongest planks in his platform was an accusation that the McKinley Tariff was fraudulent, and that calamities impending in the iron and steel industry would soon prove it.

2 Years later Carnegie wrote much nonsense concerning Homestead, for public consumption, in his autobiography: "The earnings of the men would have been thirty percent greater than under the old scale." "Some of the leaders . . . insisted upon demanding the whole sixty percent" of the increase in tonnage. His policy was always "that of patiently waiting, reasoning with them, and showing that their demands were unfair; but never attempting to employ new men in their places—never." (The word "always" in the place of "never" would be more accurate.) Only 218 rollers and heaters, he said, were involved; and so on.

During mid-June lesser steel manufacturers in the nearby Shenango and Mahoning valleys announced wage cuts between 20 and 60 percent—tiny straws in a big wind. Carnegie officials handed a statement to Pittsburgh newspapers explaining that the old scale had to be cancelled because of the collapsing market. Was the company truly *in extremis?*

From Republican newspapers and wealthy party stalwarts throughout the land came anxious appeals to Frick not to cut wages during the campaign. He ignored them. With sinking hearts they nominated Mr. Harrison.

On June 20, four days before Frick's ultimatum was to expire, he wrote Robert Pinkerton in New York in reference to hiring a large number of guards. Pinkerton replied affirmatively. He could furnish enough men to whip the British army. How many did Frick want? The price would be five dollars per head per day.

Chief attorney for the Carnegie company, Philander C. Knox, next asked Sheriff McCleary if he would deputize the Pinkertons when they arrived. McCleary stalled typically: mebbe he would, mebbe he wouldn't.

Meanwhile another of Mr. Frick's inspirations was in process: a great fence, a dozen feet high, three miles long, stoutly constructed of two-inch stock. Completely surrounding the works, it started where McClure Street met the Monongahela waterfront on the west, jogged east, then south for half a mile to Eighth Avenue, and eastward along that alcoholic street of dismal repute until it again met the river. Three strands of barbed wire (the workers believed them to be electrified) were stretched on top. The fence was augmented by several platforms upon which searchlights were mounted. Behind them pipes were laid, to which were attached hoses capable of throwing water under pressure. Over two hundred holes, three inches in diameter, were bored into the fence—every twenty-five feet, specifically—at about the height of a man's shoulder. Who was to peer, or fire, or throw water through so many apertures?

The employees watched these elaborate precautions in astonishment, called the finished product "Fort Frick," and laughed at a little poem, "The Fort That Frick Built":

> There stands today with great pretense
> Enclosed within a whitewashed fence
> A wondrous change of great import,
> The mills transformed into a fort.

Uneasiness was mixed with their derision and resentment, for news had leaked out that the company was cancelling orders which would have kept the plant humming for months to come. Tensions were coming to a head. A new conference, finally arranged for June 23, would have to be decisive either way. William Roberts, still the union's most active and intelligent negotiator, headed the labor committee and for the first time met Henry Frick personally. Roberts reduced the billet minimum to twenty-four dollars and discarded all requests for wage boosts, but insisted that no cuts of over 15 percent would be tolerated in any department. Mr. Frick left the room after a few minutes, complaining that the labor committee was too large to deal with. After some hours he sent a written note raising his minimum to twenty-three dollars. Nothing else would be conceded.

Amalgamated President Weihe, unperturbed to the end, was one of precious few who still believed a compromise would be evolved before the contract's expiration date. As he stated: "My experience has been in the last nine or ten years that very often when a conference took place in the beginning it looked as if no agreement could be reached, but when the day came upon which the scale expired, agreements were reached, and the work went on through conciliation." But despite his soothing words the fateful date of June 24 came and went without incident. An icy calm settled over Homestead. Next day Mr. Frick wrote Robert Pinkerton the inevitable, the predictable, letter:

> We will want 300 guards for service at our Homestead mills as a measure of precaution against interference with our plan to start operation of the works July 6th, 1892.
>
> The only trouble we anticipate is that an attempt will be made to prevent such of our men with whom we will by that time have made satisfactory arrangements from going to work, and possibly some demonstration of violence upon the part of those whose places have been filled, or most likely by an element which usually is attracted to such scenes for the purpose of stirring up trouble.
>
> We are not desirous that the men you send shall be armed unless the occasion properly calls for such a measure later on. . . .
>
> These guards should be assembled at Ashtabula, Ohio, not later than the morning of July 5th, when they may be taken by train to McKee's Rocks, or some other point upon the Ohio River below Pittsburgh, where they can be transferred to boats and landed within the enclosure of our premises at Homestead. We think absolute secrecy essential in the movement of these men. . . .
>
> As soon as your men are upon the premises we will notify the Sheriff and ask that they be deputized either at once or immediately upon an outbreak of such a character as to render such a step desirable.

Mr. Frick was not the only man to expect—perhaps even to desire—a collision once and for all. The strain of the past few months had produced a state of mind in both camps not unlike that of statesmen and generals on the brink of war. Discussions were getting nowhere. Hatreds were mounting to a level where they could scarcely be bottled up. The antagonists were each convinced that they were absolutely right; even Roberts was sick of wasting his breath on the "capitalists," as he called them. The erection of Fort Frick and the hard stand taken by management on June 23 had poisoned the air. It dawned upon the workmen that there would be no more conferences. On the other side of the fence, Frick and his aides were disgusted with the union for countering lucid company arguments with juvenile responses and token concessions. Days were slipping by like hours. There was no longer time to convene a neutral board of arbitration. As June neared its end, there was no longer time, really, for anything but direct action.

The union awoke to reality, formed an Advisory (strike) Committee of five delegates from each of the eight Homestead lodges, and named Hugh O'Donnell chairman. Intense, quick-thinking, an excellent speaker, handsomely attired, both cautious and aggressive in nature (depending on circumstances), he was exceedingly admired by the rank and file. He was also envied for having the prettiest wife in town. O'Donnell was tall, slim, and pale-complexioned. His stiff black hair was cut short and stood straight up. Descended from one of the most notable families in Ireland, the history of which is studded with Hugh O'Donnells, born in America about 1863, he had worked during boyhood as a newspaper reporter before he unaccountably drifted into steelworking. By 1892 he was a heater on the eight-hour turn, averaging $144 per month. He owned his home clear. It was one of the most pleasant in town, with a Brussels carpet in the parlor, a piano, and an extensive book collection which included a set of the *Encyclopaedia*

Britannica. He had never failed to vote Republican. A few other members of the Advisory Committee were less stable in nature. Hugh Ross, a shearman, was clever but much too fond of fighting. Jack Clifford was the most dangerous man in town; unless carefully watched he was certain to go wild under stress. William Roberts, Burgess McLuckie and the benign William Weihe were appointed as a matter of course. Would they help curb the more unruly youngsters?

The last days of June were frantic, kaleidoscopic; to sort their components into precise chronology would be futile. It has been said, perhaps debatably, that the matter of survival is not negotiable. Thus the week has a nightmarish tinge, full of sound and fury, accompanied by a realization that the issue is finally and truly joined. In a fury the employees moved to protect their work, their very existence (for they knew no other); the great company prepared to crush its mightiest and most tenacious opponent —that very group, paradoxically, which helped produce its goods and create its profits. These men knew the Pinkertons were coming; reports from Amalgamated spies in Chicago and New York had already reached Homestead. Moreover, the non-union employees—even the day laborers (who guessed wrong, as it happens)—were now convinced that if the strike were to be lost they would be put on the cheapest possible tonnage rates.

It remained to be seen if this dire apprehension would be justified. Meanwhile the men worked on. They joked about Fort Frick, peered curiously through the loopholes, told each other half in jest that it was only the bottom half of the ninth and the ball game wasn't over, that the last card still hadn't been dealt, that the fat wasn't yet in the fire. Thus, in the idioms of the day, they pretended there would still be one more conference to solve everything.

Strangely enough, the mills went wild with activity on June 25–27, especially in the armor plate division. Thundering, shuddering, belching smoke and flame, the converting department, too, broke all production records for a three-day stretch. This brief, hysterical period of maximum output created a surface illusion that nothing was really wrong. At the Upper and Lower Union Mills in Pittsburgh the company signed routine contracts, ending June 30, 1895, with the Amalgamated Association. The Homestead men marveled—was a break at hand? But to the newspapers Francis T. E. Lovejoy stated unequivocally that negotiations were at an end. Stores and saloons were nearly deserted now; the townspeople were commencing to hang onto their cash. It occurred to them that the 33rd Street Union Mill was capable of filling contracts for structural steel, the inference being that the company was preparing for a long siege.

Tuesday, June 28, without warning, the armor plate mill and open-hearth department were shut down, an action which put eight hundred men out of work. That night effigies of Frick and Potter were hung from a telegraph pole within the works. A clerk sent to cut down the figures was driven away with a water hose. It was the last straw; as one historian writes, "Frick had patently tried to force the workmen into opposition, and he had succeeded." He began firing men in other departments, one or two hundred at a time. The Advisory Committee responded boldly by passing a resolution demanding that all non-union employees refuse to return to work July 1. O'Donnell submitted the request before a hot, tumultuous, noisy meeting of three thousand workers jam-packing the Opera House. He asked for a vote and explained that the decision would be binding on all, regardless of union affiliation. It was passed overwhelmingly. Another speaker told of a rumor that two hundred scabs were en route, disguised as Pinkertons. The word went around: "Watch the depots."

The strike vote was a blow to Carnegie officials, who had never even remotely considered fighting anyone but a few hundred Amalgamated people. More men were laid off wholesale. At union headquarters O'Donnell fought back with a statement, freely circulated, which amounted to a declaration of war: "The Committee has, after mature deliberation, decided to organize their forces on a truly military basis. The force of four thousand men has been divided into three divisions or watches, each of these divisions is to devote eight hours of the twenty-four to the task of watching the plant. The Commanders of these divisions are to have as assistants eight captains composed of one trusted man from each of the eight local lodges. These Captains will report to the Division Commanders, who in turn will receive the orders of the Advisory Committee. During their hours of duty these Captains will have personal charge of the most important posts, i.e., the river front, the water gates and pumps, the railway stations, and the main gates of the plant. The girdle of pickets will file reports to the main headquarters every half hour, and so complete and detailed is the plan of campaign that in ten minutes' time the Committee can communicate with the men at any given point within a radius of five miles. In addition to all this, there will be held in reserve a force of 800 Slavs and Hungarians. The brigade of foreigners will be under the command of two Hungarians and two interpreters."

Firing continued at an accelerated pace until July 2, when the last several hundred men were dismissed. The process took six hours, seventy thousand dollars were disbursed at the offices just inside the main gate on Eighth Avenue, and for a time the scene almost turned into a riot. A final, official note was distributed by Lovejoy to Pittsburgh reporters: "Hereafter the Homestead steel works will be operated as a non-union mill. . . . There will be, no doubt, a scale of wages; but we shall deal with the men individually, not with any organization." He added, "There will be no further conferences with the Amalgamated Association."

Deserted, except for some striking watchmen and government inspectors, the great plant lay idle now, and silent. Not a furnace burned, not a wheel turned, not a puff of smoke drifted skyward. It was an unnatural condition, much different from the normal shutdown last Christmas. It was fantasy come true, difficult for the men to comprehend. A few still felt, or hoped, that a last-ditch compromise might be worked out. Still not thoroughly organized (except on paper), they milled around in confusion, while hundreds streamed toward the depots on the outskirts of Homestead and Munhall. As yet there had been no violence, except for a small scuffle between a few men blocking the main gate and Superintendent Potter, who was refused admission. Pickets surrounding the plant spoke to each other in low tones.

Full of forebodings, saying little to their menfolk, women of the town bent over their chores. The days of animated discussion were over. Only the children, playing in the streets and yards, and on the skating-rink grounds near the top of the hill, were not quite aware that anything had changed. When they asked why father wasn't working they were answered gruffly. Some of their fathers were already packing pistols. They gave their children pennies to buy fireworks for next Monday, the Fourth of July. It would be celebrated as usual, although perhaps not too enthusiastically; and all the men would be off work—as usual on the Fourth.

On the swinging doors of saloons, in grocery stores and other places of business, in the lobby of Homestead's one fleabag of a hotel, a placard was posted: "All Discussion of the Wage Question in This Place is Positively Forbidden. By order of the ADVISORY COMMITTEE." The lock-out was on. Both sides, in fact, were locked out.

From the complexity of the arrangements and the speed with which they were put into effect, it seems clear that the strike leaders had devised their tactics well in advance, as Frick had also done. They were certainly alert to the possibility of a naval invasion, and had put into service a fleet of their own. Its chartered flagship was a small paddle steamer, the *Edna,* fitted with steam whistles for calling the alarm. Day and night she cruised slowly up and down the Monongahela, escorted occasionally by skiffs. There were about fifty of these in all, manned by two men each; they could and sometimes did mount little sails, but were usually rowed. The *Edna* and all skiffs carried flares, and some crewmen carried weapons. To guard further against a waterfront landing, fires were lighted at intervals on both banks of the river, patrols walked back and forth along the shoreline, and sentries were posted upon the old Smith-field Street bridge, which intersected the works west of the landing entrance.

Atop the Electric Light Works in Homestead proper the strikers placed a steam whistle. By the number of blasts it emitted the men could ascertain where to assemble to meet the enemy.

Every road leading into the borough was blockaded. No person was allowed to enter without a satisfactory explanation. Newspapermen were issued badges for entry and departure, and those whose reports were derogatory were debadged and hustled out of town. Telegraph communications were set up at union headquarters. Railway depots were surrounded by armed guards. As days passed, the picket line along the waterfront was increased to a thousand men who patrolled the river on both sides, five miles upstream, five miles down. Flags and fireworks were in large supply due to the proximity of Independence Day; they were widely distributed and a simple signaling system was worked out. Vigilantes, some of whom were mounted, were placed on the surrounding hills.

"Quiet Homestead," headlined the Pittsburgh *Commercial Gazette* on page one. Other subheads were equally placid: "The Company Apparently in No Hurry to Employ Men," "The Liquor Question One That Gives the Leaders Much Concern," "Sunday Sermons on the Relations Between Labor and Capital."

But those relations were now nonexistent, or, one might say, negative. In Boston, St. Louis, and Philadelphia the Carnegie company was openly placing advertisements for steelworkers to apply for Homestead jobs, and measures were being taken by cable to import others from Europe. The plant itself was barred to visitors. Only twice were officials permitted inside to see that all was well, in line with the Advisory Committee's stated policy of protecting the property. At its suggestion, mechanics were allowed to repair a leaky natural gas cock and main. Another gas scare occurred July 3, when one of the mill chimneys was seen to be sending up a bit of smoke. The Advisory Committee sent a note to the Pittsburgh office that the matter "caused

considerable excitement among our men" and added that
"if the gas is not turned off we cannot be responsible for
any act that may be committed." It was turned off.

Rain fell heavily that evening, drenching the unhappy
multitudes on patrol, many of whom unmilitarily deserted
their posts for congenial saloons. Booze and beer flowed
heavily and a few fights flared up. It was the sort of development the Advisory Committee feared most, for their
cause would be ruined if four thousand ugly-tempered
men were to degenerate into a mob. Burgess McLuckie
visited every bar in town and warned the owners not to
serve drunks and noisy customers. Next day they were told
to close at 8 P.M. Suddenly there followed a printed order
to shut down altogether. Saloonkeepers were furious, nor
were the strikers thrilled. In a flash, speak-easies sprang up
and beer wagons began clattering through the streets, selling their wares openly and without license. Some of them,
commented the *Commercial Gazette*, "were running
around at 2 o'clock Sunday morning." Nevertheless union
chiefs kept the alcohol problem under control for the time
being; only one saloon stubbornly stayed open.

By July 4 all executive functions of the boroughs of
Homestead and Munhall were being administered by the
Advisory Committee and its lieutenants, who worked the
water, gas, and electric stations, enunciated *ad hoc* laws,
and kept the peace. No further entries into the plant were
permitted whatsoever, aside from designated strikers who
regularly inspected the premises. The situation was, of
course, fundamentally unstable. It was close to anarchy,
even revolution; nor could it long endure by any stretch of
the imagination. In all economic history there had never
been a two-way lockout on such a scale. Their first flush of
enthusiasm having somewhat paled, the men of the Ad-

visory Committee were now worried over the immensity of their act and its illegality. To attempt further dealings with Frick was hopeless; but what about Mr. Carnegie? Perhaps the champion of the workingman would intervene.

Where was he? He had said vaguely, when he left New York, that he intended to travel "on the Continent." Between July 1 and 6 the Advisory Committee tried repeatedly to communicate with him, and so did Mr. Frick. Neither was successful. Mr. Carnegie and his wife were secluded at a lonely lodge on Loch Rannoch, Perthshire, Scotland, thirty-five miles from any railroad or telegraph connection. Having shut himself off from the outside world, he killed time by firing at grouse from a shooting box.

Henry Frick's state of mind may be imagined during this remarkable period, so alien to his orderly, autocratic philosophy of life. The Pinkertons, fortunately, were due on Wednesday. Meanwhile he decided to get Sheriff McCleary moving. When that languid gentleman reached his office in the Allegheny County courthouse the morning of July 4, he found a paper from company attorneys Knox & Reed formally demanding that he furnish one hundred deputies to guard the works. It further advised him that the county (he, in effect) would be held responsible for any damage that might occur. He replied without joy that he would do what he could, and appointed Samuel B. Cluley and eleven assistants to perform their duty. While McCleary remained in his office to await developments, Cluley and his unarmed force boarded a train which reached the Homestead depot at five in the afternoon. Upon stepping off the platform they found themselves surrounded by a thousand men. A spokesman asked, "What do you fellows want here?"

"I am a special officer representing the sheriff of Allegheny County to put deputies into this mill to act as a guard and to protect the property for the company."

"No deputy will ever go in there alive."

Cluley turned to his men and remarked, "Boys, you keep close to me." They moved forward for a short distance, and then stopped. The strikers were tense and persistent; as yet nobody had been hurt or scarcely touched, but it was evident that the deputies were not about to proceed further. When Hugh O'Donnell appeared, Cluley said, "I am here in a tight fix."

"Yes, what are you going to do?"

"It is a matter of impossibility for me to put these deputies in here," Cluley confessed. O'Donnell waved his men away. The two spoke privately and agreed that Cluley should report the facts to his sheriff. O'Donnell and other committee members walked them to the waterfront and politely placed them aboard the *Edna*. The deputies crossed the river in some dejection, boarded a trolley car, and returned to the courthouse.

Even McCleary realized that it was about time for him personally to visit Homestead, and quickly. When he got there, the Advisory Committee provided him a guided tour of the plant, showed that they were guarding it and that it was undamaged, and offered to have as many as five hundred of their own people sworn in as deputies, under bail, to watch the mill and keep out trespassers. The final phrase, no doubt, had a double meaning. McCleary refused: he wished to install his own choice of men, who would act in the company interest. After all, he explained, the firm had a legal right to guard and utilize its own property. Following a lengthy discussion, the Advisory Committee agreed to allow the sheriff a *posse comitatus* of fifty deputies to take over the works.

The concession, breathtaking and containing the seed of a possible solution, startled McCleary. The date was Tuesday, July 5. He knew the Pinkertons were due some time next day; previously, as we have seen, he had been requested by Carnegie's attorney to deputize them on or before arrival. Time was running out, but there was still a fair chance to assemble a posse, enter the plant, take possession, and telephone Frick to call off his army. He rushed back to Pittsburgh.

One regrettable feature of the Homestead lockout is McCleary's inability to secure deputies adequate in number and quality. If he had done so, the character of the lockout would have changed completely and the strike might have taken a pacific course leading to a decent solution. One may doubt it; but the possibility existed, however unlikely. Given a week, McCleary might have succeeded; but he had less than a day, and few men in Allegheny County wanted any part of the miserably paid job. Under the law, technically, he could deputize any male citizen of voting age whom he desired. Under the circumstances, his threats and entreaties were useless. A handful of men agreed reluctantly to be sworn in, but the conditions under which they would do so were ridiculous. They would not bear arms, they would not intrude within the Carnegie company area, they would not interfere with the picketing, they would not escort scabs or detectives into the works, and so on. In other words, they were willing to stand around outside the plant and do nothing. McCleary, a feeble law enforcement officer at the end of his rope, could only count the hours. The newspapers that day had not been helpful. They carried a new report of the sort that was becoming familiar: Superintendent Potter and twenty foremen were scouring various cities for 260 skilled steel men to start up the works. Everyone knew what would happen when Potter tried to ram them into the mill grounds. By late evening McCleary possessed nothing resembling a posse. When he left the courthouse he must have known that the Pinkertons had long since left Ashtabula by train. Perhaps they were already afloat. He could therefore console himself with the realization that he had not been given nearly enough time anyway; and, although he had again failed, in this case the fault was hardly his. Why, in other words, had Frick waited until July 4 to request deputies?

Independence Day in Homestead had been observed with a paucity of firecrackers and gaiety. The men, it seemed, were more concerned about their own independence than their country's. "The mill-workers," reported the *Gazette,* "passed the day as they have spent every day since the company notified them of their discharge, in guarding the works against any attempt to introduce men in their places." Only one striker was released from duty, upon presentation of a doctor's certificate. The newspaper dispatch continued: "Information was received at Pittsburgh that a Hungarian Jew was busy at Frankstown engaging workmen. He offered a premium of $1.50 to each man in the same way as a recruiting sergeant for the British service levies men by passing a shilling into their palm. . . . Amalgamated scouts took him in hand and bounced him out of town."

It was a beautiful day in all Eastern states. At Coney Island the Fourth was celebrated by the largest crowd on record. Also in New York there were the usual parades and fireworks displays, plus interminable speeches (fortunately not preserved for posterity) by Murat Halstead and Whitelaw Reid. Striking union men in Detroit marred the

occasion by jumping a gang of stevedores who were un-
loading the *Lone Star* freighter at her dock. That elderly
battler for agrarian rights, James B. Weaver, was nominated for the Presidency by Populists gathered in Omaha.
Some kind of trouble, big trouble, was reportedly brewing
among the silver miners at Coeur d'Alene, Idaho. Generally, however, the holiday was normal enough in most
areas except Pittsburgh and its troubled suburbs.

Tuesday was also quiet. In Pittsburgh the Pirates won,
four to two, before a poor attendance of 1,503; while as for
New York: "The Giants Made Too Many Errors. Part of
the Team Seemed to be Half Asleep." Stocks tumbled.
The New York *Tribune* indignantly blamed the fact upon
Senate passage of a free silver coinage bill. And, among
other items in a world not yet gone completely mad, a
large headline proclaimed: "Decisive Triumph for Liberals in English Election."

At dusk, "on little cat feet," fog crept into the Monongahela valley.

SEN. GALLINGER: *In this sweeping condemna-*
tion that you make of labor organizations,
Mr. Pinkerton, have you on the other hand
in your long capacity as a detective ever dis-
covered that there is oppression or intimida-
tion practised by the employers of labor, or
in your judgment is the fault always on the
side of the workmen? Have you ever been
employed by labor organizations to look
after their interests in times of trouble,
strikes, and so on?
ROBERT PINKERTON: *I don't call to mind any*
case of that kind.
GALLINGER: *Have you ever been employed*
by labor organizations to spy out the business
and character and doings of employers?
PINKERTON: *I don't call to mind any case of*
that kind. I think in the different cases we
have always been employed by the employer.
GALLINGER: *Then let me ask you this ques-*
tion, and of course you understand it is done
in the best humor, whether or not you have
any feeling against labor organizations?
PINKERTON: *No, sir. My belief is that or-*
ganized labor is a good thing for the laboring
man with conservative leaders.

—Senate testimony

V *Invasion*

The opening phase of Mr. Frick's maneuver proceeded
like clockwork. A total of 316 men were collected in New
York and Chicago. Mostly unemployed, or drifters, a few
college lads trying to earn a little money between semes-
ters, a hard core of Pinkerton regulars, some hoodlums and
out-and-out criminals on the run, they comprised a typical
group of agency guards. The superintendent of the Chi-

cago office had tried to be reassuring. "You men are hired to watch the property of a certain corporation, to prevent it from harm," he told them. "The element of danger which is usually found in such expeditions will be here entirely lacking. A few brickbats will be thrown at you, you may be called names or sworn at, but that is no reason for you to shoot." He refused to answer the question, "Where are we going?"

John W. Holway, a twenty-three-year-old medical student, was one of many who began to feel qualms. Shoot whom? With what? No weapons were visible. But the papers were full of stories about the great Homestead lockout, and Holway had a feeling he was going there, and that there would be gunplay. After dark he and the others were placed aboard (smuggled aboard, one might say) a train standing at the Lake Shore depot. As it rolled east, Pinkerton detectives stood guard to prevent anyone from departing, particularly during stops at Toledo and Cleveland. The thought struck Holway, annoyingly, that he was a sort of prisoner. An identical procedure was meanwhile taking place westward from New York. Both journeys, no doubt, were sufficiently gloomy.

Ashtabula, Ohio, on Lake Erie, lies halfway between Chicago and New York and a hundred miles roughly north of Pittsburgh. The darkened coaches full of Pinkertons met there on July 4, were sidetracked, recoupled, and placed behind a different engine. Unlabeled crates of weapons and ammunition, which had been on the Chicago train, were transferred to the last car. Through gentle farmlands and harsh coal country the train clattered south, nonstop and at a good clip. Near Youngstown it crossed the Pennsylvania border. Not a man was armed—the letter of the law was intact. Last stop was Davis Island Dam, at

Bellevue, five miles down the river from Pittsburgh. When
the men detrained there at sunset they saw the barges,
looming motionless in black waters which lapped at the
wharf. They looked somewhat the same as any other river
scows. The Carnegie company owned them and had long
used them to move steel rails, supplies, and sundry equipment for short hauls. Both the *Iron Mountain* and the
Monongahela were about a hundred feet long, broad of
beam, and their only noticeable difference from others
working the river was the heavy wooden decking which
completely covered them a few feet above their waterlines.
Decking on such barges was rather abnormal, for it hampered the amount of freight they could load. Large boxlike
structures emerged amidships. Hatches had been built into
them, from which ladders led below.

It is not entirely clear what Frick planned to do with his
Pinkertons after they were landed at the waterfront and
deposited within "Fort Frick"; perhaps it was merely an
instinctive desire to regain physical possession of his property. The elaborate work which had gone into reconstruct-
ing the interiors of the barges, however, affords the only
real clue concerning his long-range intentions, when we
bear in mind that the trip from Bellevue to Homestead—
even upstream—would consume four hours at most. Beyond question his plan was to use the scows repeatedly.
Their hulls and decking were partially reinforced by metal
plating. The *Iron Mountain* had been converted into a
dormitory containing cots and tiers of bunks, the *Monongahela* into a huge dining hall supplied by a kitchen aft.
She was intended to carry a cook and twenty waiters. It
had not been possible to keep these preparations secret.
People in the vicinity had watched them with uncommon
interest for over a week, and had asked questions which

were answered with a simple explanation: the barges were being refitted to accommodate laborers for dam construction near the town of Beaver, on the Ohio thirty miles northwest. At Amalgamated headquarters this statement had been received with skepticism, nor were the union men now pleased by a telegraph message announcing the sudden gathering of several hundred strangers at the Bellevue shoreline. Tentatively the strikers assumed that they were faced by a naval invasion. The river patrol was intensified, and an alert was sent to lookouts on the Smithfield Street bridge. Cautiously the side-wheeler *Edna* headed downstream. The hour was ten. At the same time, the Pinkertons and the nailed-down crates—containing two hundred and fifty Winchester rifles, three hundred pistols, and ammunition—began to be put aboard the scows. By midnight they were ready to cast off.

Pinkerton Captain Frederick H. Heinde, forty-two and head of the expedition, took his place on the *Iron Mountain* with the New York contingent. His deputy, Charles Nordrum, a tough professional detective of long standing, age thirty-five, commanded the Chicago men in the *Monongahela*. Nordrum was in a morose frame of mind, feeling that surprise was utterly impossible, nor was he thrilled over the quality of his men. Most of them had never participated in a strike before, and, as he later remarked, "there were some of the worst cowards on that barge I ever saw in my life." A good deal of squabbling, too, had occurred during and after the boarding. The men wanted to know where they were going and what they were to do; but still, even at this late hour, they were officially kept in the dark. By now they all were fairly certain, however, that they were assigned to Homestead. They discussed the prospect glumly as they donned their Pinkerton uniforms, consisting of slouch hats with gaudy bands, blouses with metal buttons, and dark blue trousers with lighter stripes running down the side seams. On both barges some of the more sophisticated volunteers asked when they were to be deputized. Heinde and Nordrum ignored them.

If the men were to be sworn into the service of Allegheny County, Colonel Joseph H. Gray would have to do it; but he had not yet stepped foot on either barge. Nobody even knew where he was. Sheriff McCleary had deputized him to act as his representative—a vague title—and Knox & Reed of the Carnegie company had given him a communication to present to Superintendent Potter: "This will introduce Col. Joseph H. Gray, deputy sheriff. . . . You will understand that Col. Gray, as the representative of the sheriff, is to have control of all action in case of trouble." An aging warrior with a Civil War limp, armed with broad instructions, generally confused, uninterested in this tomfoolery about swearing in 316 potential gunmen, Gray was a perfect complement to his somewhat imperfect superior.

It was all in the day's work to William Rodgers, who operated the Tide Coal Company, which was not a coal company but a tugboat service employed by the Carnegie company and other industrial firms in the neighborhood. The only difference in this case was that he was to haul men rather than merchandise; he had therefore taken out a passenger license for the occasion. Two tugs would handle the job: the *Tide* and the *Little Bill*. Each powerful little steamer took one barge in tow. From the pilothouse of the *Little Bill*, Mr. Rodgers led the way, followed by the *Tide*. Colonel Gray finally made his appearance in another boat, which intercepted the *Little Bill*. He was taken aboard. Ready and anxious, Superintendent Potter in the *Tide* was already carrying his pistol in a holster.

Nothing unusual had yet taken place. Rodgers left the wheelhouse and walked around the deck, talking softly to his crew and to a Pinkerton officer named Anderson. At about 3 A.M. the fleet passed through Lock No. 1 near the Baltimore & Ohio bridge. They were now nearing the mouth of the Monongahela. Lights from Pittsburgh spectrally illuminated the surface of the water, but the fog was quite dense. Haze and darkness veiled the river. As they approached the Smithfield bridge in downtown Pittsburgh, a union lookout was struck by the sight of dim red and green lights coming his way. He strained his eyes and hurried to a telegraph shack near the northern end of the bridge, where he wired: "Watch the river. Steamer with barges left here."

Off Glenwood, the last bend in the Monongahela before Homestead, the *Tide*'s engine broke down. A few minutes were spent trying futilely to get her under way, but there was no time to waste. She dropped anchor, while Potter and her crew climbed aboard the *Little Bill,* which took both barges in tow on short lines, the *Iron Mountain* to port. It was an awkward arrangement. The scows scraped and jostled against each other, awakening the men inside and jarring their nerves. What the hell was going on? they asked apprehensively.

In the pilothouse of the *Little Bill,* Rodgers applied full power. The three vessels struggled against the current, and several union lookouts in a skiff were almost run down by the tug. Startled, they reached for revolvers, fired blindly at the cabin, and missed. The enemy armada chugged ghostlike beyond their range and vision.

The time was nearly 4 A.M. when, at the Electric Light Works, Hugh O'Donnell yanked the steam whistle. The

long, steady, moaning sound, indicating that a river landing was in progress, awakened and electrified the town.
In homes, shacks, tenements, and rooming houses a myriad
of lights were snapped on. Thousands of men, women, and
children began to get dressed. A mounted sentry clattered
across the bridge and burst into Homestead à la Paul
Revere, shouting "The Pinkertons are coming!" Within
minutes the streets were a surging mass of yelling, cursing,
laughing people. Some women carried babies in their
arms. Stolid, inexorable as doom, the *Little Bill* pushed
on. Mr. Rodgers changed course slightly to starboard, to
bring the scows into the landing area parallel with the
shoreline. As yet none of the vessels could be seen from
land, and it would appear that the operation was proceeding almost according to plan.

But pandemonium was reigning aboard the tug and
within the barges. The shots fired from the skiff had indicated that a dangerous reception was likely, and Captain
Heinde, disgusted at the turn of events, had already authorized (with Potter's consent) a dozen rifles to be distributed to Pinkerton regulars. Crates of weapons and
cartridges were pried open. Suddenly the *Edna* spotted the
enemy and emitted a series of piercing blasts. They were
answered by the yowling of every steam whistle in Homestead and the crackle of firecrackers. A roar went up from
the crowd when the *Little Bill* and her barges, running
close to the shore, were detected a mile west of town. The
strikers opened up with a rifle, pistol, and shotgun fusil-
lade which did no damage, except for one bullet which
shattered windows in the tugboat's pilothouse. As the
three vessels continued on their way, swarms of men followed them by running along the shore, firing from close
range. The crack of small arms, the scream of sirens, the

shouts of strikers and their families could clearly be heard inside the barges, where morale was sinking fast.

All the Winchesters and pistols were distributed, and each man given fifty rounds of ammunition. A few refused these gifts. They were not hired to fight, they complained; they had signed up simply for guard duty. Indifferent to them, Pinkerton officers walked through the barges and tried to calm the inexperienced men, many of whom were bordering on panic. Nordrum cornered Colonel Gray and demanded that everyone be deputized. The colonel was evasive and Nordrum fumed. They were under heavy fire, he pointed out; wasn't it time for Gray to act? "If you are sheriff of this county, why don't you deputize us, give us authority?" Heinde also entered the argument, but the colonel would not be budged. He had not been instructed specifically to swear anyone in, he said; furthermore, there would be plenty of time to do so when the Pinkertons were inside the company grounds. Nordrum remonstrated with Gray a few minutes later, and again Gray rejected him: the Pinkertons would not be deputized, and that was that.

The point was fast becoming academic. Mr. Rodgers reduced power, brought the *Little Bill* in front of the mill entrance, and then deliberately ran both scows aground with a soft, crunching sound of gravel under their keels. It was journey's end for the Pinkertons.

Dawn was breaking when the barges hit the beach, and Mr. Rodgers' crew, working fast, secured the inshore *Monongahela* (containing the Chicago men) against her sister ship. They were safe for the time being, but the matter of disembarking the Pinkertons was a race against time. They were within the mill grounds, adjacent to the company pumping station. It had been assumed, or hoped, that Mr.

Frick's fence, which curved down to the low-water mark so as to block access to the entrance by land, would keep the mob away. The people in question now numbered ten thousand, some of whom had taken positions on the opposite bank of the river; and they were heavily and strangely armed. The exact number of armed strikers will never be known, but several hundred of them carried weapons dating back to the Civil War: carbines and rifles, some shotguns, but mostly pistols and revolvers. Thousands more, including women and young boys, moved toward the excitement with sticks and stones and alarming-looking nailed clubs torn from fences.

The barbed-wire fence at the water's edge stopped them only for moments. It was knocked over like matchsticks. Wild with excitement, they swarmed into the mill and came to a stop at the landing. They were met by a lone figure, Captain Nordrum, standing on the *Monongahela*'s deck. There was a pause, a fragile moment of silence, broken by his commanding words, "We are coming up that hill anyway, and we don't want any more trouble from you men." He walked to the stern of the barge and helped his men throw out a gangplank reaching to the shore. Again bedlam broke loose. Nordrum retired below, and cautioned the men not to shoot. Nobody had been hit yet, he observed. "It's no use returning the fire until some of us are hurt." His advice was hardly inspiring. Meanwhile Captain Heinde, within the offshore barge, was recruiting some forty reluctant volunteers to walk the plank.

The crowd did not know who was coming ashore. Some thought correctly that the entire enemy force was composed of Pinkertons, some figured that they were almost all scabs, but the most widely held opinion (later verified by O'Donnell) was that one barge contained strikebreakers

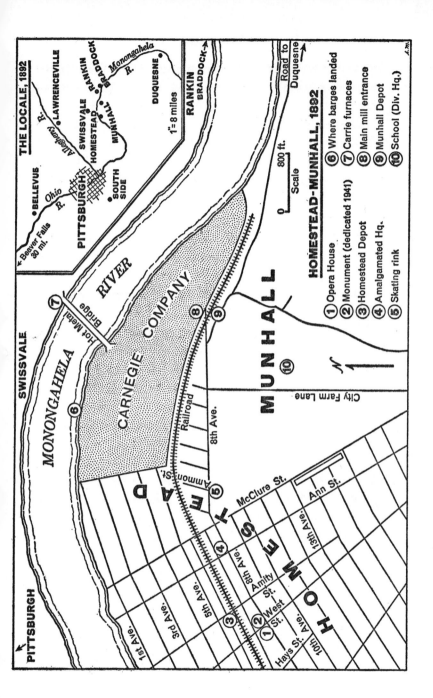

THE LOCALE, 1892

Beaver Falls 30 mi.
Ohio R.
BELLEVUE
Allegheny R.
LAWRENCEVILLE
SWISSVALE
RANKIN
Monongahela R.
BRADDOCK
DUQUESNE
PITTSBURGH
HOMESTEAD
MUNHALL
SOUTH SIDE

1" = 8 miles

RANKIN

BRADDOCK

Road to Duquesne

Scale
0   800 ft.

HOMESTEAD-MUNHALL, 1892

① Opera House
② Monument (dedicated 1941)
③ Homestead Depot
④ Amalgamated Hq.
⑤ Skating rink
⑥ Where barges landed
⑦ Carrie furnaces
⑧ Main mill entrance
⑨ Munhall Depot
⑩ School (Div. Hq.)

PITTSBURGH

SWISSVALE

MONONGAHELA RIVER

CARNEGIE COMPANY

Hot Metal Bridge

Railroad

8th Ave.

Ammon St.

MUNHALL

City Farm Lane

HOMESTEAD

1st Ave.
3rd Ave.
5th Ave.
8th Ave.
10th Ave.
13th Ave.

McClure St.
Ann St.

Amity St.
West St.
Hays St. Ave.

and the other their Pinkerton guards. In the event, these viewpoints were irrelevant. Amid the uproar, cries of "Don't let the black sheep land!" and threatening gestures, Heinde and Nordrum emerged, followed by Pinkertons carrying 45–70 Winchester magazine-fed repeaters. Tenseness, or desperation, was written on their faces as they walked toward the plank. Once more, in this curious alternation of quiet and tumult, there was a dead silence. Heinde addressed the crowd, announcing that his men were taking over the works and advising the strikers to disperse. The reply was a chorus of jeers and a shower of stones which fell around the Pinkertons like hail. They hesitated. "Don't step off that boat," someone from the shore said distinctly.

Three strikers ran forward; two grabbed the end of the gangplank while the third deliberately lay down upon it, as if to dare the enemy to cross his body. Led by Heinde and followed by the other volunteers, seven Pinkertons stepped on the plank. As Heinde was trying to shove the prone man aside, the latter pulled a revolver and shot him through the thigh. The heavy cartridge knocked him over backward. A torrent of gunfire swept the men on the plank. Heinde was hit again, this time in the shoulder, a guard named Klein was killed instantly by a bullet through the head, four of the others were wounded; and only Nordrum found himself untouched. A swarm of Pinkertons rushed topside, joining those already there. Firing steadily into the crowd, they could hardly miss; and with stunning celerity over thirty Homestead men went down. The first casualty was Martin Murray, a rougher, who fell wounded into a pile of ashes. Joseph Sotak came to his aid and was killed by a bullet in the mouth. Somewhat farther up the hill a worker named Streigle, firing at the barges, was in turn shot through the throat and died instantly. His body, lying in a clearing, was riddled with bullets from the barges.

There was no letup in the massed firing from the shore, and it was augmented by scattered gunplay from the Braddock bank. The *Little Bill* got more than her share. Bullets swept across it like hail, aimed mainly at the cabin. One struck a crewman named John McCurry and wounded him seriously in the groin. Everybody there hit the deck, including William Rodgers, who tried to steer the tug from an almost prone position. She began going around in small circles. On the barges all Pinkertons dived below, dragging most of their wounded comrades and the body of Klein with them. Again the firing stopped. The engagement had lasted no more than three minutes, and already several men were dead and scores wounded.

The strikers retreated in confusion up the bank, and scattered. They began throwing up barricades of steel and pig-iron scrap, while Hugh O'Donnell, a dynamo of activity, beside himself with anxiety and realizing that he had no influence over his men at this stage—especially the impetuous and semi-hysterical Slavs—herded all the noncombatants away from the firing line. The women, in the words of one historian, "screaming in twenty-two languages and dialects, then grabbed their kids and took to the near hills, the better to see their men shot down." The dead and wounded Homestead men (a few of whom were not strikers but had come to the scene as interested observers) were carried to their houses or doctors' offices. At the same time, Rodgers managed to get the *Little Bill* alongside the *Iron Mountain*. He took Klein's body and fourteen other wounded men aboard. One of them, Captain Heinde, said to him, "I don't feel like lying here and bleeding to death." Superintendent Potter, carrying both a rifle and his pistol, and somewhat overwrought, begged Nordrum to attempt another landing. Nordrum refused. He was not keen on the idea personally and he doubted if he could coax any sizable number of men to accompany him; anyway (he told Potter) Captain Heinde was in charge—neither Potter nor himself.

They dashed across the *Little Bill,* where they encountered a depressing spectacle. Aside from Klein's corpse, the wounded were huddled in and around the cabin. Heinde was in pain and bleeding profusely, and other men were in an equally bad way. Nordrum crouched next to the Pinkerton commander and told him he had vetoed Potter's demand for another rally. "Suit yourself, use your own judgment," murmured Heinde.

Rodgers, furious in general and impatient over the delay, wanted to leave for Pittsburgh at once with Potter, Gray, and the rest of his wretched cargo. He promised to come back as soon as possible. Nordrum returned to the offshore scow, while the lines between the two vessels were cast off. As soon as *Little Bill* got under way she was raked by another concentration of bullets and buckshot; and again Rodgers, at the wheel, tried to steer while lying on his stomach. The effort was hopeless, and at length he simply let the little tug drift. The current slowly brought her away from the shore, moved her downstream, and when she was a mile and a half away from the landing Rodgers came to his feet, applied power, and headed for the city. En route another Pinkerton died.

It was almost daylight now, and gradually the fog was being burnt off by the slanting rays of a newborn sun. From shattered windows atop the barges the Pinkertons watched in despair as the *Little Bill,* with maddening lassitude, crept away. When would she return? Below decks the temperature was rising; it was going to be a scorcher. Like sitting ducks, the two hulks lay stranded. On shore the Homestead men were accumulating sticks of dynamite and hauling a small cannon into position about halfway up the hill south of the river. The opening skirmish was over, leaving both antagonists in a dilemma. The Pinkertons were trapped. Another landing in force was out of the question, and, even if the tug should come back, it was difficult to imagine her fastening lines to both scows under heavy fire—the attempt would be suicidal.

The strikers, on the other hand, were baffled by the problem of extracting the enemy from the barges so that they could be killed, or beaten to a pulp, or at least captured. For half an hour, while the Homestead men pondered and continued their lethal preparations and consolidated their defense, not a shot was fired. O'Donnell called out for the Pinkerton commander. When Nordrum emerged, O'Donnell asked him if he were "man enough" to come ashore for a conference. Nordrum walked the plank and was asked by O'Donnell how the affair might be settled. "I am not in command here," replied the Pinkerton. "You will have to come and see other people." He suggested a talk with Potter and Gray. O'Donnell, who was angling for a total surrender of the men in the barges, was apologetic; he admitted that there were many hotheads among his people who would not consider a drawn engagement. Nordrum made one more try at influencing the throng. "Men, we are Pinkerton detectives," he shouted. "We were sent here to take possession of this property and to guard it for the company. . . . If you men don't withdraw, we will mow every one of you down." Receiving no response, he turned abruptly and walked back to the *Monongahela*. Courage, if not tact, was Nordrum's forte.

Shortly before eight, some of the regular detectives

made a final effort, astonishingly enough, to get ashore. Four were shot down in a flash. The others wounded several more strikers before retiring. For two hours ragged firing continued, while most of the Pinkertons hid under tables and behind mattresses and piles of life jackets. Regular detectives and Grand Army of the Republic veterans tried to keep them cool, but a few managed to dive into the river and swim toward the other shore. As time went on, about a dozen made their escape in this fashion. Meanwhile an exodus was taking place from the inshore barge. One at a time, the Chicago men rushed into the *Iron Mountain,* until by late morning the *Monongahela* was almost empty. Firing from the shore became more selective. The workers tried to pick off individual men who exposed themselves, directed glancing shots along the aisles of the superstructure, and concentrated on the offshore scow. More Pinkertons were wounded, and pools of blood began to collect below.

"Big Bill" Weihe hurried to the scene from Pittsburgh, and found matters so plainly out of control that he decided, for the time being, not to address the strikers. From the county courthouse Sheriff McCleary wired Governor Pattison in Harrisburg: "Situation at Homestead is very grave. My deputies were driven from the ground and watchmen sent by mill owners attacked. Shots were exchanged and some men killed and wounded. Unless prompt measures are taken to prevent it, further bloodshed and great destruction of property may be expected. The striking workmen and their friends on the ground number at least 5,000 and the civil authorities are utterly unable to cope with them. Wish you would send representative at once."

Pattison responded laconically: "Local authorities must

Henry Clay Frick

Andrew Carnegie

Hugh O'Donnell

Governor Robert E. Pattison,
of Pennsylvania

I

Homestead from the Pittsburgh side of the Monongahela

Slavic laborers

Converter in action   The Bessemer blow

WORKMEN ATTACKING THE BARGES.

SOLDIERS IN CAMP.

WORKMEN CANNONADING THE BARGES.

GREAT BATTLE
OF HOMESTEAD.
Defeat and Capture of the
PINKERTON INVADERS.
July 6 & 1892.

PINKERTONS CAPTIVES ON THEIR WAY TO DEPOT.

SURRENDER OF THE PINKERTON MEN.

Strikers at the Homestead depot

The battle at the landing

Francis T. E. Lovejoy

John McLuckie

William Weihe

Sylvester Critchlow

The attempted assassination

Alexander Berkman

The building where the attempted
assassination occurred

The condemnation of Iams

"Jack" Clifford

General George R. Snowden

exhaust every means at their command for the preserva-
tion of peace."

And the battle, a rather one-sided affair now, continued.
From Pittsburgh more arms and ammunition reached the
strikers, who moved closer to the shoreline as though to
close in for the kill. They were reinforced by armed non-
strikers from Braddock and Duquesne. A swarm of skiffs
surrounded the *Iron Mountain,* which was fired at incessantly from point-blank range. Sticks of dynamite weighing about half a pound were tossed at the barge. They
exploded on or near the target without creating any appreciable damage at first. Carrying a basket of dynamite
sticks, one huge workman ran toward the river, followed
by about twenty men. With pocket knives they scraped
holes for cartridges and short fuses. They threw the sticks
simultaneously, and most of them landed on the *Iron
Mountain,* which almost leaped out of the water. Boards
and metal plating whipped through the air. Two bombs
which hit near the bow tore open substantial holes
through which Pinkertons could clearly be seen. Riflemen
got to work on them. Several wounded Pinkertons were
lying still on deck, and when other guards tried to pull
them below they also were fired upon. Two more were
shot during this flurry.

Every time a Pinkerton was seen to be hit a shout issued
from the dense mass of people packing the slopes on both
sides of the river, hundreds or thousands of whom had
hastened there from Pittsburgh and various suburbs to
watch the fun. They were treated to a rare sight, and their
mood was gay, as though they were at a carnival. The dy-
namiting was best of all, but it dwindled as time passed, for
the strikers were running out of the "stuff," as they called
it, it was dangerous to operate so close to the shoreline and

several of them had been wounded; furthermore, despite its spectacular noise and occasional impacts, it was too slow. The barges were still fairly intact—it would take a week to sink them by explosives. There would have to be another way.

When a guard shoved a white flag of surrender through a porthole, it was shot to ribbons. By noon hundreds of additional workers were armed, and had erected clusters of steel and coal forts almost at the water's edge. Firing commenced even from within the Braddock area across the river, where the strikers could get a good bead on the outer barge. There was very little response from it. The Pinkertons huddled together, complaining bitterly and waiting for the *Little Bill,* or evening, or a miracle. Another guard leaped into the river. No shots were fired at him, and it was believed that he drowned before reaching the north bank.

The heat within the barge was brutal, but whenever a man gasping for air showed himself at a porthole or hatchway he was greeted by bullets. From the G.A.R. Hall in Braddock strikers hauled out a brass cannon dating back to Antietam—a twenty-pounder used since then for holiday celebrations—and mounted it on the hill behind a camouflage of bushes. The first shot tore a hole in the roof of the outer barge. Meanwhile the smaller cannon was firing from Homestead. Except for the first direct hit, these weapons proved ineffective. Since they could not be depressed sufficiently, every subsequent shot went long; and when a striker named Silas Wain, sitting innocently on a pile of beams, was beheaded by a stray cannonball, the Braddock gun was abandoned. A formula for getting at the Pinkertons still eluded the men of Homestead.

Another telegram sped from the sheriff to the governor:

"The works at Homestead are in possession of an armed mob. . . . The boat . . . was fired on from the shore and pilot compelled to abandon pilot house. I have no means at my command to meet emergency; a large armed force will be required. . . . You are, therefore, urged to act at once." The governor, caught like the Pinkertons between two fires and stalling for time, inquired: "How many deputies have you sworn in and what measures have you taken to enforce order and protect property?" McCleary, who had sworn in nobody and taken no measures of any kind, departed at last for Homestead.

The strikers' next move was to pour hundreds of gallons of oil, pumped by a hand engine attached to an oil tank, into the river upstream from the barges. Repeated efforts were made to set it afire. This scheme failed also; the wind was wrong, the oil was a lubricating type which burned feebly, if at all, and even when it came into contact with the scows they remained unscathed.

They loaded a raft with oil and greasy scraps, set everything aflame, and let it drift toward the enemy. There was a low moan of fear from the *Iron Mountain* when the Pinkertons saw it coming. An officer aboard stated that he would blow out the brains of anyone else who jumped ship. Another said, "If you surrender you will be shot down like dogs; the best thing is to stay here." The raft passed the barge at a snail's pace without touching it, and continued on its fiery but harmless way.

Some of the more enterprising men hacked out holes in the sides of the barges; these, coupled with the portholes and other cavities caused by cannon and dynamite, gave them plenty of openings through which they could fire. They cut loose again sporadically, and caused a few more casualties. An old Amalgamated member and Civil War veteran named George Rutter was shot in the thigh, and another worker, John Morris, was also badly hit. Both later died. Only a few Pinkerton regulars were continuing the battle. The rest lounged about, silent and inert and sweltering. A few sipped tepid coffee. Directly overhead, the July sun beat down on the decks and converted the interior into a human hothouse. Except for an active handful of riflemen, the remainder—almost three hundred able-bodied men—had set aside their weapons.

The sight of them made John Kennedy's blood boil. A Pinkerton regular, he could not fathom their docility, their apparent unwillingness even to defend themselves. He cried out, "What in the name of God did you men come here for; now is the time to make a strike!" He received the usual muttered answer: they came for guard duty, not to fight.

Their lethargy was disturbed by the strikers, whose ingenuity seemed to know no bounds and who were still intent on setting fire to the barges. This time their weapon was a small rail car, resting at the top of a long incline which led, coincidentally, on a direct line toward the *Monongahela*. It was loaded with barrels of oil which were set aflame, and released from its switch. In horror the Pinkertons watched it gather speed and hurtle toward them. When it reached the end of the line it soared feebly through the air and crashed to earth, far short of its target.

One of the strikers next conceived the plan of enveloping the barges in natural gas from a large main adjacent to the pumping station. Fourth of July rockets were then fired into it, and a small explosion actually took place which did no damage except, perhaps, to the nerves of the trapped men. The workers were running out of ideas. There were those like Hugh Ross and Jack Clifford, both of whom, needless to say, had been in the thick of the fighting all morning, who advocated boarding the barges and finishing the job with no more nonsense. Conceivably such an assault might have succeeded, but the carnage would have been severe, and very few had any stomach for it. The concept was never seriously considered.

A lull set in, broken by the occasional dry, echoing crack of a rifle. Hot and bored, the huge audience blanketing the Braddock and Homestead hills awaited developments. Men on the firing line behind breastworks were served lunch by friends and women of the town, while at union headquarters on Eighth Avenue the entire Advisory Committee, a concerned group of men, assembled and deliberated. Shortly after midday they were aroused by a new cacophony of gunfire and thousands of voices shouting with joy and excitement. The detested *Little Bill,* flying the Stars and Stripes from bow and stern, was returning to the fray.

Eight strikers were dead or dying, scores were wounded, and the men of Homestead were seeking an eye for an eye, or more. Hugh O'Donnell had not yet made the slightest attempt to curb them. Throughout the morning he had been strolling about within the Carnegie grounds and watching the show. Occasionally he mounted the new converting mill for a better view, along with a few local newspapermen. The streets of the town were full of anxious women begging for news of their men. One of them, an English girl named Mary Jones, had fainted and was now delirious; the man killed by a stray cannon shot had been her fiancé, Silas Wain.

The heat and stench below decks within the *Iron Mountain* were intolerable by early afternoon, and water was running low. Even some hardened Pinkerton regulars were willing to throw in their cards. Few shots were fired from the barge after midday, although it continued to be peppered by strikers hidden behind barricades. While several guards received light flesh wounds from ricochets, the major damage was done. Having reached Homestead (where he was ignored), Sheriff McCleary ricocheted back to Pittsburgh and fired off a new telegram to Harrisburg along familiar lines: "The guards have not been able to land, and the works are in possession of the mob, who are armed with rifles and pistols and are reported to have one cannon. The guards remain on the barges near landing, having been abandoned by the steamer which towed them there. The civil authorities here are powerless to meet the situation. An armed and disciplined force is needed at once to prevent further loss of life. I therefore urge immediate action on your part."

To this plain request for militia support, Governor Pattison, a patient gentleman, responded: "How many deputies have you sworn in and what measures have you taken to enforce order and protect property? The county authorities must exhaust every means to preserve peace."

There was no reply from McCleary. The governor wired again in phrases more irate: "Your telegram indicates that you have not made any attempt to execute the law to enforce order, and I must insist upon you calling upon all citizens for an adequate number of deputies." But the recruitment of deputies was out of the question, and the only current problem that really mattered was not to land the Pinkertons, nor to put them in possession of the works, but to extricate them.

Mr. Rodgers craved only a few moments to bring the *Little Bill* alongside the port bow of the barge, attach a single line, cut her loose from the deserted *Monongahela,* and get under way. If he had hoped that the "mob" (to employ his later description), possessed by "fiendish delight," would nevertheless abstain from desecrating a vessel showing two American flags, he was wrong. Some five hundred small arms, plus the little cannon on the Homestead side of the river—which as usual missed repeatedly—opened up on the tug the moment she came within range.

Two crew members were wounded at once. It was clear that nobody in the pilothouse could expose himself to such a swarm of bullets from both flanks and remain alive. The earlier episode repeated itself. Rodgers, Potter, Gray, the two wounded employees, and four others on board dropped to the deck and let the *Little Bill,* a splendid target, turn in slow circles. Mr. Rodgers, remarked one writer, "lay down and steered by dead—or at least dazed—reckoning" until the tug floated past Homestead and returned to Fort Perry, near Pittsburgh. Despairingly the Pinkertons within the shattered scow stared after her: their last and best hope, gone forevermore. Cheered by this latest success, the strikers again concentrated on the outer barge. A Pinkerton picked this unfortunate moment to wave a white flag and was shot down. Another guard, Thomas Connors of New York, was caught in an open doorway and hit through the right arm; the main artery was severed and he died later that afternoon. He was, perhaps, the last casualty of the formal engagement. A. L. Wells, a student from Bennett Medical College in Chicago and a volunteer guard on the expedition, was caring for the wounded Pinkertons as best he could.

The Advisory Committee continued its conference in a turmoil. Superficially the situation seemed good. It was known that the governor had refused, thus far, to turn out

the Pennsylvania Guard. Sheriff McCleary had thrown in
the sponge. The *Little Bill* was *hors de combat*. Already,
only about ten hours after the battle had begun, news of it
had crossed the nation like wildfire. Messages of sympathy
from other Amalgamated members were pouring in from
as far as Texas. Yet somehow the Pinkertons had to be
dealt with. Some conservatives uneasily suggested allowing
the *Iron Mountain* to be floated down the river and out of
harm's way. They were hooted down as defeatists and even
traitors. But what *was* to be done with the enemy? O'Donnell insisted that they should be allowed to surrender. He
was unconditionally rejected; but, as the afternoon wore
on, the idea of accepting the Pinkertons' capitulation gradually took hold—at least at union headquarters.

O'Donnell walked to the shoreline, where the shooting
had all but stopped and the workmen were amusing themselves by throwing Roman candles, skyrockets, and other
fireworks at the barges. In plain view of the Pinkertons he
addressed part of the throng with a plea for peace. Reactions were generally unfavorable. Majority sentiment was
still for destroying the enemy by some brilliant method
not yet concocted. O'Donnell was answered by cries of "No
quarter!" "Not one must escape alive!" Nobody paid
much attention to him—military discipline had collapsed.
He gave up and awaited the arrival of other union officials,
mainly Bill Weihe, vice-president G. H. McEvoy, William
Garland, and Burgess McLuckie.

It was three o'clock, and within the barge sentiment for
surrender was mounting. A captain of detectives named
Cooper asked the men to hold out until six, when he expected (for reasons unknown) another company attempt
to haul the *Iron Mountain* free. Sullenly the Pinkertons
cooled down, while another miserable hour passed. Those

suffering from gunshot wounds could not hold out indefinitely. The *Little Bill* had already failed twice, and surely no one expected Captain Rodgers to make another try. As for salvation by the sheriff of Allegheny County, that was even more out of the question. No more white flags were put out. Even Nordrum, watching the shore for any sign of truce or trouble, had relapsed into apathy and appears to have turned over his command to Cooper. It was up to the strikers to break the stalemate.

An impromptu meeting held within the mill grounds, attended by about a thousand workers, came to nothing. The commotion was such that Weihe could not be heard. He stepped down and was followed by president-elect W. M. Garland, a heater who was scheduled to take command of the local in November. Mounting a boiler, Garland begged the strikers to disperse. "We have positive assurance," he yelled, "that these deputies will be sent away and all we want is the statement that you will not do any more firing." The reply was a babble of boos and imprecations: "Burn the boats, kill the Pinkertons, no quarter for the murderers." He continued, "For God's sake, be reasonable. These men have killed your comrades, but it can do no good to kill more of them." Thunderous disapproval silenced him.

McEvoy was next, and he began, "This day you have won a victory such as was never before known in the history of struggles between capital and labor. But if you do not let these men go, the militia will be sent here and you will lose all you have gained." The word militia had a sobering effect, but he was interrupted by a crash of dynamite from the river. No further attention was paid to him, and in disgust he allowed the meeting to break up.

The union officials and Hugh O'Donnell were in a quandary caused not only by their own strikers, who were shockingly out of control, but by other factors which had not been anticipated. A few anarchists had arrived from Pittsburgh and were mingling with the men, and the ranks had also been infiltrated by an assortment of hard-boiled outsiders looking for a fight. Many women, especially those whose men had been killed or wounded, were wild with hate. They were a nuisance and potential troublemakers. Hundreds of Slavs who did not understand English could not be reasoned with, and were the most bloodthirsty of all. Half a day had slipped by, with time working against the Advisory Committee, in that the forces of law and order were certain to coagulate before long. It was essential to end the affair quickly; further destruction of the enemy would do more harm than good. The strike leaders walked among the workers and tried to reason with them individually. By five o'clock the peace faction was in fair control.

Waving an incongruously small American flag, O'Donnell harangued the throng, demanding a cease-fire and safe conduct for the Pinkertons. His suggestion that he be allowed to fly a truce flag was scornfully refused—the enemy would have to make the overtures. "What will we do then?" he asked, and a striker replied, "We will hold them in the boats till the sheriff comes, and we will then swear out warrants for every man on a charge of murder." The idea—a most unrealistic one—nevertheless received overwhelming support; more important, it indicated that both antagonists were now willing to stop the war.

The men trapped and stifling within the *Iron Mountain* had just voted, almost unanimously, to give themselves up. When a white handkerchief was dangled from a porthole it was not fired upon. O'Donnell ran down the embankment, came aboard the outer barge, and was met on deck by Captain Cooper. "This is enough of the killing," said O'Donnell; "on what terms do you wish to capitulate?" Cooper asked for assurance that there would be no violence toward his men, and also requested permission to box the Winchesters in order to carry them to the railway depot. O'Donnell agreed and departed. The Pinkertons donned their blouses and slouch hats (ridiculous, but it seemed important to make a decent appearance), and nailed up the rifle crates.

One hundred armed strikers swarmed aboard the *Iron Mountain*. The situation was delicate, for the guards were carrying pistols and a murderous battle at close range might easily have been precipitated. However, the disembarking was nonviolent. As each man emerged from below, his pistol was taken from him, his jacket removed and tossed into the river. The Pinkertons submitted passively to this outrageous treatment and raised no objection even when their crates of rifles were seized. One by one they were shoved across the gangplank to congregate on the shoreline. A few of the younger guards were weeping. The three hundred waited there, surrounded, while the strikers looted both barges. Cases of food were pried open and their contents passed out to women and children; mattresses, tools, cooking equipment—everything portable and of the slightest value—were confiscated and distributed.

After dousing the barges with barrels of Mr. Carnegie's oil, the workers put the torch to them. Hot, dry as dust, they blazed beautifully, the process being accelerated by light northerly breezes. The crowd cheered the great flames and billows of black smoke, and cheered again when the nearby company pump house also caught fire. With surprising speed the *Iron Mountain* and *Monongahela* burned down to their waterlines, the pump house down to the ground.

Temporarily these diversions had distracted the onlookers, but now they turned their hard, collective attention upon the prisoners forlornly awaiting escort to the Homestead depot. They were marched around the western edge of the plant toward deliverance, about half a mile away, fortunate that Mr. O'Donnell was an honorable man and that the crowd, at long last, was under control. They were sneered at, laughed at, sworn at, even threatened; but as they started up the long slope not a man had been touched in anger.

A DAY OF RIOTING

BLOODY WORK AT HOMESTEAD

TWENTY KILLED IN A BATTLE BETWEEN
STRIKERS AND PINKERTON MEN

THE DETECTIVES BROUGHT UP THE RIVER IN
BARGES TO PROTECT THE CARNEGIE WORKS
— STRIKERS GATHER IN FORCE TO PRE-
VENT THEIR LANDING — BOTH PARTIES
WELL ARMED AND SHOOT TO KILL —
DYNAMITE, CANNON AND BURN-
ING OIL USED — THE PINKER-
TON MEN COMPELLED TO
SURRENDER AND TER-
RIBLY MAL-
TREATED

—*New York* Tribune, *7 July 1892*

VI *The Militia*

Bedlam did not break loose until the first captives were halfway up the hill, when a few were slapped across the face. Next clubs were used, children pelted the prisoners with rocks, and then the women started in. One shoved an umbrella into a man's eye and poked it out. When a guard dropped to his knees in tears and begged for mercy he was kicked sprawling; while trying to flee he was clubbed into unconsciousness. Blocked right and left by the mob, no Pinkertons were able to break through and escape. One striker carefully slugged each of them behind the ear with a large stone wrapped in leather, tied to the end of a short rope. An elderly grayhaired man, already streaming with blood, was shown no more mercy than the others; and while those suffering from bullet wounds were generally spared, a few took additional whacks for good measure.

Reluctantly young John Holway started up the embankment, appalled at what was taking place ahead of him. Three strikers knocked him down. "You have killed two men this morning," said one; "I saw you!" As they shoved him up the hill, he was hit in the head by a stone and decided to make a break for it. He bulled his way through the crowd and began to run, pursued by a hundred people. In his words: "I ran down a side street and ran through a yard. I ran about half a mile, I suppose, but was rather weak and had had nothing to eat or drink, and my legs gave out, could not run any further, and some man got hold of me by the back of my coat, and about 20 or 30 men came up and kicked me and pounded me with stones. I had no control of myself then. I thought I was about going and commenced to scream, and there were 2 or 3 strikers with rifles rushed up then and kept off the crowd. . . ." Peculiarly, Holway does not appear to have fired a shot all day.

Sand was thrown into some Pinkertons' eyes, temporarily blinding them. Most of the Slavs disdained weapons; they simply grabbed men around the neck and punched their faces with bare fists. Over forty victims, pounded to a pulp and unable to move, were dragged toward the skating rink and its adjacent theater, while the rest staggered on. A few were divested of their money and watches. One striker pumped a bullet into a guard named Connors and then clubbed him; another bashed in the head of a wounded man (Edwards) with the butt end of a musket. Both victims died that evening. One "detective" may have lost his mind as a result of his beating, for he killed himself with a pocket knife after reaching the theater.

In tiny print the New York *Tribune* next day meticulously listed other dead and wounded: "Peter S. Prash, kicked in the back and badly cut back of right ear. . . . J.

Emmet, New York, shot in the body in three places with buckshot, and struck on right ear with a club. . . . Edward Milstead, Chicago, mouth terribly bruised and lacerated. . . ."—the list went on for 120 lines. Not a man avoided injury. Hugh O'Donnell and other Amalgamated members were struck and bruised in attempting to protect the Pinkertons, but they were able to save many of them (such as Holway) from further and possibly fatal mistreatment.

Without food or water the Pinkertons were shoved into the town theater, which was surrounded by armed strikers. Their job was to keep the prisoners in and the mob out. The Slavs, by and large, were in favor of murdering them all, a solution rejected as too extreme. Meanwhile members of the Advisory Committee were in earnest conversation with Sheriff McCleary at the county courthouse. Time was of the essence; it was important to hospitalize the more severe casualties, and the possibility of another violent outbreak still existed. Early in the evening they agreed that the sheriff and twelve unarmed deputies would be allowed to escort the Pinkertons to the West Penn Hospital in Pittsburgh. McCleary, William Weihe, and Amalgamated attorney W. J. Brennen left for Homestead by train, after the sheriff had tried without success to round up a single deputy.

The debate outside the theater was still in lively progress. Assuming that all the Pinkertons were not to be slaughtered, which in particular should be selected for a mock trial and then hanged? How many others should be held as hostages? Eventually Weihe managed to stop all this puerility, but it was after midnight when the Pinkertons were placed, not without difficulties and further unpleasantness, aboard a special five-car train which carried them to Pittsburgh and out of history. As it huffed and puffed from the station its battered occupants were given three sarcastic cheers.

It is difficult to estimate the casualties emanating from this episode, one of the most sanguinary in American labor annals. Sources differ, and men continued to die here and there for weeks to come. Bullets, beatings, drowning, and suicide brought death to approximately nine strikers and seven Pinkertons. Some forty strikers and twenty invaders were shot, and nearly three hundred of the latter were harmed in varying degrees while running the gantlet. The workers had won the battle but not the war.

The specter of the Pennsylvania militia haunted the wiser strike leaders, who were otherwise optimistic about bringing Messrs. Frick and Carnegie to terms. Concerning McCleary they had no fears. True, he had managed to swear in twelve men the morning after the fight, but his so-called posse was unarmed and amounted to no more than a token. Interviewed in Harrisburg, Mr. Pattison commented in words that cheered the strikers: "The information received up to this time does not warrant the interference of the State. The local authorities have not exhausted all the means in their power, as they clearly ought to do. Sheriff McCleary up to this time has employed only twelve deputies. If the emergency is such as he says, he ought to have 1000 deputies."

Badgered by newsmen who wished to know why he had not acted and why he apparently did not intend to act, McCleary stated, "I believe it would be suicide to take my men there. Five hundred deputies could do nothing more than a dozen. Besides, I have been unable to secure them. They all refuse to go." His hands were tied, whether the

governor believed him or not. A day passed during which
pressures were exerted on Pattison from both sides. Business leaders, political conservatives, and many an editorial
writer were incensed over his refusal to summon the state
guard instantly. In a terse wire Mr. Frick requested him to
do so. On the other hand, scores of telegrams and letters
beseeching him to abstain accumulated on his desk.

Reporters swarming in and around the executive mansion were a nuisance, but he dealt with them patiently and
spoke several times for publication. "It is not the duty of
the soldiers to do police work. They cannot be called out
as private watchmen for the Carnegie works." He expressed regret over the threat to national security which
might be caused by a shortage of armor plate, noting that
"the strike of the metal workers at the Homestead Mills
will delay work on the armored cruiser *Maine*."

His sharpest barbs were flung against officer McCleary,
whose latest effort had been to distribute a printed proc-
lamation requesting all worthy citizens to come to his office
bearing arms. The number who reported was zero, whereupon the sheriff relapsed again into a state of lethargy and
frustration.

"Why, the Sheriff of Allegheny has not done a single
thing," complained the governor to newspapermen. "He
has neglected his duty and every citizen of Allegheny
County knows it. He has sent out a few notices, requests
for people to become members of his posse, and his request
has been virtually ignored. He will never get a posse by
following that line of action." He concluded with an interesting, if debatable, assertion: "I am of the opinion that
there would not have been a drop of blood shed if the
proposition had been accepted to let the locked-out men
guard the premises." McCleary was stung into action and

issued five hundred summonses Friday, July 8. When he called the roll, only twenty-three middle-aged business and professional men replied; all were unarmed and all refused to be deputized. In disgust he waved them away. Home they went, or back to work, or to the ball game in Pittsburgh, where the Pirates licked Philadelphia four to three, for the record, before a skimpy audience of 1,183. Excellent games like this were being all but ignored.

On that date several members of the Advisory Committee reached the state capital and were received by the governor. They had repelled an armed invasion, they argued, and thus were not to blame for the riot. As for the sheriff, they were willing to submit to him and any number of his deputies—why, therefore, call out the militia? Mr. Pattison listened attentively without committing himself. A telegram from Burgess McLuckie reported that Homestead was quiet; there was no longer any disorder for the state guard to quell. Mr. Pattison did not respond. While his silence may have been construed as ominous, the workers by and large felt that he did not intend to summon the troops. By Saturday the governor was still undecided. Homestead was indeed peaceful—the Amalgamated people were seeing to that and realized that they were treading on eggs—but it also was a fact that the company was being forcibly and unlawfully barred from its property and prevented from operating it.

He had a variety of unpalatable choices. He could do nothing, and hope for some kind of a spontaneous solution. He could assemble the militia and, in effect, break the strike. With the support of President Harrison he could convene a neutral mediation board—a slow process lacking in legal force. (The President, by the way, had already been approached and had declined to intervene.)

Or the governor could announce that the state guard would definitely not be summoned, and that it was up to the Carnegie company and the Amalgamated to make their peace, aided, perhaps, by his personal prodding and advice. Logically there were merits and demerits in each approach, and one may sympathize with Mr. Pattison in his perplexity, faced as he was by political, moral, legal, and economic considerations of the first magnitude. Three days had passed since the harrowing affair. Had he made the do-nothing choice?

They had been three funereal days in Homestead. Preceded by musicians playing *The Dead March,* an undertaker picked up the bodies of John Morris, Silas Wain, and Peter Fareis and took them to a chapel where joint services were held. The bitter sermon by Methodist Reverend S. J. McIlyar was received in silence, broken only by the sobs of women. "This town is bathed in tears today," he said, "and it is all brought about by one man, who is less respected by the laboring people than any other employer in the world. There is no more sensibility in that man than in a toad." (The gentleman in question, Mr. Frick, refused to comment or be interviewed. Private detectives were said to be guarding his palatial East End home at night, and accompanying him to the downtown Carnegie offices each day.) An estimated three thousand people followed the funeral wagon on its long, hot, dusty trip to the cemetery. There the widow of John Morris, dead at twenty-four, spoke to a newspaperman. "Our little home was almost paid for and we were so happy. I was afraid John would meet with some terrible calamity and I begged him not to go out. . . . I feel sorry for the widows of those guards and wish I could give back to them their husbands."

Henry Streigle, Joseph Sotak, and Thomas Weldon were

buried the next day, the services conducted for Sotak, a Hungarian, by Reverend John Kovacs being especially grim. At their conclusion several hundreds of his compatriots sang a Slavic dirge. The days that followed were punctuated by the deaths of three more wounded strikers; and it was during this time that the Pinkerton agency received much free, if unwelcome, publicity in the form of a little song that caught the nation's ear: "Father Was Killed by the Pinkerton Men." Robert Pinkerton would not speak, but William granted Chicago reporters a few comments in accents far from affable. "We held off until the last moment on the business, but our company, having done Carnegie's work for years, they insisted that we supply the watchmen." He denied that he was sending five hundred additional men east. "We are not recruiting men and don't expect to. We have enough in service to answer calls."

The strikers, however, considered it possible that the Pinkertons would try another invasion. Again rumor after rumor swept Homestead and the system of armed patrols remained in effect; the atmosphere was much the same as before the battle. From Buffalo this telegram (another false alarm) reached Amalgamated headquarters: "Three cars of Pinkertons and two cars of ammunition passed here at 9 o'clock last night for Pittsburgh. Be on guard." Hugh O'Donnell denied publicly that two more cannon were being shipped to the strikers, and scoffed at a report that a huge load of dynamite was in readiness to blow up the mills, as a last resort. Through Saturday Mr. McCleary did nothing. "The Sheriff Will Await Developments," a typical headline ran. In Pittsburgh the Window Glass Workers union adopted a resolution calling upon the mayor to return to Mr. Carnegie $1 million donated for a city library. Mayor Gourley refused. It was reported that a strong force of Pinkertons was approaching Homestead on the Baltimore & Ohio with the intent of filtering into the plant from the northeast. A new line of scouts was therefore drawn up to intercept them; but they did not arrive, and it may be said, once and for all, that no more armed Pinkertons would ever be sent to Homestead.

Like Dr. Frankenstein's monster, the strike threatened its own maker—the Amalgamated Association—and frightened the more responsible leaders. In a spectacular concession, Hugh O'Donnell sent word to Mr. Frick that he was willing to drop all wage demands. He requested only that the contract termination not be changed from June to December. Another union official confided to Sheriff McCleary that the strikers would be content merely to "confer with" the company. The survival of the local was now all that really mattered, and in a conversation with a newsman Frick stated that, as far as management was concerned, it was finished.

Terms were no longer the issue, he said, so long as the company was deprived of its property. "We today are turned out of our plant at Homestead and have been since the first of July. There is nobody in the mills up there now; there is simply a mass of idle machinery with nobody to look after it. . . . I may say with the greatest emphasis that under no circumstances will we have any further dealings with the Amalgamated Association as an organization. That is final."

"What of the future?"

"That is in the hands of the authorities of Allegheny County. If they are unable to cope with the situation, it is clearly the duty of the Governor of the State to see that we are installed in our property and permitted to operate our plant unmolested." His mood was worsened by a personal problem; his wife was ill and about to give birth. That night when their second son, Henry Clay, Junior, was born, it was disclosed that both mother and child were doing poorly. Everyone was now in difficulties: the Amalgamated, the family of Mr. Frick, the strikers as a whole, Andrew Carnegie personally, the sheriff, the governor, the Pinkerton agency, and the locked-out company—not to mention battle casualties and their mourning survivors. Was there any decent way to settle the mess, or would it deteriorate into a process of attrition?

The events of July 6 and the continuing strike jolted America. Hundreds of reporters converged upon the town, including several Englishmen and Germans hitherto based in Washington and New York. The news each day, the comments, the editorials, the sermons, the cries of indignation pro and con, the analyses, the predictions, the babble of talk, all swelled in crescendo and riveted attention upon what had been one of the world's more obscure working boroughs, even drowning out the sound and fury of the upcoming November elections. Both the Senate and the House of Representatives, one day after the battle, appointed investigatory committees to take testimony and deliver official reports. Specifically they were to inquire into the use of private armies by large corporations. Political lines were drawn rather distinctly from the beginning, with most Democrats and Populists backing the strikers and Republicans assailing them. Very few of any party affiliation, however, came to the Pinkerton agency's defense. The New York *Tribune* headlined:

DEMOCRATS FOOLISHLY ELATED
Absurd Assumptions and a Discreditable
Display of Satisfaction over
the Bloodshed

Said Samuel Gompers, "I am a conservative man and everyone knows me as such. I am opposed to strikes, but in this case I believe it would be better for the men to die heroically than starve to death slowly." In the *American Journal of Politics* Reverend W. M. Jones wrote that "it is doubtful if, save in the presence of a large armed force, the mill owners could resume their work without violence, if they sought to do so with other men than the strikers. Why? Because public sympathy is with these lawbreakers and against the enforcement of law in this case." The typical antilabor viewpoint was lengthily stated in the American *Review of Reviews;* admitting that Mr. Frick could have used "a little more of tact, humor and friendliness," it asserted that the burden of blame lay heaviest upon the workers. "Of course the strikers made haste as fast as possible to put themselves in the wrong. They almost invariably do so. . . . When as strikers they possessed themselves of firearms, they forfeited all title to sympathy. . . . Pinkerton watchmen are no better and no worse than other watchmen. The strikers had no just grievance against them. . . . The workmen at Homestead had better abandon their insane and criminal resort to weapons. . . . Their remedy is at the ballot."

An astonishing opinion was expressed by *Cosmopolitan,* coming as it did from the pen of its wealthy editor, John B. Walker: "For if a man hire 300 poor devils ready to shoot down their brothers in misery, there is no reason why he may not hire 10,000." A patently subversive type of capitalist, he advocated an income tax upon the affluent, and even went so far as to suggest "that when men employ many laborers, their business ceases to be a purely private affair, but concerns the State, and that disputes between proprietor and workmen must be submitted, not to the brute force of so many Pinkerton mercenaries, but to arbitration." But from London the magazine *Blackwood* referred to United States unions as lawless and tyrannical, and commended Carnegie officials for not surrendering to "agitators."

In Congress Senator Palmer of Illinois called the Pinkerton invasion an insult to the Commonwealth of Pennsylvania, and Senator Voorhees of Indiana derided the Republican tariff, which had deceived the workmen into believing they would get their share of its benefits. The Pinkertons, he added, had been killed by men acting in self-defense; he regretted that Mr. Carnegie had not been leading them personally "instead of skulking in his castle in Scotland." Republicans defended the McKinley duties, but they too repudiated "Pinkertonism." A majority of newspapers throughout the country deplored Carnegie's and Frick's harsh methods and demanded legislation forbidding the use of a Pinkerton "standing army" during labor disputes.

The men of Homestead read these speeches and articles avidly, recognizing for the first time that their strike was of national, perhaps world-wide, significance. Outraged by statements they considered untrue, once more they began ejecting from town sundry newspapermen considered hostile to their cause. It did develop that a few were in the pay of the Carnegie company, although others who were ousted were merely writing the news as they saw it.

English trade unions beseeched Mr. Kier Hardie, a Labour M.P., to return one hundred pounds given to him by Carnegie for election expenses. He sent the money not to its donor but to the Homestead people who, he said, had more right to it. Meanwhile Mr. Carnegie was located by an American reporter near Loch Kinloch, where he had rented a shooting box at a cost of ten thousand dollars. The newsman observed in his article that Carnegie had nothing to say and that he (the writer) had been received in a "contemptuous and insulting" manner, as though the "intrusion upon his ducal magnificence" was something to be resented.

He received the nickname "Baron Carnage-y." Democratic congressmen assailed him as well as Frick and the Pinkertons, and pointed out that while the firm was attempting to cut wages it was simultaneously enjoying fantastic profits due largely to an indirect subsidy in the form of a 70 percent tariff on steel and a 55 percent tariff on iron. Many radicals did not see the issue in such factitious terms. Mr. Daniel DeLeon of the Socialist Labor Party abstracted their position some days after the now-famous battle: "These troubles at Homestead will result in some extraordinarily fallacious reasoning on the part of our Democratic friends; they will ascribe it all to the protective tariff, forgetting or wilfully ignoring the fact that in free-trade England workmen have been shot down like dogs in scores of strikes. It is the old struggle between capital and labor, which has been carried on and will be carried on in all parts of the world for a long time."

Emma Goldman and Alexander Berkman had no use for DeLeon, a relative moderate, but for once they fully agreed with him. Too fully, one might say; for they had decided to carry the class struggle far beyond the moderate stage. To dramatize, to accelerate that struggle in the minds of workers everywhere there was nothing to do but murder Henry Clay Frick.

In Worcester they had been closely following strike developments since late June, and had made tentative plans for agitational activity in Homestead. "We continued our daily work," wrote Emma, "waiting on customers, frying pancakes, serving tea and ice-cream; but our thoughts were in Homestead with the brave steel-workers." At night they could talk of nothing else. About July first, inflamed by a newspaper story ("FAMILIES OF STRIKERS EVICTED FROM THE COMPANY HOUSES"), they determined to close up shop, leave for New York, print inflammatory leaflets translated into English, and distribute them in Homestead. The landlord of their restaurant was bewildered; why hurry, when they were on the road to riches? They placated him with a fable about a dying relative, worked until 1 A.M. ("We never before had so many customers," complained Emma), and left on a morning train with the day's receipts: seventy-five dollars.

While struggling in New York with the task of composing and printing their leaflets, they were stunned by the news of July 6. Virtuous workmen had been slaughtered by the hirelings of evil capitalists—the time for manifestoes was over, the moment for action had arrived. In their East Side flat Berkman announced, "Frick is the responsible factor in this crime; he must be made to stand the consequences. . . . I will kill Frick, and of course I shall be condemned to death. I will die proudly in the assurance that I gave my life for the people. But I will die by my own hand. . . . Never will I permit our enemies to kill me." The girl listened enthralled to the purple prose. Her "Sasha" was right, as always. He would go to Pittsburgh alone, after constructing two time bombs.

There was no problem about it. An anarchist friend in Staten Island would sell him dynamite, and detailed plans for making bombs were spelled out and illustrated in Johann Most's *Science of Revolutionary Warfare* available at

the New York Public Library. Train fares, living expenses,
dynamite and other bomb materials, however, brought
their savings down to forty dollars. Cash was becoming a
factor for, among other expenses, Berkman would need
new clothes in Pittsburgh. Through political canvassing
on the streets, Emma received donations of twenty-five dollars more. Meanwhile Berkman was working madly on the
bombs in their flat at night, while Emma stood lookout. As
soon as one was completed he took it to Staten Island for
testing. When he returned she could tell from his look
that something had gone wrong. The worst was true; the
bomb had not exploded.

Why not? Berkman insisted testily that Most's instructions were no good. Or perhaps the dynamite had been
damp, or perhaps Berkman's mechanical aptitude was low
—what difference did it make? Was there any sense in
completing the second bomb? No, it would fizzle like the
first. Therefore Mr. Frick would have to be killed with a
gun. A cheap one could be bought, of course, in some
pawnshop, but their present fortune consisted of only fifteen dollars. Berkman computed that he would need at
least twenty more for the gun and a new suit; his proto-
beatnik wardrobe was impossible. Already it was Saturday
and the psychological moments were ticking away. Emma
promised to raise the balance somehow, and mail it to him
later. She gave him the entire fifteen dollars. That evening
a farewell dinner was held with several jolly friends, who
had no idea of what was going on, and afterward they
accompanied Berkman to the Baltimore & Ohio station.
The conductor sang out, "All aboard!" With Berkman
standing on a bottom step, the train slowly moved away.
Emma ran after it, waving, and called, "Sasha, Sashenka!"
She peered after her lover until he was out of sight, went

back to the flat, slept fitfully, and awoke next morning
with a perfect plan for raising money fast.

"Mob law is absolute," a special correspondent tele-
graphed the *New York Times*. He reported that the strikers possessed all the Pinkerton guns and ammunition, and
that additional weapons had been furnished by a Polish
gun club and a Pittsburgh organization called the Hibern-
ian Rifles. The writer (who had just been kicked out of
Homestead) also claimed that reinforcements were pouring into the borough—"lawless, desperate, murderous
characters," many claiming to be workmen. (In at least one
case he was ever so right.) Mr. Potter and Mr. Childs tried
to enter the plant but were stopped at the railway tracks.
"You know who I am?" asked Potter. "Yes, but we have
orders not to allow any one to enter the works."

More stringently than ever the Advisory Committee
ruled the town and controlled the flow of news. "Strikers
Prepared to Dynamite Any Incoming Train," asserted the
Pittsburgh *Commercial Gazette*. Even the adjutant general
of Pennsylvania experienced difficulty in entering Homestead and wiring Governor Pattison, who had sent him
there for an unbiased report. The former's opinion was
that troops were not yet needed. Yet a state of siege was certainly in progress. Suspicious-looking strangers were
barred. Outgoing telegrams were censored, including those
of a private nature. Journalists were required to carry
credentials from the strike committee and to wear a con-
spicuous badge. Those without them were either hustled
out the Homestead-Munhall limits on foot or refused lodg-
ing by hotelkeepers acting under stern instructions. Various citizens were arrested without warrant and brought
before the Advisory Committee for admonishment or dis-

missal. Burgess McLuckie reiterated that the saloons would remain closed.

People of the Pittsburgh area were interested to learn through their newspapers that they possessed the finest militia in the land. Since certain railway riots in western Pennsylvania during 1877 it had been reorganized and brought to a high state of efficiency. Between that year and 1892 it had subdued many disorders and strikes with its full divisional allotment of artillery, three troops of cavalry, and six Gatling guns. All infantrymen carried the same .45 Springfield rifles used in the regular United States Army. The total complement of officers and men was well over eight thousand, divided into three brigades of 2,500, 3,100, and 2,800 men respectively. Some from adjacent counties were known to be friendly toward the strikers, and had been heard to say that if they had to make an appearance they would do so, but that they would not use their arms at Homestead under any circumstances. Following a rumor that the battery guns would be spiked, extra guards were placed around them. But Sunday, July 10, dawned and still the troops had not been summoned from their civilian pursuits.

The citizenry discovered, too, that the commander of the Pennsylvania National Guard was one Major General George R. Snowden, a Civil War veteran. Several pictures and descriptions of him in the local press revealed a tall, long-nosed man of about fifty, wearing a large mustache, gold-rimmed glasses, and an expression of bleak, professorial disapproval.

That his imposing force might be ordered to Homestead was the major topic of printed and oral discussion over the weekend, as Alexander Berkman noted upon arrival (with one dollar bill in his wallet). Using the alias Rakhmetov, he rented a room at the Merchant's Hotel in Pittsburgh and dashed off a letter to Emma. Money was needed without delay, although he had two anarchist friends in the city who might be helpful if necessary. The scenery depressed him. "Thick clouds of smoke overcast the sky, shrouding the morning with sombre gray," he wrote. "The air is heavy with soot and cinders; the smell is nauseating. In the distance, giant furnaces vomit pillars of fire, the lurid flashes accentuating a line of frame structures, dilapidated and miserable. They are the homes of the workers who have created the industrial glory of Pittsburgh, reared its millionaires, its Carnegies and Fricks. The sight fills me with hatred. . . ."

He had time, as well as Mr. Frick, to kill, and appears to have penetrated the Homestead blockade without difficulty. There he saw the cannon, the board fence with its barbed wire, empty shells, oil barrels, piles of breastworks, charred remnants of the barges: all the aftermath of war. Tense, grimy men carrying shotguns and Winchesters hurried by. He listened disgustedly to Hugh O'Donnell address a meeting in "ingratiating" phrases, begging the workers not to offend the militia. O'Donnell was followed on the platform by a tall, dark man. "Soft words these, Mr. O'Donnell," he shouted. "They'll cost us dear. Remember what I say, brothers. The soldiers are no friends of ours. . . . Don't let the soldiers come, I tell you. First *they'll* come; then the blacklegs. You want 'em?" The crowd roared disapproval. "Well, if you don't want the damned scabs, keep out the soldiers, you understand? . . . We have sweated and bled in these mills, our brothers have been killed and maimed there, we have made the damned Company rich. . . . Keep them out, I tell you!"

He stepped down amid clamorous applause. John McLuckie, the big-boned, easy-going burgess of Homestead, spoke next. "I haven't prepared any speech, but I want to say, I don't see how you are going to fight the soldiers. There is a good deal of truth in what the brother before me said; but if you stop to think on it, he forgot to tell you just one little thing. The *how?* How is he going to do it, to keep the soldiers out? That's what I'd like to know. I'm afraid it's bad to let them in. The blacklegs might be hiding in the rear. But then again, it's bad *not* to let the soldiers in. You can't stand up against 'em; they are not Pinkertons. And we can't fight the Government of Pennsylvania. Perhaps the Governor won't send the militia. But if he does, I reckon the best way for us will be to make friends with them. Guess it's the only thing we can do. That's all I have to say."

In dejection the meeting broke up. Berkman returned to Pittsburgh. During his youth in Vilna, the son of a wealthy druggist, he had attended Odessa University (where he had been expelled for outrageous views and writings), but now as he strolled through the fashionable East End he was consumed by detestation for the rich, the broad avenues lined with stately trees, their grand residences, the carriages with uniformed flunkies. He had turned absolutely against his class and his past. Even the women annoyed him. "And the fine ladies on horseback smile and laugh. . . . Well, it may soon be our turn to laugh." He walked back to his lonely room. There was much to do—when would Emma reply?

It was three days since Sheriff McCleary had last corresponded with the governor. He now wired Harrisburg: "The situation at Homestead has not improved, while all is quiet there." He reaffirmed that the strikers were in complete charge and that he was still helpless. "Only a large military force will enable me to control matters. I believe if such a force is sent the disorderly element will be overawed and order will be restored. I therefore call upon you to furnish me such assistance."

Governor Pattison's reply was curt: "Have ordered Maj. Gen. George R. Snowden with the division of the National Guards of Pennsylvania to your support at once. Put yourself in communication with him. Communicate further particulars." News of the governor's capitulation reached the men of Homestead late that evening.

Morning arrived, forbidding and overcast, hinting at rain; and it found the dismayed strikers at a loss how to receive their visitors. In a speech at the skating rink Burgess McLuckie tried to make the best of a deteriorating situation. "This man Pattison is acting quietly and rightly. He understands our position. He does not cater to monopolies. . . . Your friends are about to come; the safest, the best people that can come. We don't want Pinkertons here. We want the militia . . . any man who insults the militia shall be taken to the river and ducked." His euphoric interpretation was received with little enthusiasm. There was a good deal of unhappy talk all day, adding up to a general agreement that the troops should be welcomed as fellow workingmen. A brass band would greet them. What tune should it play? Among various mordant suggestions were "See, the Conquering Hero Comes," "The Rogue's March," and "Hold the Fort."

In the grocery store below Amalgamated headquarters McLuckie began rehearsing a speech for the benefit of General Snowden. A bulletin posted on its window evoked faint cheers: "No. 23 was wrecked above this place last night; trains are blocked and troops are delayed." Headlines blared all over America:

TROOPS FOR HOMESTEAD
GREAT EXCITEMENT IN HOMESTEAD
The Conservative Men Counsel No
Violence to the Militia

One worker when interviewed said hopefully, "But they will have to go away sometime, and when they do we would like to see them run the mill non-union." O'Donnell, too, was quoted in words he perhaps did not believe: "We are really glad that the troops are coming."

"What will be the result?"

"How do you mean?"

"Will not the next step be the bringing in of Pinkertons and non-union workingmen?"

O'Donnell remarked that the climate would be unhealthy for Pinkertons. As for scabs, he laughed and said, "Non-union men are not got so easily as you may think. That is a question not for this summer but for next. We are not worrying." Nor was Mr. McCleary. "A Load Off the Sheriff's Mind," observed the New York *Tribune,* to which newspaper the officer had granted an expansive statement. He said he would personally accompany General Snowden to Homestead, and that the mere sight of the soldiers would disarm the mob. And in that same issue: "ANOTHER PINKERTON DIES"; his name was James O'Day, he had been wounded in the fight, had become delirious on the train, from which he had jumped as it neared Chesterton, Indiana, fracturing his skull.

Throughout Monday the guardsmen assembled at their armories while Snowden completed his plans for the occupation. When told of arrangements for a public reception he brushed them aside as "most improper. . . . It would be an amazing thing if the National Guard of Pennsylvania was not welcome in any part of Pennsylvania." Stories, bulletins, gossip, and screaming headlines swamped the Pittsburgh region: "Troops Moving," "The Governor Acts," "A Last Telegram from the Sheriff Determines Him," "The Civil Arm Powerless," "Only the Military Able to Properly Maintain the Peace," "Eight Thousand Armed Men," "They Are to Be Massed at Brinton Station and To-Morrow a Large Force Will Take Possession of Homestead." Drifting crowds gathered at the Homestead depot and provided fine pickings for whores and pickpockets; but it was still not known definitely when and where the militia would arrive.

At the state capital, Governor Pattison, piqued at the way his hand had been forced and at criticisms concerning the four-day delay, explained his position: "The law is very explicit on this point and left me no other way to act. Besides, Sheriff McCleary had not demanded military aid as yet. He had only suggested it. The statutes expressly provide that military aid shall not be furnished the civil authorities until the latter have exhausted every means in their power to quell an insurrection. . . .

"It is a very easy matter to talk about calling out the militia, but it is not so easy to call them in again. Witness the coke riots of last year when the militia was out for more than two months. The militia have a very salutary effect on turbulent strikers while they are present, but their withdrawal is exceedingly likely to cause a renewal of hostilities."

Which raised the obvious query: Was an insurrection in progress? In New York Samuel Gompers denied it vehemently. A labor-management dispute was not an insurrection, he said, and the state of Pennsylvania had nothing to do with it. He added, "If Governor Pattison was right in refusing to send the state militia to Homestead last week, he must be wrong now, as the state of affairs was more urgent then." And at Union Square the Socialist Labor Party held a mass meeting wherein it was resolved that Henry Frick and Robert Pinkerton be execrated as murderers. The *Tribune* took a dim view of the proceedings and complained furthermore, "The speeches were terribly noisy and accompanied by much gesticulation and perspiration, and they lacked that calmness of diction and logic which is so desirable."

So it went that turbulent Monday, even as the troops were speeding toward their destination. It turned out to be the Munhall station—not Homestead—and they arrived at about ten the following morning. Thrown slightly off balance, the crowd surged from Homestead to meet them, and arrived just as Snowden, six of his officers, and McCleary stepped out of a parlor car. Behind them were more locomotives hauling ninety-five coaches, from which rifles, knapsacks, and the heads and shoulders of soldiers protruded. The workers' grand rush startled Snowden, who assumed that trouble was brewing. He conferred rapidly with his staff. Company E of the 18th Regiment emerged and advanced. Not a word was spoken as the crowd was shoved back about a hundred yards. Several strikers, however, eluded the skirmishers and approached the general, hats in hand. One of them began, "General, we welcome—" When Snowden waved them away they turned to a Major Heidekooper, who asked for their names. "We don't care to give our names. We are a committee to welcome—" The major also turned away.

Into this atmosphere arrived Hugh O'Donnell and other members of the Advisory Committee. Snowden deigned briefly to speak with them. He told them, first of all, to disband their band; he was there on business and had no

need for irrelevancies, including Burgess McLuckie's prepared speech. The musicians did not play and John Mc-
Luckie did not speak. With Snowden staring at him,
O'Donnell said, "On the part of the Amalgamated Association, I wish to say that after suffering an attack of illegal
authority, we are glad to have the legal authority of the
State here."

"I do not recognize your association, sir. I recognize no
one but the citizens of this city. We have come here to
restore law and order and they are already restored."

"But we wish to submit—"

"Then, sir, submit to the gentleman behind you."

O'Donnell turned and saw Sheriff McCleary. "I do submit to him. We have never questioned the sheriff's order."
Smiling glacially, Snowden repeated that the strikers must
take care to obey the sheriff. "But we have obeyed the
sheriff. Haven't we, Mr. McCleary?"

"No, you have not. You refused to let my deputies enter
the works." He and O'Donnell bickered; and after an awkward pause O'Donnell concluded, "Well, I believe we
have nothing further to say." He and the rest of the Advisory Committee retired in defeat toward union headquarters, while the troops detrained and began taking up
assigned positions on the surrounding hills. Only one incident marred the proceedings: when strikers tried to stop
Battery B's cannon from being unloaded from its open
freight car, the Sheridan Cavalry galloped to the rescue
with drawn carbines.

The soldiers pitched tents and stacked their bayoneted
rifles. By noon the artillery had been wheeled into position, trained on the mill grounds and the strikers' homes.
The choicest and highest spot around Homestead—Munhall Hill—had been reserved in advance for the 18th Regi-

ment, Snowden's special pride and joy. Other units were stationed to the west, and one brigade made camp on Shanty Hill across the river near Braddock. Temporarily General Snowden set up headquarters in a schoolhouse. There, using field glasses, he surveyed the boroughs of Homestead and Munhall, the mills, and his bivouac areas. Again, for what reason only heaven knows, O'Donnell and others approached him, and again they were dismissed. "The State of Pennsylvania needs no help from the Amalgamated Association in preserving peace," proclaimed the general, who was enjoying the situation immensely and could see no flaw in the chesslike disposition of his troops. He seemed under the impression that they were on the eve of battle, and with no regard for military security divulged to a New York reporter how he would squeeze the enemy toward the river. "That," he explained, "was the secret of Sheridan's success—in knowing the country."

From the moment of his arrival Snowden showed himself acutely aware of the meaning of public relations and was ever available to correspondents. He could not, in fact, stop talking and writing for publication, and a time was to come when his ceaseless utterances would embarrass even the governor of the state. That first day, when asked, "General, is it intended to use your troops for the protection of non-union men?" he responded in a manner indicating that he intended to formulate policy: "The gates are open, and you may enter if the company permits it." The people of Homestead fathomed the man in a flash and, one and all, by nightfall despised him.

He had neglected to bring up rations for his troops, and for a day and a half they were permitted to live off the land. When they poured into Homestead for food they were treated rather amiably. All the saloons opened and soon were crammed with soldiers and strikers. The fraternization perturbed Snowden, who instructed his provost marshal, Colonel Charles Greene, to clear the soldiers out of town; henceforth they would be given leave only in groups, escorted by an officer, and would not be allowed to consort with the workers. The guardsmen settled down in thousands of poncho tents which, like mushrooms, sprouted upon the slopes north and south of the Monongahela; and how long they would stay no man could say.

One after the other, all neighboring Carnegie plants went out on sympathy strikes—Beaver Falls on July 14, the Upper and Lower Union Mills next day, then Braddock, Lawrenceville, and Duquesne—after their workers had warned Mr. Frick in writing to negotiate with the Amalgamated at Homestead. The company response was irreducibly brief: "Mr. Frick declines."

As to speculations that he might be in danger, the *New York Times* asserted, "There have been published numerous statements to the effect that Mr. Frick is constantly guarded by detectives. There is no sign of a guard in his office. He can be seen at his desk from the public hall of the building, and anybody can reach the hall by going up in the elevator." Indeed he had many callers, many meetings, and much planning to do, although there was no current business to transact. From a production standpoint the entire Carnegie Steel Company, Limited, had ground to a standstill. Only bugle calls and booming sunset guns from historic Braddock Field disturbed Pittsburgh's uncanny peace.

REP. EZRA B. TAYLOR (*Rep., Ohio*): *You understand by reducing the tariff you were paid less wages directly or indirectly?*
JOHN MCLUCKIE: *In this case lower wages were paid.*
REP. CHARLES J. BOATNER (*Dem., La.*): *It gave them an excuse to do it.*
MCLUCKIE: *It was to their interest at the time. The Duquesne mill is not a union mill. At any time this company sees fit to reduce these men they have no possible defense, and they can run billets down to almost any price.*
TAYLOR: *Now, it appeared to me that those houses, as I looked at them yesterday, were very comfortable, well painted and looked as if they were large; that is true, is it not?*
MCLUCKIE: *Let me ask you a question—but you are not on the stand.*
TAYLOR: *Well, I will go on the stand.*
MCLUCKIE: *Do you think they are too comfortable?*

—*House testimony*

VII *Berkman and Frick*

Judicially Emma Goldman surveyed herself in a mirror. Complexion excellent. Blond hair, blue eyes. Features adequate. Hips too wide; figure otherwise good. A corset and high heels, neither of which she had ever worn, would provide a taller, slimmer silhouette, and convert her into one of the better-looking streetwalkers. The prospect was nauseating, she had cried half the night, but she consoled herself by thinking of Sonya, in *Crime and Punishment,* who had also sold her body for a cause. Years of radical agitation, strike work, sweatshop toil, visionary zeal, a brief and hideous early marriage, the ideological tutelage and

sexual love of Johann Most and Alexander Berkman—all
these, and more in her family and psychological background, combined to make the step both possible and
plausible.

She borrowed five dollars from a servant in the apart-
ment building and purchased some tawdry articles Saturday morning. That evening she joined the other girls
plying their trade on Fourteenth Street; but when interested men approached her she ran away. By eleven her
high heels were killing her, she was exhausted from running, her head ached, she was distraught by her moral
weakness. She decided positively and definitely to go with
the next man, who turned out to be a tall, well-dressed
person some sixty years old. "Not here!" she screamed
when he led her to a wine house on Union Square where
she was known. They went to another saloon, crowded and
noisy. Almost speechless with shame, she asked for a stein
of beer. He examined her closely. "You're a novice in the
business, aren't you?" "Yes, this is my first time. . . . But
thousands of girls are driven by economic necessity."

"Where did you get that stuff?" he asked in surprise. She
had no knack for prostitution, he said. "You haven't got it,
that's all there is to it." He handed her a ten-dollar bill
and told her to forget the whole idea, unless she cared to
become his mistress.

"For always?"

"There you are!" he exclaimed, and walked away, refusing to divulge his name. She returned to her room bewildered, a professional failure, but ten dollars richer. Next
morning she wired her sister for a loan, which came immediately, whereupon she sent twenty dollars to "Sasha."

The funds reached him in the nick of time. He was dead
broke and had certain purchases to make—food to keep

himself alive, a suit of clothes, a gun, payment on his room, and faked calling cards identifying him as Simon Bachman, the owner of an employment agency. The cards when printed were neat and impressive, regrettably the gun was a small rusty revolver of such vintage that whether it would fire was problematical, the suit was medium gray with thin stripes, conservative and businesslike. After several postponements, he arranged a short appointment with Mr. Frick at his second-floor office in the *Chronicle-Telegraph* building on Fifth Street in Pittsburgh. Frick was interested to hear that "Bachman" could deliver large numbers of skilled and semiskilled steelworkers, but since he was too busy to discuss the matter another date was set up for several days hence: Saturday, July 23.

The visit showed Berkman that Frick left early for lunch and returned before the rest of the office force. At one o'clock the victim would probably be alone at his desk. Unable to wait, a bundle of nerves, Berkman called twice on Friday but got no further than the anteroom, where other callers were seated. Tomorrow would be the day.

The special House committee of three Republicans and two Democrats arrived at the Monongahela Hotel in Pittsburgh the same day the militia reached Homestead, labored for several days, heard dozens of witnesses, and gave birth to a mouselike document ("Employment of Pinkerton Detectives") calculated to offend no person of normal political sensibilities. It reached two conclusions and their attendant corollaries:

1. It would be best if Pinkerton agents were not employed in labor disputes.
   a. It was perfectly legal, however, to employ them in labor disputes.

    b. Therefore it would be advisable to deputize them, so if they killed anyone that would be legal too.

2. Impartial arbitration of labor-management disputes was to be recommended.

    a. But neither voluntary nor compulsory arbitration has legal force, since:

    b. Strikers cannot be forced to work, management cannot be forced to produce, the element of contract cannot exist, and there is no law against peaceful picketing; ergo:

    c. Arbitration was not to be recommended too strongly and should not be built into mandatory statutes.

Gravely the committee chairman, William C. Oates of Alabama (soon to become governor of that state, a tall, courtly former Confederate colonel of fifty-seven who had lost his right arm at Fussel's Mill in 1864), presided over spirited testimony that was flashed daily to every corner of the nation. Mr. Powderly scoffed at arbitration as a hopeless process that might even be "fixed" in advance by wealthy companies, and he lashed out at so-called detectives. "When the Pinkertons fire upon the people they do so from behind the breast-works of capital. Those upon whom they fire are too poor to indulge in litigation. The law protects the rich without question, but the poor must pay for the justice they obtain. . . . The Governor of Pennsylvania may also assert that he did not send armed men to Homestead, or that the militia 'did not go armed.' The men rode in one car and the arms were transported in another . . . mere quibbling . . . simply intended to deceive." He derided William Pinkerton's testimony that his employees were all "sober, industrious, reliable men," and referred by name to several notorious individuals who had been hired for the Homestead job. One of them, it seems, had killed his wife; another had recently been released from jail, and so on. When asked by Charles J. Boatner (Louisiana) if strikers should interfere with non-union scabs, he replied innocently, "We agree with Andrew Carnegie—'Thou shalt not take thy neighbor's job.' "

Tense and withdrawn, Mr. Frick proved a stubborn witness. The manufacturing cost of a ton of billets was as crucial to the problem as the known price of labor, but he refused to divulge it. "I hardly think that is a fair question," he told Oates. To Mr. Boatner's semi-query, "You do not feel disposed to give away any secrets of the trade?" he frankly agreed. Time and again Boatner asked if he had requested the Pinkertons to be armed. Frick's memory was hazy. He kept sidestepping, and finally replied, "No, sir, I think not." Boatner gave up. "Well, that is all. He has evaded this question all through."

The congressman then turned to Frick's haste in requisitioning the Pinkertons as early as June 25. Why had he not worked earlier and more vigorously with Sheriff McCleary? "You did not believe that 300 men could be found in the county of Allegheny who would protect this property?"

"Such as the sheriff would have furnished."

"Did you have any reason to believe that the sheriff would select deputies from the class who would not protect you?"

"Only the experience of three years ago when the sheriff took 100 men up into our property and they were driven off, their hats and coats taken from them, and they were driven back to Pittsburgh."

"And because the sheriff failed three years ago you took it for granted that he would fail now?"

"We thought it was better to secure our own watchmen." The subject was dropped; after all, McCleary had been unable to round up a decent posse, as everyone knew.

McLuckie referred to Pinkertons as "a band of cut-throats, thieves, and murderers in the employ of unscrupu-lous capital for the oppression of honest labor." O'Donnell called them armed invaders antagonistic to labor. He lied in stating, "I am sure the crowd near the water had no guns." "Who fired the first shot?" "I cannot say." "Do you know anything of the attempt to fire the barges with oil?" "I decline to answer." Concerning passage by Congress of an arbitration bill, William Weihe was unimpressed: "From the experience we have had with arbitration it seems it is almost always against the workman."

The meeting room in the hotel where the hearings were conducted was too small, stuffy, and jammed with over fifty people each day. The majority of them were re-porters. Testimony on both sides was quite contradictory and it soon became apparent that not much pure truth was likely to emerge from it. The committeemen were anxious to wind up their chore and get on with the job of running for re-election. Questions and answers were rapid-fire, and the stream of witnesses was bewildering in their quantity and attitudes. William Roberts, official of the Amalga-mated and worker in the armor plate department, fur-nished most of the figures from the union perspective. The following exchange provoked a violent rebuttal by com-pany officers and was given unusual press coverage:

Boatner: "Do you think if the manufacturer is protected to an extent of 50, 75 or 100 per cent, there ought to be some means to divide it up?"

"I certainly do."

William D. Bynum (Indiana): "That would be a divi-sion between the laborer and the capitalists, and the poor consumer would be left out in the cold. Who will take care of him?"

"I understand the laborer is largely the consumer."

Oates: "I will ask you another question. Are you familiar with the wages paid for similar kinds of work in other mills?"

"Yes, sir; in the structural department, and the difference in favor of Carnegie is fully 30 to 40 per cent."

"To what mills do you allude?"

"I will take first the 23-inch structural iron mill to compare with Jones & Laughlin. The roller at Jones & Laughlin receives 70 cents per ton. The roller on the 23-inch mill in Homestead receives about 22 or 23 cents per ton."

"Is there any difference in the productive capacity of the machinery?"

"The difference is in favor of Jones & Laughlin."

"Do they compete with Homestead?"

"They have to compete in the market with Carnegie, Phipps & Company."

Round and round went the charges, countercharges, evasions, discrepancies, denials, truths, and half-truths, until the heads of the patient congressmen began to swim. They could not even agree on the height of the famous fence (which was still standing), and Mr. Frick averred that the holes bored in it were for "looking out." John Kennedy, the Pinkerton officer, called his entire force a pack of cowards for not bursting forth and fighting the enemy on land. Robert Pinkerton swore that his people had no quarrel with organized labor and that the workingman had no just complaint against them. William McQuade of the Amalgamated denied under oath that any new machinery had been installed at Homestead in recent years—a statement demonstrably fictional—and as to Mr.

Frick's proposed wage scale he said prophetically, "You understand this will affect some three hundred and some odd, according to the statement he has made to you. Cranemen, pull-ups, marker, gauger, stamper, painter, line drawers, helpers at scales, millwright, millwright's helper, scrap crew and greaser. These men heretofore have not been paid tonnage rates, but as soon as this new scale gets in vogue he will compel all these men to accept tonnage rates."

"About how many in number would it add to the tonnage rates?"

"By Mr. Potter's own statement to me, it would affect every person he could possibly put under it who handled a ton of steel."

Deputy Sheriff Gray insisted that the first shot came from the shore. Kennedy called Gray "as big a coward as any of them." Various strikers testified that the first shot came from one of the barges. Recalled to the stand, Frick said the company would be forced out of business under the old wage scale. Roberts responded with statistics showing that net earnings on various manufactured items ranged from 33 to 66 per cent, and that over-all profits had been increasing steadily every year. In a curious *non-sequitur* Frick next claimed that due to increased productivity the Homestead men would earn more under the new scale than under the old. So, by inference, the mill would thus go bankrupt even faster than under the former pay rates.

Reeling in confusion, the committee adjourned and hurried back to Washington. Late in the month Oates issued his majority report (from which the minority document did not greatly differ), a lengthy and innocuous affair showing much random thinking and no trace of bias. He fairly described the borough, the mills, their value, their products, the background of the dispute, the measures and countermeasures taken by both sides, the ensuing violence, and the morals to be drawn:

But in the negotiations we do not think that the officers of the company exercised that degree of patience, indulgence, and solicitude which they should have done, by way of minute explanation of reasons why the company proposed a reduction in their wages. Mr. Frick, who is a business man of great energy and intelligence, seems to have been too stern, brusque, and somewhat autocratic. . . . There was nothing in the laws of Pennsylvania to prevent Mr. Frick from employing Pinkerton men as watchmen in the works at Homestead, yet we do not think, under the circumstances, he should have done so. He made no direct appeal to the county and State authorities for protection in the first instance, but began to negotiate for the employment of Pinkerton forces before negotiations for the re-employment of the workmen of the Amalgamated Association were broken off.

Many newspapers and periodicals, such as the *North American Review,* published Mr. Oates's views in full. They received close scrutiny and were interminably analyzed by commentators holding one attitude or another. On the floor of the House, for example, Congressman Stockdale, a member of the Committee on the Judiciary, asserted, "I dissent from the conclusion of the majority that Mr. Frick and Mr. Potter were careful not to violate the law. . . . naming these men 'watchmen' does not alter their character. . . . Pinkertons are not usually hired at $5 per day each to do the drudgery of watching, but are hired for their fighting qualities."

Observations by Mr. Oates, a Democrat, concerning the McKinley Tariff and other related issues were, of course, politically suspect:

Mr. Frick claims that over-production has caused a most remarkable decline in prices within the last three years. . . .

The high protection . . . disturbs the laws of trade—of supply and demand—and by thus producing more than there is a demand for, prices are driven down and a necessity is created for cutting down the expenses of the manufacturer, and it may be the wages of labor. . . .

They did not violate any law of Pennsylvania; but they knew that the hostility to the Pinkerton men on the part of all labor organizations was calculated to produce a breach of the peace. . . .

The sheriff may be a very inefficient officer and lacking in that pluck and energy that is so essential . . . but had Mr. Frick gone to [the governor] in person and laid the facts before him, there is no doubt that Governor Pattison would, as he finally did do in obedience to a sense of official duty, have supplied a sufficient force to enable the sheriff to take possession and deliver the works to the officers of the company. . . .

The Pinkerton men . . . were brutally and outrageously maltreated. The injuries inflicted upon them, in some cases, were indecent as well as brutal. Whether these men were of good or bad character, the offence which they had committed against the feelings of the people of Homestead could in no way justify the indignities. . . .

I think that Mr. Frick, like many other manufacturers, is not infatuated with labor organizations . . . and had no very great desire to contract with his workmen. . . . I am persuaded that if he had done so an agreement would have been reached and all the troubles which followed would thus have been avoided. . . .

I have no doubt that the Amalgamated Association . . . may be very useful to its members in many ways if properly limited and directed . . . [but] there is such a thing as over-organization, to the extent of making the members thereof zealots, and then its unreasonable demands, like a boomerang in its rebound, injure its devotees more than the blow injures the supposed enemy. . . .

Congress . . . has no power to interfere by legislation in the labor troubles at Homestead, nor in any similar ones. . . . A voluntary arbitration law was passed by Congress, applicable to railroad strikes, and there is also one in Pennsylvania applicable to her own affairs, but neither of them is of any practical utility. . . .

Nor is a compulsory arbitration law practicable. . . .

The legislature of every state should be diligent in enacting wise, conservative and just laws for the protection of both labor and capital, so that demagogues may have a narrower field for agitation. Unless something of this kind be done, within the next decade we may reasonably expect a revolution. . . .

Congress can contribute much towards allaying agitation by repealing all class legislation and greatly restricting foreign immigration.

The reactions to this hazy (except for the last phrase) and often meaningless rhetoric moved along customary political lines. Nothing was solved; and the sterile war of words soon ended, to be instantly forgotten. Worse yet, the Senate interrogators were still to come, to ask the same questions and receive the same irreconcilable answers, to rehash the same tasteless stew.[1]

Hot, bored, pestered by insects, the troops on the hills napped, played cards and shot craps, patrolled Homestead in squads, and waited to be sent home. Perspiring in their heavy blue uniforms, they marched and countermarched aimlessly, in accordance with Snowden's orders that drill practice be conducted daily. They were assigned other unmilitary duties, such as disinfecting with lime the streets adjoining the plant, and helping to remove garbage and decomposing matter which had accumulated there for months or years. Nothing, as far as they could see, was happening. The last trace of civil authority ended on a

[1] They arrived late in November, when the strike was over. Of the seven men appointed to the committee only two—Senators Jacob H. Gallinger and William A. Peffer—showed up.

note of low comedy when a cow wandered into one of the bivouac areas to defecate. A borough constable who stormed the site to capture and intern her with the honors of war was seized and incarcerated in the guardhouse. One evening a thunder and wind storm blew down innumerable tents and coverted the roads into mud, impeding the commissary wagons and the flow of food supplies. Children sold ham sandwiches to the troops for a nickel apiece. Mail reached the men slowly, their post office consisting of a wagon drawn by one plodding horse, which made the rounds of the camp at irregular intervals. Sunlight glinted against the polished cannon, everywhere flags flew, each evening the cavalry paraded, but the general scene was sufficiently dreary. There was one barber for eight thousand men, and one hospital: a bench within a little tent under a tree.

When one of the hearths was fired up, strikers assembled threateningly at the main gate. There they were stopped by drawn bayonets. Relationships between "the town and the hill" had become increasingly strained; the honeymoon was over. The men of Homestead agreed among themselves that their personal arms and captured Winchesters would under no circumstances be surrendered. Picket lines continued in effect—as long, as heavily armed, as dense, as vigilant, as impenetrable as ever—and in an official report General Snowden observed, "Pennsylvanians can hardly appreciate the actual communism of these people. They believe the works are theirs quite as much as Carnegie's."

Over six hundred offers of financial assistance had reached the strikers and their morale was high. A letter sent by Superintendent Potter to former employees in the repair shops and mechanical departments was received indifferently: "Dear sir: Repairs will be resumed on Monday morning, July 18, 1892. We invite you to return to your old position. Work to commence at the usual time." Not a soul returned. A member of the Advisory Committee told a New York reporter, "I regard the whole thing as a confession of weakness on the part of the Carnegie Company."

"How long can you keep up the fight on these lines?"

"Five years. Look at the figures. The idle mills are costing the Carnegie Company $50,000 a day. The militia is costing the State about $24,000 a day, a total of $74,000 a day. Say that the support of each of the 3,800 workingmen amounts to $2 a day, there is $7,600 a day the lockout costs us. Well, we believe that we can pay $1 as often as the Carnegie Company pays $10. . . ."

But his reasoning left something to be desired. The company was not paying for the militia, and its financial resources were, for all practical purposes, unlimited. Furthermore, new men—contrary to Mr. Carnegie's philosophy—were trickling into the works. By the latter part of July about a hundred workers were on duty and living inside the plant; but since they were known to be merely repair and maintenance men they caused little stir among the strikers.

A nervous young man with a bucket of paste, a brush, and an armful of posters splashed the firm's final ultimatum all over Homestead. The deadline for strikers to return to work, it announced, was 6 P.M., July 21, and Frick added, "It is our desire to retain in our service all of our employes whose past record is satisfactory, and who did not take part in the attempts which have been made to interfere with our right to manage our business." When that date passed with no response the lockout technically became a strike. The men were convinced that the United

States did not contain enough unemployed shearers, rollers, heaters, and other skilled workers to operate a plant the size and complexity of Homestead. Anyway, how could they pierce the picket lines, and would any of them dare try?

Mr. Frick reasoned differently. He intended gradually to bring in semiskilled and even unskilled men, and teach them how to make steel on the job. A day after the final deadline the *Little Bill* and *Tide* began ferrying small groups of "black sheep" into the mills from Pittsburgh. Never were vessels more thoroughly hated, and never were their names mentioned without an accompanying curse. As more strikebreakers filtered into the plant, faint whorls of smoke began issuing from several chimneys, and again rancorous incidents flared up on the periphery of the great plant. No steelworkers were on hand as yet. All these early arrivals continued to be maintenance men, waiters, cooks, clerks, foremen, and several dozen carpenters building one hundred temporary housing shacks near the pressing mill. The exact purpose of these structures was not clear at the time.

General Snowden and his staff, having moved into three cottages owned by the company on Eighth Avenue not far from the main entrance, planned to dine at the nearby Frick Hotel. Shortly the head waiter resigned; he would not bring food, he said, to the "enemy." When the cooks and waitresses also quit, a crisis arose which the general met with military firmness and alacrity. He commanded that substitutes be rounded up who would swear fealty to him and the Commonwealth of Pennsylvania, and this was done. The divisional commissary also furnished personnel to help feed their officers.

Sheriff McCleary was now a changed man, speaking with

authority to contemptuous crowds of men, striding through the streets with a pistol at his hip, surrounded by deputies and troopers, evaluating people and problems for the benefit of newsmen. Those individuals who had fought the Pinkertons, he predicted with satisfaction, would soon be prosecuted. Hugh O'Donnell concurred—he personally expected to be arrested soon for murder. True, he had murdered nobody, but Mr. Lovejoy clarified the matter in a published statement: "We have good cases against 1000 of these men. . . . twelve to fifteen informations will be lodged every day. The laws of Pennsylvania are very broad on this subject. Persons on the premises at the time are liable not only as accessories, but as principals." But would the Amalgamated not retaliate? After all, more strikers had been killed than Pinkertons. Lovejoy admitted, "It is, of course, possible that we or some of us may be arrested." He further claimed (July 17) that the mills would be operating efficiently within a week.

The ax fell next day when, through the company law firm of Knox & Reed, warrants were issued against Mc-Luckie, O'Donnell, Ross, and four other members of the Advisory Committee who "did of their malice afore-thought feloniously and riotously with force and arms and deadly weapons kill and murder one T. J. Connors. . . ." Carrying these redundantly phrased documents and guarded by two full companies of infantry supplied by Snowden, three constables proceeded to Homestead to serve them. All the accused had gone into hiding except McLuckie and O'Donnell, who surrendered and were taken to a Pittsburgh courthouse. The judge fixed bail at ten thousand dollars each. They were locked up until the money could be procured, which was overnight in the case of the burgess. O'Donnell, however, languished in his cell for five days until being sprung on bond. Mr. Brennen, the Amalgamated attorney, began preparing similar informations charging Frick, Lovejoy, Potter, three other company officials, Robert Pinkerton, and William Pinkerton with murder.

So began the tortuous legal proceedings which were to drag on for months in various forms, as we shall see, straining the union treasury, making a mockery of the state's judicial machinery, and causing the protracted imprisonment of many strikers. It may here be divulged that subsequently bail was quickly furnished for all company and detective officers, that not one spent a moment in jail, and that the discrepancy in treatment caused great indignation among the rank and file. When released, McLuckie remarked, "I had a good rest in jail." Fifteen hundred strikers gave him a triumphal reception when he reached Homestead.

That morning, during a driving rain, Governor Pattison also arrived in the borough. After being greeted by a seventeen-gun salute, he reviewed the troops and conferred with General Snowden. Next he was visited by members of the Advisory Committee, who asked him to withdraw the militia. He politely declined. The governor stayed two days, saying little and doing nothing; he seemed depressed by his handiwork and anxious to be gone. Meanwhile, although the works were relatively deserted, the stacks continued smoking, screeching noon whistles announced a nonexistent lunch period, and work proceeded on the frame buildings. Even as they were being built they were stocked in advance with cots, blankets, and food. Dining halls with adjoining kitchens also arose. Mr. Frick had become something of an expert in such preparations, first on the barges and here within the mill grounds. At the moment, seventy labor agents were combing the Eastern states for "labor replacements," otherwise known as black sheep or rats or scabs, who were offered cash bonuses and free railroad tickets to Pittsburgh. It was evident now where they were intended to live.

Skipped Friday paydays brought sobering reflections, especially to the impoverished former day laborers. The average Amalgamated handout to non-union strikers was less than a dollar per day, varying with the number of dependents—thin gruel indeed, even in 1892. Men inside the works could be plainly seen from higher ground—was the jig already up? A few strikers secretly inquired of the militia what protection they would receive if they went back to work. But except for these isolated, clandestine contacts the soldiers and strikers mutually kept their distance, uttering nothing but occasional warnings and insults, despising and fearing each other. Such was their relationship after ten days of military occupation which had commenced with a welcoming committee and a brass band.

A large three-story tenement near the river at the east end of the mill housed scores of Hungarians. Troops watched it as a probable place for gunfire to start. Next to it stood rooming houses where many unmarried strikers lived. This area was considered the most dangerous of all, and troops were instructed to patrol it with fixed bayonets. Both Homestead and Munhall were filled with company detectives, spying and reporting to their headquarters. Strikers avoided talking to strangers. Women berated the militia shrilly as the latter walked the streets. Near the Upper Union mill in Pittsburgh, around Thirty-third Street, fifty non-union strangers were surrounded by a mob of strikers. Savage fighting took place, and the former group was turned away from seeking employment.

From Amalgamated headquarters, one afternoon, men spat upon the militia below. A messenger carrying a rifle, bayonet affixed, walked upstairs and said, "Gentlemen, Colonel Greene presents his compliments and says that if any more spit is spat out of any of these windows, on anybody, the whole building will be shut up." Accordingly a solemn notice was posted on the ground-floor grocery window "to expectorate on the floor and not on the street." It was all most unpleasant, most of all the evictions; for there was a loophole in each lease covering each company-owned house. According to the fine print it was possible for the company to turn out tenants at any time, without cause, whether or not their rent was in arrears. This had been going on for well over a week, except while the governor was in town. As homes were vacated, a few strangers and their families moved in. More fights, of course, broke out, until troops were finally assigned to escort these people inside with their belongings. Moving wagons did a thriving business, although some evictees without money found themselves huddled on the street, surrounded by pots, pans, children, weeping women, a pile of clothing, and a few sticks of furniture. By the weekend starting Saturday, July 23, all eighty-odd eviction notices had been served and the last tenants had departed—some permanently.

Alexander Berkman arose early that morning, breakfasted sparsely in his room, and walked to the Carnegie offices downtown. His ensuing actions indicate a perfect agony of indecision; out the window went his planning and timetable concerning Frick's routine. He arrived much too soon, found the place a beehive of activity, walked out, and paced the streets. Meanwhile Frick left for lunch at the Duquesne Club. Berkman spotted him when he returned. He dashed up the stairs and nearly collided with Frick emerging alone into the hall from the elevator. At that moment he could have killed him with ease, but Berkman recoiled. The two men, opposites in everything but their respective brands of fanaticism, a study in contrasts, faced each other. Berkman stammered out a question about another person's office. Frick told him it was several floors up, and entered the reception room, which was separated from his private office by an oak and glass partition and a swinging door. Except for Frick and a Negro attendant, both rooms were empty.

Unaccountably Berkman went downstairs and waited on the sidewalk—for what? Company employees began returning from lunch, among them Vice-Chairman John Leishman, who proceeded into Frick's private office. It was almost two o'clock and everything was going wrong. Berkman pulled himself together, hurried upstairs, and accosted the attendant. "Take this card in to Mr. Frick. I am in a great hurry and must see him at once." The Negro boy went in and spoke a few words to Frick, who murmured, "Tell the gentleman I will see him in a moment." When so advised, Berkman left the waiting room, then swiftly turned and brushed past the startled attendant. At first he was dazzled by sunlight pouring through the windows. There sat his prey at the end of a long table, one leg dangling over the arm of a chair. Frick's back was toward Berkman and he was talking to Leishman. The faint, unorthodox noise of Berkman shoving the attendant aside caused Frick to swivel around.

"Fr—," began Berkman. Frick rose, with fear on his face. Exultantly Berkman thought, "He understands." He drew his gun from a distance of twenty-five feet. "Perhaps he wears armor," he reflected, aiming at the head. Frick tried to dodge when the trigger was pulled. With a roar and a flash that echoed in the high-ceilinged room like cannon fire, the bullet entered his neck at a downward angle and lodged between his shoulders. Frick sagged to his knees and leaned motionless against the armchair.

"Dead?" wondered Berkman. He had to make sure. While walking closer, he was jumped by Leishman. Quick as a leopard, Berkman flung the little man to the floor, moved closer to Frick and pumped another slug into the right side of his neck.

Once more Leishman threw himself on the assailant and shoved his arm upward. The third shot went into the ceiling. Frick crawled dazedly toward Berkman and helped pull him down. The exertion caused blood to spurt from his wounds. As yet hardly a sound had been uttered, even as the three men swayed and struggled in front of the window, watched by a few transfixed people on the sidewalk below. All three fell to the soft carpeting in a tangle of limbs, with Berkman underneath. Using his left hand, he managed to pull a sharpened file from a trouser pocket; with this he stabbed Frick in the hip, the right side, and near the left knee. For the first time Frick cried out in pain.

It all had lasted less than half a minute, and now the room was turbulent with shouting clerks, workmen in overalls, the door attendant, and one or more policemen. A carpenter slowed Berkman down with a glancing blow from his hammer at the base of the skull, but he continued half-consciously slashing away at Frick. His arms were pulled and twisted and he was lifted to his feet. His necktie had been ripped off. Gone was his battered derby, and his light suit was disheveled and spattered with Frick's blood. When an officer dragged his head back by the hair, for an instant Berkman and Frick stared at each other. The older man looked the picture of death, his face ash-gray, the black beard streaked with red, blood oozing from his neck. "Mr. Frick," he was asked, "do you identify this man as your assailant?" He nodded without a word.

Berkman was thrown into a chair, his jaws moving strangely. A deputy sheriff who tried to get a clear shot at him was waved away by Frick, who finally spoke: "Don't shoot, leave him to the law; but raise his head and let me see his face." They pried Berkman's teeth open and extracted a capsule containing fulminate of mercury. Perhaps it was not (as some writers have stated) enough to blow the room to bits, but it was sufficient to tear off the top of his head, fulfilling his vow not to be executed by the enemy. Police dragged him downstairs, where they were surrounded by a mob estimated at two thousand. There were cries of "Lynch him! Shoot him!" but Berkman was either uncaring or in shock. A civilian inquired, "Are you hurt? You're bleeding." Berkman passed his hand over his face and replied vaguely, "I've lost my glasses." An officer snapped, "You'll be damn lucky if you don't lose your head."

They took him to Central Station in a paddy wagon—a short, nasty trip during which he was not treated too gently—and locked him in a cell. He collapsed on a wooden bench and fell asleep for a few minutes, dreaming kaleidoscopic dreams of the carpenter who had slugged him from behind, of his mother and his childhood, of Mr. Frick, of being hanged for murder. He jumped up and pressed his head against the cold bars. Was Frick alive? "Have I failed?" he asked himself miserably.

Mr. Frick was alive and resting on a couch. He conversed quietly with those around him, and even made a small joke about Berkman's surprising strength. Doctors came, removed his outer clothes, and prepared an anesthetic. He refused it, remarking that they could probe better if he were conscious. He helped guide the instrument into both neck wounds and twice said, "There, that feels like it, Doctor," as the bullets were located. After the holes were plugged with cotton, his neck bandaged, his leg and body wounds dressed, he asked to be propped up facing his desk. Mr. Frick's business day was not yet over.

He wired his mother and then cabled Mr. Carnegie: "Was shot twice but not dangerously. There is no necessity for you to come home. I am still in shape to fight the battle out." He signed letters previously dictated, specified the terms of a certain loan in the process of negotiation, and dictated a statement for the press: "This incident will not change the attitude of the Carnegie Steel Company toward the Amalgamated Association. I do not think I shall die but whether I do or not the Company will pursue the same policy and it will win."

It was dusk when they laid him on a stretcher and took him home in an ambulance. His wife called to him from her sickroom as they carried him by, and he replied, "Don't worry, Ada, I'm all right . . . how is the baby?" The following morning he dictated a "NOTICE: —To all men who entered our employ after July 1st, 1892: In no case and under no circumstances will a single one of you be discharged to make room for another man. . . . Positive orders to this effect have been given to the general superintendent."

He remained in bed for ten painful days. A telephone was installed at his side; a battery of secretaries was in constant attendance; he conducted company affairs as usual during a blistering heat wave. It was an astounding performance. On August 3, his month-old baby died. Next day he attended the funeral, sat up almost all night at the side of his anguished wife, and slept for an hour or two. Then he breakfasted, took a streetcar to the office, arrived at eight o'clock sharp, and pressed a buzzer for his morning's mail.

Returning to Alexander Berkman in prison after the assault, a detective forced open his mouth and found another capsule. Asked what it was, Berkman responded sarcastically, "Candy." It proved to contain nitroglycerin; and with it went his last chance to avoid the due process of law. The net result of Berkman's moronic act was to brand anarchism and nihilism, once and for all, in the eyes of all reasonable citizens as philosophies akin to lunacy, to harm both Frick and himself, to stain (unfairly) the image of the Amalgamated, and to make Mr. Frick even less amenable to a strike settlement than before, if such a thing were possible. There was no longer the slightest doubt that it would be a fight to the death.

New York headlines stunned Emma Goldman: "YOUNG MAN BY THE NAME OF ALEXANDER BERGMAN SHOOTS FRICK— ASSASSIN OVERPOWERED BY WORKING-MEN AFTER DESPERATE STRUGGLE." But why would workingmen overpower Sasha, their devoted friend? Surely this was a lie of the capitalist press. And Frick—was he dead? That was the prime issue, for Emma loved her Sasha second only to the Cause. Early editions gave the impression that Frick was dying, and Berkman had told her that his sharpened file would be coated with poison. When it developed that Frick would live, she became alternately depressed and violent, even planning with the aid of another gentleman friend to blow up the Allegheny Courthouse the day her lover was executed. Sullenly she awaited the trial and verdict.

Andrew Carnegie was handed Frick's cablegram while

riding in his carriage. In consternation he scribbled back: "Too glad of your escape to think of anything. Never fear, brave and dear friend, my appearing on the scene. . . . Be careful of yourself is all we ask." Pell-mell he clattered back to Rannoch Lodge. Later in the day he changed his mind and cabled Frick that he was coming home. In commanding phrases Frick insisted that he stay where he was. Subsequent cables from company officials pointed out, similarly, that his return before the strike was beaten would imply the repudiation of Frick. Reluctantly Mr. Carnegie remained in seclusion.

A visitor at Frick's bedside found him steaming with wrath. He denounced the strikers as murderers and declared that even if Carnegie showed up along with President Harrison and the entire United States Cabinet he would not settle the strike. Right or wrong, he feared that Carnegie's return might lead to a weak-kneed compromise with the strikers. Probably he was wrong, in view of one of Carnegie's earlier messages: "All anxiety gone since you stand firm. Never employ one of those rioters. Let grass grow over works. Must not fail now. You will win easily. . . ." But Frick was not thoroughly appeased, and to an associate named Milholland he wrote, "If he interferes, every manager that he has will resign and of course I will get out of the concern."

Alone, distraught, kept at arm's length, Carnegie gave vent to his emotions in a stream of letters and cables. To William Gladstone he deplored "the false step made in trying to run the Homestead Works with new men . . . a test to which workingmen should not be subjected. . . . The pain I suffer increases daily. The Works are not worth one drop of human blood. I wish they had sunk." And months later he wrote Whitelaw Reid: "The guards were intended only to protect them. . . . This has been the hardest trial I ever had to endure. . . . I have been in misery. . . . No one knows the virtues, the noble traits of the true workingman who has not lived with them, as I have, and there's one consolation in all my sorrow; not one of them but said, 'Ah, Mr. Carnegie, if you had only been here it never would have happened.' " These words, however, may be balanced against another private communication in which he remarked coolly that it was absurd to have attempted a river landing July 6; in other words, Frick was merely guilty of poor tactics.

In prison before his arraignment Berkman was allowed to speak to a few selected newspaper reporters. He flaunted his anarchism, insisted that he had no accomplices (the New York police, incidentally, were then searching for Emma), and regretted that Frick was not dead. If he were, argued Berkman, Carnegie would make a deal with the strikers. In view of information, letters, and cablegrams published later, the assumption appears incorrect. But Carnegie remained in Europe until it was all over, and we shall never know what he might have done. Eventually, though, he would come home to face the music, which was already swelling in volume.

*Three months ago Andrew Carnegie was a
man to be envied. Today he is an object of
mingled pity and contempt. . . . He has
not only given the lie to all his antecedents,
but confessed himself a moral coward. One
would naturally suppose that if he had a
grain of consistency, not to say decency, in
his composition, he would favor rather than
oppose the organization of trades-unions
among his own working people at Homestead . . . if he had a grain of manhood,
not to say courage . . . he would at least
have been willing to face the consequences
of his inconsistency.*

*But what does Carnegie do? Runs off to
Scotland out of harm's way. . . . A single
word from him might have saved the bloodshed—but the word was never spoken. Nor
has he, from that bloody day until this,
said anything except that he "had implicit
confidence in the managers of the mills."
The correspondent who finally obtained this
valuable information expresses the opinion
that "Mr. Carnegie has no intention of returning to America at present." He might
have added that America can well spare
Mr. Carnegie. Ten thousand "Carnegie
Public Libraries" would not compensate the
country for the direct and indirect evils resulting from the Homestead lockout. Say
what you will of Frick, he is a brave man.
Say what you will of Carnegie, he is a
coward.*

—*St. Louis* Post-Dispatch

VIII *Private Iams*

Overnight Mr. Frick became a subspecies of hero, respected for his quiet valor by people of all political views

within the spectrum of common decency. Even the men of Homestead, relieved to learn that his assailant was not a striker, expressed formal regrets over the incident and were politely thankful that Frick would soon be up and about, presumably to continue his task of destroying them. And if there were those who darkly muttered that Berkman might have done better, it was only natural to find a few rotten apples in a carload. The switch in public opinion was not to last long, but momentarily one of the most disliked men in American life found himself treading the paths of glory, a detour which may have surprised Mr. Frick without much interesting him. The villain of the piece was now Andrew Carnegie because he gave the impression of having fled, leaving his dour subordinate to face the music.

Like most snap judgments concerning big men immersed in bigger events, this was an oversimplification. It is true that Frick had handled himself admirably in the Berkman affair; but from the standpoint of culpability for the strike—the employment of Pinkertons, the measures taken that led inevitably to the July 6 disaster, the evictions, the use of permanent scabs, and the refusal to negotiate with the union after June 21—nothing had changed and Frick stood alone as the hatchet man. When he spurned the Advisory Committee's capitulation in mid-July he sealed the case against himself.

Legally the strikers were wrong in locking out the company and resisting the Pinkertons' landing, although it is hard to see what alternative they had, except to go back to work tamely July 1 on Frick's terms and to dissolve the Amalgamated lodges in Homestead, a line of action (or inaction) which may be dismissed under the circumstances as inconceivable.

The role played by Mr. Carnegie, however, was more complicated. He could not in all honesty say, as he plaintively did, that he was no longer engaged in business and that the strike was out of his hands; for he was far and away the majority shareholder and most assuredly guided high-level policy while in Pittsburgh or New York for several months each year. When he sailed in March he knew with fair certainty that a strike was coming, although it had been his custom for years to visit Europe at about that time. Possibly he would have handled the matter much differently than Frick; the hiring of such a large number of Pinkertons and the melodramatic way they were to be smuggled into the mill was not his style. But all this is theorizing. The fact remains that the actions taken by the Carnegie company were in gross violation of the prolabor principles he himself had stated so passionately for so many years. He was—or appeared to be—the hypocrite supreme, after the attempted murder of Frick. Governor Grosvenor of Ohio called him "the arch-sneak of this age." Ben Butler suggested extraditing him for murder. In Little Rock and other cities he was burned in effigy. Temporarily the reputation he had spent years to erect had collapsed.

The backlash extended to England, where the London *Times* expressed itself with rare acerbity: "Mr. Carnegie's position is singular. The avowed champion of trades-unions now finds himself in almost ruinous conflict with the representatives of his own views. He has probably by this time seen cause to modify his praise of unionism and the sweet reasonableness of its leaders. Or are we to assume that this doctrine is true in Glasgow but not in the United States, or that it ceases to be applicable the moment Mr. Carnegie's interests are touched?" Day after day, disconsolately from morning until night, he fished Rannoch's streams and evaded newsmen. The nation roared in derision when he emerged once to announce that he could not interfere with his managers even if he wanted to; and coldly the London *Financial Observer* noted: "Here we have this Scotch-Yankee plutocrat meandering through Scotland in a four-in-hand, opening public libraries and receiving the freedom of cities, while the wretched workmen who sweat themselves in order to supply him with the ways and means for this self-glorification are starving in Pittsburgh." At length Mr. Carnegie departed for Italy, determined to say no more.

Overshadowed by other events, the amusement and resentment directed against him soon faded away, although still another scandal was to break over his aging head near the close of the year.[1] The economic collapse beginning early in 1893 also helped divert attention from the tarnished idol of the workingman.

Among the militiamen was Private William L. Iams, Company K, Tenth Regiment, a strapping blond in his twenties from one of the better-known families in Greene County. Lolling on the grass when news reached camp of Berkman's attack, he jumped to his feet and exclaimed, "Three cheers for the man who shot Frick!" The egregious remark was overheard by his commanding officer, Lieutenant Colonel J. B. Streator, who emerged from his tent to demand an apology. Stubbornly Iams refused; "I hate Frick," he said. He was escorted to the guardhouse while his fate was debated. As a preliminary measure it was de-

[1] Secretary of the Navy H. A. Herbert reported that the Carnegie company "had failed to temper armor evenly . . . had plugged and concealed blow-holes, which probably would have caused a rejection . . . had re-treated, without the knowledge of the inspectors, plates which had been selected for ballistic tests . . . ," charges which President Cleveland later upheld. The firm was fined $140,000.

cided to hang him up by the thumbs; and this was done late in the afternoon under a hot sun, by kicking a box out from under him.

Iams chewed tobacco while hanging from the limb of a tree. Regimental officers looked on; a surgeon occasionally tested his pulse, and another medical officer checked his heartbeat. After twenty-eight minutes it was so faint that the surgeon ordered him cut down. Iams slumped to the ground unconscious. Revived by whiskey and ammonia, he was returned to the guardhouse. The episode was reported to Snowden, who approved the punishment and further ordered that he be discharged in disgrace, drummed out of camp, and sent home. The general was in a hurry, fearing that Iams' presence might draw open sympathy from other troops and perhaps infect his entire regiment.

Awakened next morning, Iams was jammed into a suit of blue overalls so small that it barely covered his knees. The left half of his mustache and head was shaven bare, and he was made to wear a five-cent straw hat. In this mode he was brought out to face the members of his brigade assembled on the parade ground, while the band sounded doleful strains. All visitors were barred. Colonel Streator galloped to the scene on a white charger and selected twenty men to shoot Iams, should he try to escape. Lengthy charges and penalties were read to him by the regiment adjutant. (The dishonorable discharge meant disfranchisement.) He was put in the center of a hollow square formed by the brigade and walked out of camp to the tune of "The Rogue's March." After reaching Pittsburgh (where he was lionized) he changed clothes, shaved off the rest of his hair, and vowed revenge. He would shoot Streator on sight, he said; as for Snowden, "I will get even with that four-eyed son-of-a-bitch on the hill." He wasted no time filing suit against Streator and the two medics.

There was, it seemed, no end to the marvels emanating from Homestead, and this juvenile incident was the last straw. The army of reporters gathered in the borough and Pittsburgh, writing about the sensational strike in several languages for a dozen countries in both hemispheres, made the most of it. In America reactions concerning the military were almost unanimously hostile, and they were inflamed by unique statements from the loquacious General Snowden: "His [Iams'] conduct was that of aiding, abetting, and giving comfort to our enemy"; and "I have my own opinion as to the character of the punishment that should be meted out to a soldier guilty of treason in time of actual revolution." Thus he concurred with the English *St. James Gazette,* which asserted that Iams deserved "shooting, not torture."

The treatment received by ex-Private Iams was termed barbaric, capricious, tyrannical, unjust, and ferocious; and it was noted that the constitution of the land expressly forbade cruel and unusual punishment, which brought up the basic issue of civil rights for men in active militia service. There was much unhappiness in army and navy circles in Washington, D.C., where the transaction was considered a blow to the prestige of the armed forces. Most officers felt that a routine court-martial would have been more circumspect. "I think that Colonel Streator is worse than Berkman," declared one Captain Hugh Coleman, and a full colonel in the New York Guard was quoted as saying in some bewilderment that he had never heard of a United States soldier being hung up by the thumbs. The Bishop of Harrisburg, Thomas McGovern, denounced the act as a "disgrace to our civilization. . . . If the National Guard is unwilling to restore the tortures of the Inquisition, let them drive Col. Streator out of their ranks." Concerning Iams' chastisement this eastern headline was typical: "It Is Pronounced Too Severe. Soldiers and Civilians Strongly Criticize Col. Streator's Action."

Young Iams testified aggressively in court, denying nothing and belaboring the uncomfortable defendants with raucous witticisms. Witnesses were divided as to whether his punishment had exceeded the alleged crime. To the question "Have you hung up men by the thumbs in your regiment?" Colonel Norman M. Smith of the Pennsylvania Guard responded, "I have never had occasion, but if I had, I would cheerfully do so—I mean I would do so. I wish to strike out the word 'cheerfully.'" After eight days of spirited testimony and gavel pounding, the judge directed the jury to find all three officers not guilty unless it was decided that they had acted "with malice." Upon this basis Streator, Grimm, and Hawkins were at once acquitted.

In the case of Alexander Berkman the issue was cut and dried; it was simply a matter of pronouncing sentence. This formality, whatever it would be, did not appear to concern him. Frick's recovery precluded the death sentence and state laws authorized a maximum sentence of seven years for attempted murder. Berkman had little to say. He criticized the prison food, stated that he would refuse counsel and as an atheist would not be sworn in court, and wrote several letters to Emma Goldman that stunned her with their distant, icy tone. The movement would gather strength from his "instant of righteousness," he predicted; he was under the delusion that an *attentat* in the United States would galvanize the masses as it might have done in chaotic, explosive Mother Russia.

A rebel to the end, he blamed himself repeatedly for not having finished Frick off. Evidently the fault had been in the cheap, small-caliber revolver of low penetrating force;

although, for one whose only training had been a few target sessions while attending school, his marksmanship had
been fairly good. Still, he had failed to kill Frick or himself. He began toying with the idea of escape.[2] Meanwhile
in lieu of a defense (which he disdained because he expected his trial to be a mockery in any event, nor would he
degrade the anarchist cause by pleading for mercy personally or through a hired, capitalist-licensed lawyer) he
worked on an explanation of his motives. His English was
poor, so he prepared it in German. Its thesis was that his
act of pure idealism could not be categorized or judged by
the slanted laws of a rich ruling class. Thus in Pittsburgh's
Murderer's Row the days dragged on, while the taciturn
Berkman chain-smoked, brooded, and scribbled revolutionary sentiments for the edification of American workers, and for posterity.

To his credit, Mr. Frick stayed aloof from the sordid
witch-hunt that automatically followed. Scores of arrests
were made in big cities throughout the nation, especially
in Pittsburgh, which Chief of Police O'Mara discovered to
be "full of men with Anarchist principles . . . and they
were getting ready to carry out some gigantic schemes."
Most people believed that Berkman was a mere pawn in an
anarchist conspiracy. Among others, three known anarchists named Knold, Eckert, and Bauer were jailed in Pittsburgh as his direct accomplices. The charge was baseless;
Bauer, in fact, detested Berkman and had suspected him of
being a counterspy. Bauer and Knold, nonetheless, were
convicted and jailed. But "Who Furnished the Lazy and
Poverty-Stricken Anarchist with Money?" asked the New
York *Tribune,* while fifty policemen searched in vain for
Emma Goldman. It took a reporter to locate her in a sa-

2 An elaborately engineered tunnel almost freed him in 1899.

loon, drinking beer and surrounded by admiring radicals. She was as defiant as ever and, beyond admitting that she expected to be arrested and that she had been living unmarried with "Sasha," refused to answer additional questions. The persistent newsman was beaten up and thrown out into the street.

At length Emma was captured, tried on a charge of making speeches inciting to riot, and sentenced to a year in the Tombs. There she was interviewed by Nellie Bly of the *World,* who found that the ogre threatening the foundations of society was five feet tall "with a saucy turned-up nose and very expressive blue-gray eyes that gazed inquiringly at me through shell-rimmed glasses." She was intrigued by her light brown hair "falling loosely over her forehead, full lips, strong white teeth, a mild, pleasant voice, with a fetching accent." She referred to the little anarchist as a "modern Joan of Arc"—a phrase which incensed many a reader.

The Homestead strikers, too, could scarcely believe that Berkman had been a lone wolf. One of them, Jack Tinford, in jail awaiting trial for throwing dynamite at the barges, whispered to him during an exercise period, "Too bad you didn't kill him. Some business misunderstanding, eh?" When Berkman tried to explain, Tinford moved away in disgust. Even the formidable Johann Most used the incident to turn against him, partially because he and Berkman were intensely jealous of each other over Emma. He was tracked down in New York and flew into a rage at the mention of Berkman's name. "I hate him as much as I hate Frick, who is the czar of America," he exploded. "Berkman has been a botch all his life, as you can see by the poor job he did last Saturday. . . . I have done nothing, but the police, you know, must arrest someone." He referred to Emma as a "harmless creature," an unfortunate phrase which alienated her from him once and for all. A hot-tempered young lady, she publicly horsewhipped him before her arrest.

Berkman was tried on six separate counts, including assault with attempt to kill both Frick and Leishman, felonious entry into the Carnegie offices three times (three indictments here alone), and illegally carrying concealed weapons. The trial was close to a farce. Berkman was not told its date until the morning when he was taken into Judge McClung's courtroom; there he found the jury already seated. The interpreter who was to read his prepared speech was old and half-blind. He stumbled through the first third of it, one halting word at a time, until the judge mercifully stopped him and turned the case over to the jurors. They deliberated without leaving the box and found Berkman guilty on all counts.

McClung gave him the maximum, and by multiplying the charges, as noted above, handed down a sentence of twenty-one years in the Western Penitentiary for assault, plus an additional year in the Allegheny County Workhouse on the concealed weapon charge. Berkman paid dearly for refusing counsel. He had not tried to harm Leishman. The jurors had not been challenged; tripling the legal sentence could easily have been voided by any competent defense attorney; and the right of appeal was not exercised by the bemused defendant, who could only mutter after sentencing, "I did not expect justice and I did not get it." McClung overstepped the law and demonstrated pure vindictiveness, and Berkman was guilty of foolishness and false pride which ruined half his adult life for no logical purpose.

Over and over the strikers disclaimed any connection

with him. While everyone believed them, the attempted
assassination certainly did not advance their cause. Hugh
O'Donnell regretted "that the bullet from Berkman's pistol, failing in its foul attempt, went straight through the
heart of the Homestead strike," an opinion which was incorrect except in the sense that the shooting hardened Mr.
Frick's already granitelike determination to accept no terms
from his former employees but unconditional surrender.

Only the militiamen were breaking the strikers' hearts.
By early August the company was claiming seven hundred
new men at work, including fifty Negroes and a smattering
of technical school graduates. The figure was exaggerated
and the Amalgamated sneered at Superintendent Potter's
assertion that the strike was already broken. When Vice-
Chairman Thomas Crawford of the Advisory Committee
called it a gigantic bluff, Potter invited him to send a
committee to see for themselves. Next day four skilled
workers visited the plant and inspected it microscopically.
At a mass meeting (one was being held in the Opera House
almost every day) they reported that a fair number of men
were inside but that hardly any steel was being manufactured. The firm, they concluded, must be losing such huge
sums that it would have to give in sooner or later. It was
resolved unanimously, therefore, to fight it out. Unfortunately nobody could blink his eyes to the plain fact that
new strikebreakers, slowly but surely, were entering the
mill every day—fifty at a time—through the waterfront
entrance, via the shuttle service of the *Tide* and *Little
Bill*.

To operate normally Mr. Frick needed two thousand
skilled and semiskilled specialists, and he was having
trouble getting them. Common day laborers were a dime a
dozen—they were no problem, and the strikers were rela-

tively uninterested in how many scabs of this class were on the payroll. However, the Associated Press noted that in Baltimore several picked men were hired by Carnegie agents on the spot August 9 and shipped to Homestead. These were the workers the Amalgamated feared most, and they were beginning to arrive in disquieting numbers. But two thousand was a large figure, and at this stage the outcome was still a tossup. As yet not one striker had returned to his job; nevertheless, Mr. Potter, in his daily interview with the press, said he was being swamped by applicants, including strikers. "We made 5 heats last night," he averred, "and the steel was as pretty as any I ever saw." The strikers considered this propaganda and were cheered when, on the same day, superintendent Richard Nichols resigned from Upper Union and joined the Amalgamated. His situation, he said, had become "unbearable."

The fact is that no steel worth mentioning was produced in August. The A. F. of L. pondered the idea of boycotting all Carnegie products (an illegal process in several states, including Pennsylvania) and decided against it because "the firm is not turning out material enough in quantity or of a quality to justify a boycott." Mr. Leishman called this statement "amusing." Thirty-five strikebreakers quit Homestead in a body and were immediately replaced by others more tractable. At the skating rink Sam Gompers addressed fifteen hundred strikers, promised them continuing financial support which would insure victory, and commented concerning Berkman: "I don't know why I should be asked to go out of my way to give Berkman an additional kick. . . . I do know, however, that I have heard of thousands of men being shot down . . . every one of whom was a better man than this despot, Frick."

The political pot was boiling and the war of words continued undiminished. Stated the Milwaukee *Sentinel*: "The attempt to assassinate Mr. Frick is the logical result of the crazy theories brought forward by the Democratic newspapers . . . ," the idea being that Berkman had been rendered insane by the un-American seditiousness of those publications and the utterances of that fanatic, Grover Cleveland, who had recently warned against the machinations of "the favored few." The Chicago *Globe* called the Pinkertons hired assassins, not entitled to the privileges of civilized warfare. As though in reply, the *Nation* countered that their carrying of arms was "lawful and not hostile to constituted authority." The Brooklyn *Eagle* wondered editorially if Carnegie really had to cut wages in order to stay out of the poorhouse. Johann Most in *Freiheit* considered the Homestead struggle "worthy of comparison with the greatest rebel deeds of heroism of all countries of all times." On the other side of the hill Mr. Frick stated, with a passion unusual for him, that he would fight the strike "if it takes all summer and all winter, and all next summer and all next winter . . . to the bitter end. I will never recognize the union, never, never!"

It was an endurance struggle now. Sixteen more strikers were arrested for murder; the usual bail was demanded, and despairingly Weihe wrote Gompers, "It just keeps us going to get bondsmen." Contributions kept pouring in from all over America, but after six weeks the financial burden was straining the Amalgamated to the tune of fifteen hundred dollars each day, with no end in sight.

Slowly the mill grounds filled with scabs, many of whom were worthless characters looking for a few days of novelty, a few free meals, a few dollars from the company. Most of them soon deserted. Some played it both ways by then joining the Amalgamated and sponging a little aid money; upon its delivery they generally left Homestead for good. Others such as the newly recruited East Europeans stayed on their so-called jobs contentedly, living within the fenced area, doing almost nothing, smoking, napping, eating, and apparently quite ready to exist in this delightful limbo forever. Yet, somehow, by the end of the month the last slab of armor plate for the cruiser *Monterey* was being finished. It was clear now that government orders would be filled, in view of the further fact that the contract permitted deadlines to be extended in case of labor troubles.

Imperceptibly public interest waned. Homestead was becoming old-hat, so quickly do fashions in titillation change. There were other momentous events, news, and sensations in the memorable year 1892. November elections were drawing nigh. At Coeur d'Alene, Idaho, spectacular open warfare between silver miners, "black sheep," employers, and militiamen had broken out on an unprecedented scale—the strike was still in the headlines. The nation was also rocked by the case of Miss Borden of Fall River, Massachusetts, who had been most indiscreet on August 4; in the doggerel of the day:

> Lizzie Borden took an ax
> And gave her mother forty whacks.
> When she saw what she had done
> She gave her father forty-one.

A rail strike was paralyzing the East Coast. At Coal Creek, Tennessee, another violent mine strike had erupted in which impetuous militia killed many workers by spraying them with Gatling guns.

One full regiment of the Pennsylvania Guard, including considerable artillery and mounted troops, was sent home.

Surely few people could have known that the massive Homestead lockout-strike, born in bloodshed and weaned on hate, had scarcely begun.

The first break occurred in August at non-union Duquesne, where the Tenth Regiment escorted repairmen, mechanics, and assorted strikebreakers into the plant. A riot started, resulting in the arrest of thirteen strikers after a nasty man hunt on the Munhall hills. A veritable stampede took place when the others tried to get back to their jobs. By all accounts it was a sad and ignoble spectacle. At about the same time the sympathy strike at the 33rd Street Upper Union Mill also collapsed (as expected) and work was resumed non-union and without contract. There was no violence as the men returned listlessly to their jobs. Only the plate mill, however, was operated, the attempt to run the eight-inch, ten-inch, and scrap mills being temporarily abandoned due to a shortage of men. These two company victories were intrinsically minor, but they were a psychological blow to the men at Beaver Falls, Braddock, and Homestead. Without doubt some "non-union deserters," as they were called, returned to work at Homestead and Braddock late that month. Beaver Falls alone remained completely shut down, but, since it had always operated in the red, company officials lost no sleep over it.

Members of the Advisory Committee worked hard to counteract false stories concerning wages previously paid; this was necessary in order to keep contributions flowing in. Although the highest wage paid in one month (to one worker) had been about three hundred dollars, and the average salary of skilled men had been less than half that amount, fairy tales to the contrary were circulated by responsible men who probably knew better. Congressman

George Ticknow Curtis in The *North American Review* referred to wages of even the unskilled Slavs as "exceptionally high" and sadly reported that "it was impossible to shoot those firing from the shore at the barges, because the strikers had made a breastwork for themselves by placing women and children in front and firing from behind them."

Pay figures were specifically distorted on a grand scale by industrialist Lewis S. Gillette: "The 240 men who have been reduced were the head-rollers or sub-contractors, who have been making, strange as it may seem, from $10 to $50 a day; some have made as much as $13,000 a year, all owing to the improved machinery which increases the output of piecework." But as August waned, it seemed increasingly useless for the Amalgamated to fan the dying embers of controversy. With ruin facing the union members and all those who had participated actively in the July 6 battle, it was essential to win the strike and stop the bickering.

Each day hundreds of strikers filed into union headquarters to receive their subsistence allotment, and they did so more silently than heretofore. The days of bravado were gone. Mr. Pattison's state guard, the *Tide* and *Little Bill*, and even Sheriff McCleary's languid force of deputies had made a mockery of their once-powerful picket line; it was a scrawny, bedraggled affair now. In Homestead and Munhall tempers were growing short and the atmosphere was dangerously charged. More and more unpleasant incidents took place, providing mildly diverting copy for readers of the eastern press turning the pages *en passant* toward the sports section. When a confused or drunken scab named Pat Coyne entered the room of another, Max Newman, late at night, Newman awoke and drilled him with a bullet between the eyes. Hidden in freight cars crossing the Monongahela, strikers kept firing at the hated *Little Bill*. Four strikebreakers accused of larceny were acquitted but were almost lynched by a mob when they emerged from the county courthouse; they were saved by military police carrying fixed bayonets and half-cocked rifles.

Violence against the scabs had become chronic, and hardly a day passed without incident. They were waylaid, slugged, bombarded with bricks, pelted with slingshots, wounded by bullets, and pistol-whipped. Sheriff McCleary could not fathom the abysmal ineffectiveness of his men. He swore in fifty more, and a few days later enlisted ninety-one scabs as deputies. The total was well over two hundred at this stage, all armed but not inclined to act. They stood by, for example, when two outsiders named Fyock and Homer were jumped by several strikers. Fyock drew a gun, fired, missed, and hit a boy in the leg. A wagon driver, Frank Milliken, who had been moving non-union men into vacated Homestead dwellings, was seized one evening and his face battered in a protracted, noisy brawl which attracted no deputies. After a personal investigation proved to McCleary that most of his euphemistically termed "posse" had allowed themselves to be sworn in for the sole purpose of drawing pay, he fired almost half the force. He was disgusted with the whole mess, he announced, and added that any man who took his office, even at fifteen thousand dollars per year, "would be an idiot." The last of the strikers to die was George Rutter; he had been delirious ever since July 6, and on his deathbed was still raving, still imagining that he was trading shots with the Pinkertons on the water's edge. He was buried at Verona, where his widow and children were presently living.

Mr. Frick was receiving enough letters, usually deco-

rated with skull and crossbones, to fill an album. They
threatened him with dynamite and shooting, and after being perused with sour satisfaction were filed in his waste-
basket. Superintendent Potter was stoned while sitting on
the porch of his Eleventh Avenue Munhall home. The
home of one scab was burned to the ground. A large
boardinghouse where strikebreakers lived was also set afire.
At one of the Union mills a dynamite charge was set off,
which did considerable damage. Local boycotts were numerous; a butcher, for one, was blacklisted by all strikers
and their families merely for furnishing ice to the troops.

The militiamen, too, began causing trouble. Those who
remained (another regiment was recalled in August) were
fed up and clamoring to leave. Drunkenness in the ranks
increased. For the first time, fist fights between them and
the Homestead men took place. In the heat and deadly
boredom discipline sagged. Burgess McLuckie—only a fig-
urehead now, in and out of jail—prepared warrants for the
arrest of several soldiers who had been accosting and insulting women of the town. Wives and daughters of the
strikers were no longer safe, he told newsmen, as long as
troops remained in Homestead. Another scab was beaten
unconscious by two strikers near the Upper Union Mill.
The Amalgamated issued a statement that the new men
were drinking beer and hard liquor on the job and leaving the Homestead works in a state of intoxication. The
red-light district around Sixth and McClure flourished as
never before. Another riot was quelled at Duquesne by the
state troopers on August 13 when strikers tried strenuously
to induce the workers to strike again.

All these acts of violence, robbery, arson, and immorality
were symptomatic of a dying organism. In New York and
Buffalo the rail strike was crushed, and a portent of things

to come was expressed by the headline: "Luckless Switch-men Told to Get Back Their Places If They Can." On the last day of August, Henry Frick walked into the Home-stead plant for the first time since June. He was satisfied with operations there, he said. "As far as the company is concerned, the strike is a thing of the past."

This was not yet correct. Unlike conditions in the steel industry today, in 1892 a mill such as Homestead could not show a profit without running full, or almost full. Not even Frick could claim that it was doing so. Interest, fixed charges, the salaries of idle managers, and overhead and maintenance costs continued day after day, as certain as death and taxes. Even if by early September the plant was running at 50 percent capacity, which it was not, the com-pany was losing heavily in unfilled orders and cancelled contracts. Frick would never surrender; that was certain, but how long would Andrew Carnegie's volatile patience hold out? He was, in addition, a lukewarm Republican and well aware that the strike was crippling Mr. Harrison's chances.

As Chauncey Depew expressed it after the election: ". . . the Homestead strike was one of the most important factors in the presidential contest, and led to a distinct issue in the campaign. It happened at a crisis and injured us irremediably. . . . The Republican leaders attempted early in the campaign to have the strike settled and cabled Mr. Carnegie direct without consulting Mr. Frick. Every inducement was made to bring Mr. Carnegie into the can-vass, but he persistently declined to lend his influence or to pay one dollar to the campaign fund."

The attitude of many liberals and workingmen, who had formerly voted Republican under the illusion that protection would protect, was switching fast; and this graceless poem gained currency:

> The mills of the gods grind slowly,
> And they grind exceeding fine;
> And in the ides of November
> You'll find us all in line.
> Our bullets made of paper,
> We'll plunk them in so hot
> That the G.O.P. will wonder
> If they ever were in the plot.
> For we are the people and
> We'll occupy the land
> In spite of the Carnegies'
> Or Pinkerton's brigands.

With few exceptions such as Hugh O'Donnell ("I am a Republican and a Protectionist," he announced from the Allegheny County Jail, where he had been incarcerated for the third or fourth time), the men of Homestead would vote Democratic; but that was two months off. Meanwhile they had a strike on their hands which was going from bad to worse. They hung on and hoped for a miracle—Mr. Carnegie perhaps? The exhaustion of management? Could Frick be overruled? Furthermore, the mighty Braddock works were operating even more feebly than Homestead.

They pondered the simple arithmetic of the case. Assume (they assumed) that Frick had a thousand men at work at the moment (he claimed fifteen hundred). But four thousand were needed to run Homestead full, a tenth of whom had to be ultraskilled, dyed-in-the-wool experts trained from adolescence. Over half the remainder had to be semiskilled mechanics, repairmen, shearmen, assistant rollers, and so on, in addition to division foremen and their helpers. Where would they come from? How many unemployed elite of this ilk in the United States could fill the bill? Few enough, and still fewer would do the dirty job of strikebreaking at Homestead. So ran the theory. Yet production was rising, slowly to be sure, but rising. Fact was extinguishing theory but the strikers stood pat, and their obstinacy must be considered one of the most remarkable aspects of the conflict.

Bit by bit the picket lines disintegrated until they no longer existed except, in vestigial form, near the main entrance on east Eighth Avenue. Three thousand men walked the streets aimlessly day and night, most of them too broke even to patronize the saloons. Always they tried to prevent new men from entering. At times they used force—the Pittsburgh newspapers were full of such incidents—but as a rule the visual deterrent of a horde of hard-looking, unshaven men was sufficient to give pause to many an applicant. Some scabs, usually men with families, who were trusted by company officials were allowed to leave the mill grounds after work, and with considerable courage circulated in Munhall and Homestead, but the great majority never went past the gate. The unnatural conditions under which they lived will be noted later in this narrative.

Picketing had failed. There was some question, anyway, whether it had done more harm than good. Public opinion was dubious about it, and many a good citizen wondered if strikers had the right to bar (more or less forcibly) new workers from employment, not to mention the cardinal sin of locking the managers out of their own property. The quandary has existed to this day, as Samuel Yellen has underscored in his treatise on Homestead in *American Labor Struggles,* wherein he quotes Mr. Godkin's *Nation,* then a middle-of-the-road publication, as condemning strikers for depriving "rich men of their property and poor men of their right to labor." The poor men to whom Godkin referred were strikebreakers. As for the Amalgamated, it was "morally responsible for Berkman's performance. . . . If it was right to murder the Pinkertons . . . it was right and logical to try to kill the employer of the Pinkertons." Chairman William Oates took exactly the same former view in his report: "The right of any man to labor, upon whatever terms he and his employer agree, whether he belongs to a labor organization or not . . . is secured by the laws of the land."

So those who picketed were damned if they did and damned if they didn't; if they did they were morally and legally wrong, if they did not they passively accepted defeat. Religious leaders were sorely perplexed by the problem in ethics raised at Homestead. Regarding strikers the Protestant *Independent* was adamant: "They have no more right to decide how the mills shall be operated, or by whom, than a coachman has to bar his employer out of his own carriage." The *Christian Union,* however, took a roundhouse swing at any and all wage cuts, scabs, blacklists, and the minions of Robert and William Pinkerton. The *Christian Advocate* rejected picketing and stated, "This is no time to arbitrate. The battle of law and order must be fought to the end." But, argued the *Congregationalist,* enormous companies erected upon the labor of thousands cannot be considered "merely private property," an attitude echoed by the *Baptist Quarterly Review,* which blamed a society in which four thousand men controlled two-thirds of the nation's wealth and tilted the scales of legal justice heavily against the laboring man. The *Watchman* supported the Carnegie company and the Pinkertons right down the line. And if clergymen were sharply divided on the issue so dramatically crystallized at Homestead, they reflected the perplexities of all men during the hapless '90s.

In New Orleans "Gentlemen Jim" Corbett, a three-to-one underdog, knocked out bloody, battered John L. Sullivan with a right hook to the head in round twenty-one. It was a clean-cut, clear-cut, perfect solution to an issue that anyone could understand. But the Homestead strike seemed endless and insoluble, defying, as it were, all laws of economic gravity. Days, weeks, and months passed. Within the mill grounds over a thousand men worked, ate, and slept in monklike seclusion. Services were held each Sunday, one of which was described with perhaps a glint of irony by a Pittsburgh newspaper: "With for a church the biggest mill in America, boarded by a high fence and a protectorate of one hundred and fifty armed watchmen, with one thousand soldiers in easy reach, the non-union men in the Homestead plant gave thanks to God this morning." They gathered on rough benches within the beam mill while an orchestra played "Nearer, My God, to Thee" and Chaplain Adams of the Sixteenth Regiment preached a sermon on Saul of Tarsus.

Their food was none too good, and, as usual during summer, working conditions were brutally hot; but these factors could not explain the baffling rate at which they were sickening and dying. Doctors could not definitely diagnose the ailment. Whatever it was—dysentery and typhoid fever were the usual guesses—*Tide* and *Little Bill* were kept busy every evening transporting the ill and the dead across the river to Pittsburgh's hospitals and morgue. There was something very suspicious about the affair.

In Pittsburgh, Munhall, Braddock, Homestead, and Duquesne, Labor Day was not celebrated. Silence reigned, no bands played, no workers paraded, and there is no record in the local press of a single speech by any personage allied with either of the warring factions. Those at work put in their normal hours; it was not an off day. Mr. Frick, whose ardor for the holiday was probably not white-hot, spent it in his office as usual. He had more cards up his sleeve and was preparing to play them.

To all appeals for accommodation; to all remonstrance and argument; to the county of Allegheny, looking forward to an enormous bill of damages, to the Commonwealth of Pennsylvania, hurrying eight thousand soldiers from their daily vocations to protect them, at a cost of twenty-five thousand dollars a day, to the people of the United States, who gave them their monopoly and stuffed their pockets with unearned money; to the three thousand operatives at Homestead; and to the women and children whose homes are practically confiscated over their heads and who must follow their husbands and fathers into exile, they [Carnegie and Frick] answer only that they will do as they like with their own. They will have their pound of flesh . . . they will crush the "Amalgamated"; they will employ no union men; they will pocket the largest profits— but they will pay the wages that please them, and entertain no question about that.

—*Chauncey F. Black in* Forum

IX *Treason!*

From start to finish the paramount issue was recognition of the Amalgamated Association at Homestead, Beaver Falls, and the Upper and Lower Union Mills, those plants where company-union contracts had existed before the strike. A mere conversation between officials on both sides after July 1 would have sufficed to imply that recognition. Earlier in the game it had seemed worthwhile to sound out Mr. Carnegie himself, in hopes that he would influence Mr. Frick. Since the union had no way of reaching Carnegie, a prominent intermediary was needed. During a visit to Homestead, an A. F. of L. committee suggested Whitelaw Reid, publisher of the New York *Tribune,* former minister to France, presently candidate for Vice-President on the ticket with Benjamin Harrison, a man who surely would be interested in bringing peace to a tariff-assisted industry. With the unanimous approval of the Advisory staff, Hugh O'Donnell set out for New York to approach him. There he dictated a letter, ostensibly from Homestead, in the office of one of the editors. Excerpts indicate the deteriorating, supplicating position of the strike leaders:

HON. WHITELAW REID, New York, N. Y.

DEAR SIR:—I address you in behalf of the 12,000 inhabitants of Homestead, Pennsylvania. In their name I ask that you interest yourself in the unfortunate controversy still pending between them and the Carnegie Steel Company, by whom the majority of the adult population of the town is employed.

In presenting the matter to you I have no desire to dwell upon the merits or demerits of the conflict. I am looking toward the future, not the past. . . . A borough, not only one of the most prosperous in Pennsylvania but in the entire Union, whose population represents to the highest degree the thrift, industry, intelligence and morality—in short, the best tendencies of the American people, is at present practically under martial law. . . . It is in the interests of no one that this state of affairs should continue . . . there is but one, and only one, course to pursue . . . an honorable settlement . . .

It is not desirable . . . that the men who have by years of patient toil acquired a little homestead should be cut off from their employment if it can be prevented in any honorable way. . . . How shall it be done? Simply let the Carnegie Company recognize the Amalgamated Association by re-opening the conference doors, and I have no hesitation in saying that when that is done the end of the strike is at hand. I am warranted in saying that there is no disposition on the part of the employees to stand upon a question of scale, or wages, or hours, or anything else. . . .

I believe you are in a position to render more effective
service than, perhaps, any other man in this country. . . . My
appeal is not in the name of any political party, nor in the
name of organized labor, but for the sake of the men, women
and little children that make up our present distressed community.

Sincerely and respectfully yours,

HUGH O'DONNELL

Upon being handed this letter, Mr. Reid phoned Mr.
Frick and asked Mr. Carnegie's address for the purpose of
telegraphing him. It required no astuteness to smell what
was in the wind, and Frick refused to cooperate. Reid then
obtained it from John C. New, the U. S. Consul General
in London, and cabled Carnegie via State Department
cipher to accept a quick, amicable settlement. Mr. Carnegie was at first inclined to do so; he was sick of the mess
and in a mood to take any face-saving way out. "We have
telegram," he cabled Pittsburgh, "from Tribune Reid
high official London Amalgamated Association reference
Homestead Steel Works. The proposition is worthy of consideration. Replied 'nothing can be done. Send H. C. Frick
document.' You must decide without delay. Amalgamated
Association evidently distressed."

One may imagine Frick's reaction to this recommendation for a policy of appeasement. Happily for him, Carnegie changed his mind next morning and dispatched the
following: "After due consideration we have concluded
Tribune too old. Probably the proposition is not worthy of
consideration. Useful showing distress of Amalgamated Association. Use your own discretion about terms and starting. George Lauder, Henry Phipps, Jr., Andrew Carnegie
solid. H. C. Frick forever!" By "too old" he meant "too
late." But it was not really too late to deal with the union

if Carnegie, at heart, wished to do so. Another factor, without doubt, was his fear of Frick, or his unwillingness to split with him. He was dependent upon the man, whatever he may have thought of him personally, and felt that the future of the company lay in Frick's hands. By "starting" he meant "continuing." The mills were already operating when he sent off the second cablegram quoted above, and by mid-September the production curve was smoothly ascending.

Temperatures in the Pittsburgh region continued abnormally high all summer. Within Homestead's converting departments they were recorded up to 150 degrees. The shanties which housed most of the strikebreakers, called "Potterville" by the strikers in honor of Superintendent Potter, were a sea of discontent. Desertions therefrom by the day laborers were extremely numerous, and even some of the lower-paid mechanics and repairmen participated in the daily exodus. For a time, in fact, these removals, in the words of one newspaper, proceeded "at such a lively rate . . . as to threaten to depopulate the mill in a week." A few of the workers were maimed for life by machinery with which they were not fully familiar. That strange intestinal disease persisted—normal treatment for dysentery and typhoid had no effect on it. Company men tried hard, but not too successfully, to keep the fearful, unhappy men within the confines of the wooden fence. For a change in diet, deputy sheriffs occasionally escorted them into town where restaurant owners were compelled to feed them; under the Brooks law of Pennsylvania they would have forfeited their licenses if they had refused. One or more scabs usually slipped away after each meal. A certain Henry Stocher of Philadelphia made such a nuisance of himself that he was ejected by his superiors. He had been told that he was to get work as a bricklayer in Pittsburgh. "We were made prisoners in the works and guarded like convicts," he reported. "The more ignorant were told by the foreman that if they ventured outside the union men would shoot them like dogs. . . . At least half of them are sick from heat, bad water and poor food."

Petty incidents became routine and received scant attention from local papers and the wires of Associated Press. To avoid arguments and threats, a strikebreaker named Hugh Sweeney escaped by simply scaling the fence. The tiny incident was reported as a tiny news item. Information concerning illnesses and deaths was suppressed by the company, which posted signs reading "No Newspaper Men Allowed Inside." Despite this, one reporter gained entrance and wrote that practically all machinery was in action. He was nearly but not quite correct. Every department was operating to a limited degree except for the 23-inch plate mill, and mediocre steel was being produced and delivered. The Fifteenth Regiment left the area, leaving only elements of the Sixteenth. Pinkerton operatives had infiltrated the strikers' ranks by the scores and were attending secret lodge meetings. Those apprehended were not shown the quality of mercy. From a train passing over the yards on a trestle, strikers threw circulars printed in English and German; they promised all deserters good treatment and free train fare home. Company officials were furious, but hundreds of leaflets got into the hands of men inside. Then came a grand rush toward the exit, and nothing could stop a large number of scabs from departing. The *Tide* was fired upon by unknown men who had improvised a small, ridiculous cannon for the purpose.

They missed. Paul Oldshue, one of the Amalgamated officials in charge of the Slav and Hungarian strikers, noted that his men were becoming restless; he asked the Advisory Committee for extra cash to keep them in line. Brawls in the saloons became more numerous. It was advisable for strangers with soft, smooth palms to stay out of them—indeed, this characteristic had long been grounds for suspicion. And still the "black sheep" poured in.

They came on the *Tide* and *Little Bill,* and (escorted by troops) by rail from Swissvale, across the river near Braddock, their journey's end being the Munhall depot at the east end of Eighth Avenue. Due to deceptive hiring practices by Carnegie agents, these excursions were occasionally unpleasant. For example, one named F. W. Nye hired fifty-six men in Cincinnati, promising easy work and good pay in a steel plant other than Homestead. When they boarded the cars the doors and windows were locked, armed guards were found to be in charge, and later they were told their true destination. A riot commenced which continued all the way to Munhall; several men were cut by bayonets, and as one worker recounted, "plenty of black eyes were given. The doors were forced open and men began dropping off." While only twenty-one of them were brought into the mill, from Mr. Frick's standpoint twenty-one were better than none.

In truth, his major worry at the time was not the number of new men gradually augmenting his work force but the illnesses, deaths, and state of panic among them. The first step in solving the riddle was a discovery by Pittsburgh physicians that the patients responded to treatment for poisoning. What followed was another in the never-ending series of lurid episodes that marked the Homestead lockout from beginning to end.

Secretly Pinkerton detectives began investigating the food being brought into the mill, and the men who handled it. Weeks passed before they nabbed their man— Robert Beatty—who at once confessed that he had hired a cook named Patrick Gallagher to dissolve a yellowish ash into the coffee and soup of the workers. It was a mixture of arsenic and croton oil varied with powders of antimony. The plot thickened. Its mastermind, it developed, was one Hugh F. Dempsey, Master Workman, District Assembly 3, Knights of Labor, a skinny little bald gent with a straggling mustache and mocking gray eyes. Until now he had had no personal connection with the strike. Dempsey, Beatty, and Gallagher were arrested, tried, convicted, and handed sentences of seven years, seven years, and five years respectively. The verdict was slightly questionable. Since at least three workers had died as a result of the alleged poisoning, one wonders why Dempsey did not receive the death penalty. No testimony other than oral was introduced at the trial; no poison was brought into evidence.

Dempsey denied his guilt doggedly. The Pittsburgh *Post* justified the verdict but observed, "The leading witnesses against Dempsey—his paid accomplices—were utterly unworthy of belief"; and both of them later recanted their confessions. Gallagher startled the country by averring that he had lied throughout the trial, and that the whole affair had been trumped up by the Pinkertons, who had promised him complete immunity if he would talk as they directed. At any rate, the men served out their sentences after losing repeated appeals for pardon. "There is no desire to interfere," wrote Mr. Frick piously to the Board of Pardons, ". . . but the claim of innocence and unfair trial heretofore made is so manifestly untrue as to call for a protest from every well-informed and law-abiding citizen."

The Knights of Labor stood by their disgraced official, insisting that he was innocent, and not only kept him on their rolls throughout his term in the penitentiary but re-elected him as Master Workman—a gesture which accelerated the breakdown of that once-powerful organization. Guilty or not, the convicted men contributed nothing to the strikers' cause and confirmed a growing suspicion that members of labor unions were dangerous, or deluded, or demented anarchists, or a combination of all three. But public attitudes did not matter much any longer. The men of Homestead stood fast, and so did the men of Carnegie; it was late September and few—possibly none—of the strikers had applied for reinstatement. "The firmness with which these strikers hold on is surprising to everyone," Frick wrote Carnegie, adding his hope that there would be a change after the election. As yet he had neither broken their unity nor crushed their determination to resist; and three months after the outbreak he was still perplexed by a Gordian knot—how to acquire enough trained, high-quality men to run Homestead near full capacity.

On September 22 the grand jury returned 167 true bills against Homestead strikers who had participated in the battle. The indictments ranged from murder to conspiracy to aggravated riot. Total bail exceeded half a million dollars—an impossible amount—causing about a hundred of the indicted men to skip town. Jack Clifford, Hugh O'Donnell, Hugh Ross, and Sylvester Critchlow were faced with murder charges and imprisoned without bail for seven months. Others such as John McLuckie and William Roberts each put up ten thousand dollars and were freed, pending trial. The rank and file were confused by these technical maneuvers and began to acquire a guilt complex—were they, after all, nothing but a collection of killers, rioters, conspirators?

Once more the legal merry-go-round turned. Next day Burgess McLuckie made informations against Frick, Leishman, Lovejoy, Potter, eight other Carnegie officials, William and Robert Pinkerton, and five other detectives; all were charged with accessory to murder, conspiracy, and aggravated riot. They were arrested in Pittsburgh and New York, and freed on bail supplied by Pittsburgh bankers Andrew and Richard Mellon. The bonds were made out in advance. The men in question simply filled in their names, signed at the bottom, handed them to the desk sergeant, and walked out the door.

The indictment against O'Donnell was, of course, baseless, but the other three men charged with murder were definitely in trouble. Critchlow had always been a fire-eater and had been seen in action at the waterfront by any number of people. As for Ross, he was known to be another tough customer; yet it could not be firmly established that he had fired bullets or thrown dynamite on July 6. The evidence against Clifford was serious. One Pinkerton swore that he (Clifford) fired into the barges while shouting obscenities at the guards. A Carnegie company clerk testified that he saw him attach a fuse to a piece of dynamite in an iron pipe and throw it at the inboard scow, while a revolver protruded from his pocket. When the question of who had fired the first shot arose, Judge Ewing refused to hear testimony. "The parties on the shore had no duties to perform except to go away," he said. "There is no question—there *can* be no question—of self-defense about it."

In the end, these four defendants and scores of others charged with lesser crimes were acquitted. The jury deliberated only one hour in finding Critchlow not guilty of murdering the guard Connors. Ordinarily O'Donnell *et al.* would have been released on the spot; but, even as the grand jury was pondering, a new blow was directed against the strikers—the most crushing and bewildering thus far. On September 30 Chief Justice Edward Paxson instructed the grand jury to issue warrants against thirty-five Amalgamated men, including the entire Advisory Committee, for treason, under the Crimes Act of 1860. Some immediately fled. Four went to jail, or stayed there, one of whom (as usual) was Hugh O'Donnell, and one was released on the ten-thousand-dollar bail which had become automatic.

At one fell swoop this move deprived the strikers of their leadership and may be considered the most devastating single action taken by the authorities to extinguish the strike after the arrival of the Pennsylvania State Guard. Nobody had even been prosecuted, much less convicted, under the statute, which called it treason for "anyone owing allegiance to the Commonwealth of Pennsylvania, who shall levy war against the same, or shall adhere to the enemies thereof, giving them aid or comfort within the State or elsewhere . . ." In Philadelphia, General Snowden— ever voluble, obsessed as always with death and treason and conspiracy and the like—claimed credit for the master stroke. "I am the man who suggested that these men be indicted for treason. I told Knox & Reed to do it and they prepared the papers . . . the punishment, I believe, is a heavy fine and long imprisonment. It ought to be changed to death." Specifically the fine and imprisonment were not to exceed two thousand dollars and twelve years. The Amalgamated increased its legal staff to seven, and Mr. Weihe stated that the fight would be fought to the end.

The charge smacked of harrassment rather than sober

law enforcement. Only a year earlier the Pennsylvania Assembly had passed a statute making it quite legal for workers to strike "without subjecting them to indictment . . . under the criminal laws of this commonwealth"; the concept, anyway, that the Homestead men were levying war against the state of Pennsylvania was palpably invalid. In the *Chicago Law Journal* John Gibbons further pointed out that the element of intent was necessary to make a treason charge stick; and the Homestead strikers had "never intended to make war upon the commonwealth or overthrow its authority."

General Snowden to the contrary, Paxson seems to have acted unilaterally. There is no record that he interfered upon the request of any local authority, although strike leaders claimed they had proof that he was prodded by Frick. The judge asserted that he merely wished to test the applicability of the Crimes Act in strikes involving violence; he was an unprejudiced seeker after truth.

The presiding judge of the Allegheny County grand jury announced that Paxson had "kindly consented" to instruct the jury. Paxson next told newsmen that he himself would hear applications for bail and pronounce the verdicts, if and when the accused were tried and convicted. In this Alice-in-Wonderland setting the news broke upon an astonished America, to be greeted by a storm of protest. Almost all publications, legal authorities, and laymen denounced Paxson. It was not so much that his plan was novel, and had never been attempted before in any state, but that it was motivated by an antilabor bias almost embarrassingly obvious and extreme. In Homestead it came as a surprise, the greatest sensation since Berkman's assault on Frick. Business practically stopped. Anxious groups assembled and asked, "What does it mean?" How could their leaders possibly be considered traitors? While Amalgamated attorney Brennen was certain that Paxson could not obtain convictions, he too was taken aback. "Why," he exclaimed, "we were just talking about bringing suits against the Carnegie people for treason, for bringing an armed force into the community and attempting to usurp the power of the Government. . . . It seems to me that Judge Paxson should have issued warrants for the other fellows."

Paxson's charge before the grand jury, heard by an overflowing hushed audience, amounted to a long indictment of the strikers in the tone of a prosecuting lawyer:

A mere mob, collected upon the impulse of the moment . . . does not commit treason, although it destroys property and takes human life. But when a large number of men arm and organize themselves by divisions and companies, appoint officers and engage in a common purpose to defy the law, to resist its officers, and to deprive any portion of their fellow citizens of the rights to which they are entitled . . . it is a levying of war against the State, and the offense is treason. . . .
The employer cannot compel his employee to work a day longer than he sees fit. . . . It follows that the employee cannot compel his employer to give him work. . . . The men had no further demand upon its property than has a domestic servant upon the household goods of his employer when he is discharged. . . . We can have some sympathy with a mob driven to desperation by hunger as in the days of the French Revolution, but we have none for men receiving exceptionally high wages in resisting the law and resorting to violence and bloodshed in the assertion of imaginary rights. . . . It is much to be feared that there is a diseased state of public opinion growing up with regard to disturbances of this nature. . . . If life was taken in pursuance of a purpose to resist the landing of the men by violence, the offense was murder. . . .

These were not instructions to a jury but a demand for a finding of guilt. The Senate committee's report later dismissed the harangue in a single dry sentence: "Chief Jus-

tice Paxson's charge, which, in some respects, seems un-
necessarily severe in its strictures, is submitted without
further comment." The *American Law Review* called it "a
mass of stale, medieval verbiage, drawn seemingly from
some old precedents not dating later than the reign of
William and Mary."

Having been thus enlightened by the judge, the grand
jury obediently returned true bills against the Advisory
Committee members. Unable to raise bail, nine more of
them were imprisoned. When their cases came up, however, the verdicts of the jury were identical right down the
line: "Not guilty . . . not guilty . . . not guilty. . . ."
No Pittsburgh jury, in short, had yet found, or would find,
any striker guilty on any charge. In this respect the company had failed; but in a larger sense it had succeeded, for
by mid-October legal costs (added to the inexorable flow of
subsistence outlays) had drained the treasury of all eight
lodges. Even the Amalgamated national, supporting its
Homestead local to the limit, was running dry. Contributions from other sympathizers and unions were dwindling;
such donations seemed like pouring water down a bottom-
less well.

O'Donnell, Ross, and others stayed in jail until as late as
March, 1893. When acquitted on a murder charge they
were arraigned for conspiracy. When acquitted, they were
charged with riot. When acquitted, they were charged
with assault; and so on. People elsewhere were becoming
weary of the Homestead strike and its mulish antagonists.
Many were surprised to learn—such as when Paxson
brought up the treason charge—that it was still in progress.
It was fifteen weeks old now. The question being asked,
outside of Homestead and Munhall, was no longer how it
would end, but when. With our gift of hindsight we won-

der on what grounds, at this late date, the strikers still hoped to contrive some kind of settlement with the Carnegie Steel Company, Limited.

Early that October morning the Dalton boys rode into Coffeyville, Kansas, with the modest intention of robbing two banks simultaneously. Seldom has there been such a fiasco. Within minutes four of the five bandits were dead, and four of the townspeople. "DIED WITH THEIR BOOTS ON," screamed the headlines.

As the month receded into history, football became the absorbing topic. Wesleyan (closing the football gap) lost to Princeton only 60 to 0, having been beaten the previous year 76 to 0. Yale swamped Tufts 44 to 0. Harvard worked out a 30–10 win over Amherst. In a double sense there was a chill in the northern air of the nation and especially in Homestead.

A gentleman named William Morrison proceeded briskly along Chicago's streets in a carriage powered by electricity and not preceded by horses. The apparition caused so much curiosity, and alarm on the part of dogs, that he was forced to request police to clear the right of way. Surely 1892 was a year to remember.

On October 17 a heater, a mechanic, an engineer, and a day laborer applied for work and were rehired. These were grave defections, perhaps the first which could be substantiated, and they were admitted by Amalgamated headquarters. At about the same time the Homestead *Local News* asserted that two thousand men were now operating the plant, a tenth of them former employees. It concluded, "First—The Carnegie Company is gradually succeeding. Second—The great Homestead strike is gradually dying out." Much indignation followed this assessment—the

News was accused of outright treachery—but privately most strikers were discouraged and ready to call it quits. Pressed close to ruin, storekeepers were outspokenly asking for an end to the struggle. Sam Gompers came to town, was met by a brass band, and made a vigorous speech in which he lashed out at Paxson's treason charge and predicted that if the men stood fast they would win. He was followed on the stand by Amalgamated members who went even further; the company, they insisted, was practically whipped. Wonderment followed these words. Was it possible that their leaders and Mr. Gompers were right?

A great Democratic parade, including hundreds of strikers, was held in Homestead and wound its way north to the county jail, where three cheers were shouted for O'Donnell and other strikers imprisoned within. It then proceeded down Fifth Street to the Carnegie offices, which were booed. One banner showed a rooster and the inscription:

> The cock will crow in '92
> Over Fort Frick and its Pinkerton crew.

To the question of who protected the locked-out men was writ this answer: "Ask McKinley." And more poesy was raised aloft:

> Show us a man in a Pittsburgh mill
> Who has had his wages raised by the
> McKinley bill.

But the tariff issue in respect to the strike was dead as a doornail, while the problem of raising money to prevent an immediate collapse was more alive and growing larger with each passing day. When during late October a "Homestead Day" was celebrated in Chicago by ninety thousand unionists from various crafts, forty thousand dollars was contributed to the Amalgamated Association, which allocated the entire amount to the Homestead lodges. It was the biggest single financial injection yet received by the striking men; but, impressive as it was, it was no panacea, for over four thousand souls (sixteen hundred strikers and their dependents) were still on strike relief in Homestead and Munhall. At most, the sum might help prolong the agony for another couple of weeks. "We are badly in need of shoes and wearing apparel," Thomas J. Crawford of the Amalgamated wrote Gompers. In desperation the A. F. of L. decided to run another Homestead Day. Workers would contribute to the limit; theaters and other places of amusement would be asked to donate a portion of their proceeds. The rally, scheduled for December 13, never took place.

And still the Advisory Committee was swamped daily with letters and telegrams exhorting them not to weaken; unfortunately these brave words were cheap, easy to utter by those not engaged in the struggle, and seldom accompanied by hard cash. It is a fact that throughout the strike the Knights of Labor, some ninety thousand strong, contributed a grand total of several hundred dollars, amounting almost to a calculated insult to the rival A. F. of L. of which the Amalgamated was its most potent bulwark. It is not implausible to suggest that Mr. Powderly's cohorts were willing to see the strike fail. More locked-out men left the valley of the Monongahela for jobs elsewhere. More strikers asked company hiring officials for their jobs back, and in most cases they got them back routinely after signing individual agreements never again to join a labor union while employed by the firm. As yet not one member of the original hard core of Amalgamated members—those 325 who had comprised the eight locals early in the year—

had defected, and even if they had done so they had little chance (as everyone well knew) of being rehired. When Mr. Frick was asked by a member of the Congressional investigating committee if the Carnegie Steel Company had a blacklist, he replied, "No, sir," but as it happens a blacklist was very much in effect, and would remain rigidly in effect long after the strike was over, whether Frick knew it or cared to admit it.

The last soldiers had left Homestead on October 13. Sheriff McCleary, fearing the worst, almost doubled his force of deputies by swearing in new mill workers. On or about that date all scabs residing in "Potterville" who wished to leave were allowed to do so. Most of them departed and took lodgings in the boroughs, although a few stayed on for months to come. Both these events created another reign of terror within the community, including ugly cases of racism due to the considerable number of Negro strikebreakers now at work. "BULLETS FLY AT HOMESTEAD" reported the *Tribune,* when two Negroes were jumped by strikers on Fourth Avenue. The opponents drew guns, about fifty shots were fired, three men were wounded, and the Negroes were badly beaten before being taken into custody by law officers. A particularly unpopular scab named Martin Conrad, finding a large crowd gathered in front of his house, emerged in the doorway with a revolver in each hand and announced that he would shoot the first man who approached. He too was rescued by deputies who dispersed the throng. These and similar incidents, including the usual saloon brawls, were commonplace for several days. Then an apprehensive peace descended upon the Pittsburgh region. The lockout-strike was in its fourth month, and few could doubt but that the end was near.

As bullets and recriminations flew in Homestead, correspondence flew between Carnegie and Frick. Both could
sense the impending victory, and Carnegie seems to have
been genuinely concerned that Frick, and Frick almost
singly, had returned within the sphere of public opinion
to his former role as archvillain of the piece. When he
(Carnegie) suggested that he return to the States and take
his place in the closing stage of the struggle, Frick replied,
"It seems to me that you would enjoy a trip in Italy much
more . . . postpone your return till next spring. . . ."

But, complained Carnegie, "this fight is too much
against our *Chairman*—partakes of personal issue. It is very
bad indeed for you—and also bad for the interests of the
firm.

"There's another point which troubles me on your account—the danger that the public and hence all our men
get the impression that it is *all Frick*—Your influence *for
good* would be permanently impaired—you don't deserve a
bad name, but then one is sometimes wrongfully got—
Your partners should be as much identified with this
struggle as you—think over this counsel. It is from a very
wise man as you know and a true friend. A. C."

To this sensible and well-meaning advice Frick responded with his customary churlishness: "I am at a little
loss to know just why you should express yourself so. . . .
I note the counsel you give, but I cannot see wherein I can
profit by it, or what action could be taken by me that
would change matters in respect to that which you mention." In other words, he still wished Carnegie to keep his
distance, which the latter reluctantly did, proceeding
slowly to Milan, Venice, and finally Florence.

In the meantime Frick performed a shrewd juggling act.
One of the obstacles to a forced settlement was the fast-

shooting, sharp-tongued Mr. Potter, superintendent of the Homestead mill. This gentleman was now kicked upstairs to the position of consulting engineer of all Carnegie works. His place was taken by that cheery, back-slapping manager at Edgar Thomson, Mr. Charles M. Schwab, a young man of considerable executive (if not technical) ability who was liked even by the strikers. Smoothly Schwab got to work to conciliate the department heads and foremen, and within a short time had induced several to take back their jobs. They had struck along with the Amalgamated, from which they had been excluded by union rules, and their capture by the company was an important event. In turn they began coaxing their friends to return to the fold. From the strikers' viewpoint matters were becoming hopeless. Pressures put upon the Advisory Committee to surrender, on any terms, mounted to the breaking point. About half that committee was presently in jail or had left town.

Suddenly, without warning, the men at the Hartman works in Beaver Falls voted to capitulate. This left only Homestead, Lawrenceville, and Braddock still officially struck. Since total output of the Carnegie empire was running two-thirds full, and would evidently hit maximum by around the end of the year, company officials were no longer much interested in those obstinate thousands of former workers who refused to give up the ship. If they wished suicidally to go down with it—men, women, and children—that was their business.

On November 8 Grover Cleveland regained the Presidency, sweeping the solid south and seven northern states. Homestead as a weapon was used up to the hilt by the Democratic machine, with both Carnegie and Frick vilified mercilessly. One cartoon showed Carnegie, fat and leering, embracing both Harrison and his own moneybags. The caption read: "They Are Good Enough for Each Other. Are They Good Enough for You?" The bearing of Homestead upon the election should not be overestimated, but beyond question it had a telling effect upon resentful voters of the working group. Harrison lost every industrial state in the east and received less votes numerically than in his first campaign. In Homestead and Munhall not a single Republican was elected to the state legislature. Even though the Populist standard-bearer, James B. Weaver, polled over a million votes, Cleveland received a popular plurality. The great steelmakers were little perturbed. "I am very sorry for President Harrison," wrote Frick, "but I cannot see that our interests are going to be affected one way or the other by the change in administration."

Sophisticated and cynical when it came to politics and business, Carnegie answered, "Cleveland ! Landslide! Well we have nothing to fear and perhaps it is best. People will now think the Protected Mfrs. will be attended to and quit agitating. Cleveland is a pretty good fellow. Off for Venice tomorrow." And from that city he opined the following week, "I fear that Homestead did much to elect Cleveland —very sorry—but no use getting scared." To Whitelaw Reid he expressed regrets for his personal defeat and that of Mr. Harrison, and lauded "the noble effort you made to settle that deplorable Homestead blunder."

As usual, Mr. Frick kept his mouth shut. "When the election was over," noted his biographer, "he returned to business without apologizing to anybody for anything that he had done." He had plenty of business to attend to at this stage. The works were humming at a faster and faster pace, back orders were being filled, future orders were being booked, and in theory the strike—annoying but of small consequence—was still on.

Unshaven, half-starved, the remaining diehards roamed the streets, occasionally squandered a nickel for a stein of beer, and ignored that sterling, ever-framed motto of the day: "There's No Place Like Home." Any place was better than home, where they were constantly being nagged to get back to work. By and large, their womenfolk had given up the good fight. They could no longer make ends meet—only the children were eating normally—on the pathetic daily handout from strike headquarters. There was a limit to scrimping, economizing, and tightening the belt. That limit had been reached. Goaded to desperation by family problems—to make matters worse, his wife was expecting a second child—one striker committed suicide. The three thousand non-unionists had joined the fray confidently, expecting a quick, easy victory. An icy winter was approaching. Now they were whipped and everybody knew it, including the once-haughty Amalgamated people who had previously disdained them. On Thursday, November 18, the former day laborers and mechanics held an open-air meeting and voted to request the Amalgamated to release them from obligation. Union officials sullenly agreed, provided they would accept no tonnage jobs. At once two hundred applied for work. Most of them were rehired.

Next day came the deluge. About six hundred men stormed the main entrance, and two clerks were needed to make out passes for them. Mr. Schwab supervised the affair. As the men streamed through the mill office, he checked off each name against a long list and made on-the-spot decisions concerning those to be rejected. Again the majority were accepted and told to be at work next morning.

On the twentieth the combined Homestead lodges took a strike vote at the Munhall skating rink. After bitter debate, the decision to quit was close—not surprisingly, since few Amalgamated members expected to be taken back by the firm anyway.

The count was 101 to 91. What had happened to the other six hundred union men? Some were too discouraged even to attend the meeting. Some were in jail. Others had been leaving town since July. In his Pittsburgh cell Hugh O'Donnell wrote a short article, more in sorrow than anger, for the *Evening Leader.* "Great battles are rarely ever fought the way they are planned," he observed. Sunday, November 21, the few members of the Advisory Committee who were still at large assembled for the last time, voted to dissolve the committee, and announced tersely that union men would be permitted to return to the Carnegie fold. They left headquarters silently, without looking at each other, walked down the rickety stairs and out into Eighth Avenue. One of them posted an official notice on the grocery-store window below. The most spectacular lockout-strike in American history was over.

Henry Frick was personally on hand the following morning to savor the unprecedented spectacle of Amalgamated members asking for their old jobs back. Balefully he looked on, but said little or nothing. Schwab admitted them in groups of five, checked them off in the usual way, and hired a few who had apparently been inactive during the course of the struggle. As anticipated, almost all were turned away. Once they had been the elite, the skilled, the seemingly indispensable, but their jobs were filled now, and the blacklist doomed them even though the company needed them. In round numbers, only 1,300 of the original 3,800 strikers went back on the payroll. At the height of the strike about 13,000 Carnegie employees in all plants were idle. The total wage loss was $2 million. The firm never divulged its losses as a result of the strike, but they were evidently not devastating, for somehow the Carnegie Steel Company showed a net profit for 1892 of $4 million, only $300,000 less than in the previous year.

The sympathy strike at Braddock collapsed along with Homestead, but the minor walkout at Lawrenceville continued stubbornly (for reasons unknown) until the middle of 1893. Here, there, and everywhere in the Carnegie empire, former scabs feared for their present jobs. They had been promised time and again by Potter and Frick that they would never be replaced by strikers, except for incompetence. The final word, unfortunately, covered a multitude of possible sins. Foremen discovered that hundreds of them were incompetent. They were discharged during November and December to make room for experienced former workers. A cynic might define this as the double-cross supreme, but in truth the works became quite overstaffed when the strike ended, and some men had to go. Away went the black sheep, God knows where, and for months to come more were fired and more old men were rehired.

Mr. Powderly made no statement concerning the company victory, when interrogated. Congressman-elect John Davis of Kansas noted, "It teaches the workingmen this lesson . . . they can't whip Carnegie's millions while their stomach is empty." Incarcerated in Pittsburgh, Hugh Dempsey was boiling mad and not entirely logical. "Those men could have won," he said to a reporter, "if they had only held out a little longer. I don't like to surrender a bit." Editorial opinion all over the country was varied; some newspapers hailed the company for its triumph over lawlessness, others commented acidly on the methods used to achieve that triumph, but most of them reported the end of the strike dispassionately or with a trace of sympathy for the beaten workers. The issue of "Pinkertonism" flared up again; it is needless to reiterate the same arguments pro and con. In Populist-controlled Colorado the governor refused to renew the Pinkerton's Denver license. The Pennsylvania Legislature, of course, had to meet the problem head-on, and in January passed a bill which barred Pinkertons from operating in labor disputes, deputized or not. Eight other states passed mild anti-Pinkerton measures.

In Florence Mr. Carnegie was transfixed upon receipt of this cable from Frick, dated November 21: "Strike officially declared off yesterday. Our victory is now complete and most gratifying. Do not think we will ever have any serious labor trouble again. . . . Let the Amalgamated still exist and hold sway at other people's mills. That is no concern of ours."

"Life worth living again!" replied Carnegie. "First happy morning since July—surprising how pretty Italia—congratulate all around—improve works—go ahead—clear track—tariff not in it—shake."

To this hysterical communication Frick responded with a cool statement of financial matters. All expenses had been charged up, he reported, "so that we swallowed the dose as we went along." And he summed up: "We could never have profited much by any of our competitors making and winning the fight we have made. We had to teach our employees a lesson, and we have taught them one that they will never forget. . . . It is hard to estimate what blessings will flow from our recent complete victory, both to the owners and the employees of the Carnegie Steel Co.

Ltd. I am sure that I never want to go through another such fight."

Back came a letter from Rome. "Think I'm about ten years older than when with you last. Europe has rung with Homestead, Homestead, until we are all sick of the name. . . ."

As we shall see, few blessings, to which Mr. Frick alluded, flowed to employees of the Carnegie company after the strike. Thursday, November 25, Thanksgiving Day, was a singularly inappropriate holiday. It found the boroughs of Munhall and Homestead in shocking condition, most of its inhabitants pauperized, many small businesses bankrupt, rents unpaid, debts piled sky-high. Not a dime in taxes had been collected for twenty weeks, and the adjacent little mill towns were more disheveled, run-down, and filthy than ever before. Butchers and grocers were demanding cash and refusing credit. The skeleton which now comprised the Homestead Amalgamated voted to pay six dollars weekly, for as long as the money lasted, to each of its members who were still unemployed; and relief money from outside sources kept trickling in through the winter, adding up to a helpful $5,587. Workmen at McKeesport donated one thousand turkeys for Thanksgiving. From the Kaufman Brothers' store in Pittsburgh arrived boxes of candy for the children. But there was no future in this sort of thing, and obviously the ex-strike would have to die a natural, slow, painful death in the way of all lost causes.

The cost in human life (not to mention casualties, many of which were serious) came high at Homestead. Nine strikers and seven Pinkertons were killed or mortally wounded on July 6. There were several deaths in the mill due to inexperience in handling the machinery. Three or more strikebreakers died of poisoning. Some militiamen succumbed to fever. Accidental or deliberate gunplay killed several men in town. There were at least two suicides in connection with the July 6 battle and the subsequent siege. The New York *Tribune* attributed thirty-five deaths to the strike, a figure which may be low. More figuratively, another casualty of the great strike was the Amalgamated Association of Iron and Steel Workers.

Also on Thanksgiving Day, before thirty-five thousand witnesses from another world, Harvard was felled by Yale 12 to 0. Thus life went on, the bitter with the sweet; and that was the end of November.

X *Fruits of Victory*

Carnegie's triumph in the crucial western Pennsylvania region, coupled with the severe depression of 1893–1897 and its attendant slashing of wages and employment in the metal trades, crippled the Amalgamated and proved that even the world's strongest craft union could not cope with a modern, multimillion-dollar industrial giant reinforced by state military power. The decisive effect of militiamen cannot be overemphasized; one searches United States labor history in vain for a single case where the introduction of troops operated to the strikers' advantage. In virtually all conflicts before and after 1892 the state guard acted, in effect, as a strikebreaking agency by validating the right (which most organized workers deny to be a right) of employers to replace old men with new during a strike and

228

across picket lines. Yet in time, perhaps a year, even without the aid of troops the Carnegie company probably would have won. Mechanization was one reason—skill did not count as much as before. Charles Schwab claimed, for example, that he could make an efficient melter out of an intelligent farm hand in as little as six weeks. Another factor, to which we shall briefly return, was the persistent, inevitable strikebreaking effect of the southern Negro and the immigrant. Both knew little and cared less about the particular strike into which they were injected—they simply wanted and needed work, any work, even temporary work, for almost any number of daily hours at almost any pay. It is significant that the great majority of scabs at Homestead came from these two groups. Finally there was the staying power of the firm. Militia or no militia, the men of Homestead were financially finished in November. Meanwhile the company, more or less ignoring the thousands on strike, was running nearly full and profiting accordingly; and, even if every mill had still been idle at that time, the company could have held out far longer than the strikers. Frick and Carnegie were in accordance. Both men would have let grass cover the Homestead works rather than lose or even compromise there. The July 6 battle (and the attempt to assassinate Frick, irrelevant though it may have been) settled that point beyond dispute, and it may be confidently assumed that grass never would have covered the Carnegie empire in any event. A total victory was in the cards. The Amalgamated had to leave the steel scene, and it did so in a hurry. The union lost five thousand members in 1893, six thousand in 1894, and by 1895 its membership was less than half its pre-strike strength.

As the decade and the depression dwindled, fewer and fewer of those still on the rolls were listed as steelworkers.

The Association continued to be influential, and recognized, in western iron mills, in various plants of the National Tube Company, in hoop mills outside the Pittsburgh area, and particularly in the burgeoning sheet and tin plate industries. In basic steel it disintegrated until by 1910 it retained only one contract with a single, small open-hearth plant. Independent steel masters refused to deal with the union starting soon after the Homestead debacle. "Fight them to a finish with hard gloves," John ("Bet-a-Million") Gates had written a Carnegie official during that strike, "and give them no quarter after you get them in a corner and we will take the rods in 1894 if necessary." He reflected the prevailing opinion of all Carnegie competitors and customers. Jones and Laughlin rejected the union scale in 1897. One after the other—at Cambria, Republic, Bethlehem, establishments further south, near Chicago and Gary, in Ohio and Colorado—all steel manufacturers, even the smallest independents, froze out the union and dispersed its organizers. No union man was ever again knowingly hired by Carnegie employers. When detected, those who secretly held Amalgamated cards were fired on the spot; and this policy had become general throughout the industry at the turn of the century.

Intermittently the union made attempts at a comeback. An organizing drive was shattered by the Carnegie company in 1896. When three years later three hundred Homestead workers created a lodge, Mr. Frick in London cabled his officers to "stop Works if necessary to hold present position." The union failed and its local ringleaders were discharged. Under Samuel Gompers the A. F. of L. lifted not a finger to support either of these movements. The next effort of the Amalgamated to assert itself came in 1901, and again the parent organization turned its face away. Gompers would not tangle with the United States Steel Corporation, the trust formed earlier that year that included the Carnegie company and a score of lesser producers.

But the Amalgamated was desperate. While its membership had slightly increased to fourteen thousand dues-payers, scarcely any of these were employed in steel. Amalgamated president T. J. Shaffer realized that U. S. Steel must at once be challenged if the union were to survive (even theoretically) in the industry, and if the A. F. of L. were not to be excluded from the most important sector of the nation's economy. Accordingly he forced the issue. Next he requested Gompers to call the A. F. of L. into emergency conference. Gompers' succinct and incredible reply—"No"—left Shaffer in the position of having painted himself into a corner. Ineffective and poorly planned from the start, the strike melted away after six sorry weeks. Except for a minor lost strike in 1904 against steel hoop manufacturers—not to be classified as a division of basic steelmakers—and another last-gasp failure at various Pennsylvania plants starting in 1909, the Amalgamated never again struck. It was a paper tiger almost literally, in that it lived within the steel industry only as a paper structure from which, it was hoped, a new organism with teeth and claws might some day emerge. Furtively it lingered on, unrecognized and unmourned. In sheet, iron, tin, and hoops it was tolerated for a time by employers; its feeble existence was insurance against the organization of a stronger rival.

The demise of the Amalgamated in all branches of ferrous metal is dated June 1, 1909, when U. S. Steel announced that henceforth "after a careful consideration of the interests of both the company and its employees" it would operate solely as an "open" plant. It did not explicitly demand that the Amalgamated disappear. It merely served notice that even those relations still effective in some areas were at an end. In the same statement it proclaimed wage reductions averaging 5 percent.

After the 1892 strike the twelve-hour day, seven days per week, with a twenty-four-hour stretch every second week, was restored at Homestead for almost all classes of workers except the day men and trained specialists. Grievance committees were abolished. Wage scales were kept secret. Extra pay for Sunday, formerly in effect for some men, ceased. Espionage became the order of the day; it was estimated by unionists that one out of every ten workers was either a company or Pinkerton spy. During the secret 1899 effort to form a lodge, a Pittsburgh newspaper reported that "like a bolt from the blue sky, the company let the newly made union men know that it was cognizant of every move that had been made." Any workers' meeting remotely connected with plant conditions was forbidden, and those who nonetheless assembled were threatened or fired. For years the slogan, "If you want to talk in Homestead, you must talk to yourself," became an article of enforced faith.

But the matter of wages was primary. Now that Frick had the men at his mercy, what would happen to the scale and twenty-three-dollar-minimum base which he had offered earlier in the year, and his "desire to act toward our employes in the most liberal manner"? In short, scale and base were abandoned, and wages were slashed far more devastatingly than the beaten men had expected. There was, of course, no more decision concerning scales "by an agreement," as Frick put it; and with candor he told the Senate committee that now "it was brought about by our fixing the wages that we felt we could afford to pay, and they agreeing individually to accept them." If one wishes to play with words, it may therefore be argued that an "agreement" was in effect. Since the Carnegie company never again released its labor figures—its workers were not even told the basis upon which their biweekly pay checks rested—we must turn to other sources. They are stated here without comment as to reliability.

John A. Fitch in *The Steel Workers*, Volume III of *The Pittsburgh Survey*, published by the Russell Sage Foundation, lists these wages (per ton) in Homestead's 119-inch plate mill:

	February, 1892	February, 1894
Roller	12.15¢	6.00¢
Heater	9.55¢	5.25¢
Tableman	6.94¢	3.20¢
Heater's helper	4.85¢	2.22¢
Shearman	9.85¢	4.09¢

Writing fifteen years after the battle, he also observed that unskilled day laborers who formerly received 14 cents per hour had been raised to 16½ cents by 1907.

Hugh O'Donnell delivered quite different figures on the same plate mill, adding the accusation that no new machinery had been introduced there during the two years in question—in other words, there was no increase in output due to improved mechanization. These data were submitted to Professor Edward Bemis who included it in his article "The Homestead Strike" in the *Journal of Political Economy*. Again the reference is to cents paid per ton of output:

	1890–1892	February, 1894
Roller	14.00¢	6.00¢
Heater	11.00¢	5.25¢
Tableman	10.00¢	3.20¢
Heater's helper	7.50¢	2.27¢
Shearman	13.00¢	4.09¢

Very likely O'Donnell was referring in his left-hand column to the abnormally high wages paid in May, 1892, which would account for the discrepancy between him and Fitch. O'Donnell goes on to list reductions suffered by other men: screwman 11.50 to 3.70, second shearman 8.50 to 3.41, hooker 8.50 to 2.72, and so on in proportion.

(On November 23, 1892, the New York *Tribune* observed that boilers at the Beaver Falls plant had been cut from $2.25 to $1.89 per day, and that assistant rollers who had been reduced a flat one-third refused to go back to work.)

The scales listed by Fitch and O'Donnell are impossible to translate into take-home pay without knowing the tonnage output. Fortunately Fitch's following table, which deals with the six highest paid men in another Homestead plate mill, shows what happened between May, 1892 (the top production month in the company's history prior to the strike), and 1907. In evaluating it, one should bear in mind that the price level had risen 22 percent during those years. *Thus the "real" wages for 1907 should be reduced by roughly one-fifth to compare with 1892:*

	May, 1892– Daily Wage, 8 Hours	$ per Hour	1907– Daily Wage, 12 Hours	$ per Hour
Roller	$11.84	$1.48	$8.44	$ .70
Screwdown	8.74	1.09	7.30	.61
Heater	8.16	1.02	7.21	.60
Heater's helper	5.80	.72	4.09	.34
Tableman	7.75	.97	5.91	.49
Shearman	9.49	1.17	5.58	.46

Even though these six elite employees worked six days per week or less in May, 1892, their earnings were surely remarkable for that era. As previously noted, our present dollar is worth $4.20 compared to the 1892 dollar; thus, the roller cited above took home that month over three hundred dollars or the equivalent of over thirteen hundred dollars in today's money—an astounding amount, even though it accrued to one man only one time.

1907 was a year of neither prosperity nor depression. It was an average time when Mr. Fitch and Margaret F. Byington, also of the Pittsburgh *Survey* staff, visited Homestead to evaluate a typical mill town and to assess the economic damage wrought upon it largely as a result of the 1892 defeat. Miss Byington studied a fair cross-section of workers divided into ethnic groups, tabulated their weekly earnings, and found that the Slavs were averaging about twelve dollars per week, English-speaking Europeans sixteen dollars, native whites twenty-two dollars, Negroes seventeen dollars.[1] These data for an eighty-four-hour week make somewhat more melancholy reading than the "elite" table by Fitch (above) and furnish an approximate picture of the status of the rank and file.

However one may evaluate all these figures as to authenticity, there is little question but that the unorganized condition of the steelworkers allowed the Carnegie company to depress wages mercilessly. One comparison will suffice. During 1907 in the nearby unionized bituminous coal mines of western Pennsylvania, organized common laborers were being paid 29½ cents per hour while, as we have seen, nonunion "day" men working similarly in steel were earning 16½ cents. Such a difference is hard to explain on grounds other than unionization. A similar though less severe differential also applied to the semiskilled and skilled

---

[1] Miss Byington does not state these averages in her two tables, but they have been worked out through simple arithmetic and are probably fairly accurate.

in both industries. So much for the loss in leisure and the loss in cash following the loss of the strike.

When the historic fight ended, working and living conditions in Munhall and Homestead reached a new low which did not significantly improve until the boom years of World War I. Beatrice Webb visited the area during the middle of the gay nineties and found it "a veritable Hell of a place." Mr. Carnegie she termed a "reptile." Fifty-cent prostitutes abounded in the noisome Fifth Ward. A miasma of apathy, sullen indifference, and broken spirit permeated the atmosphere at work and at home. Now nothing mattered but a simple matter of survival, of retaining one's job and a bearable standard of living for one's family. Carefully hoarded savings were gone, along with the American dream. Men like Joe Reed, one of the strike leaders, swore that they would never again join a union. Passively they submitted to any terms of work and employer control. It was every man for himself. Cowed and docile, they learned to live with the stretch-out, the speed-up, espionage, the blacklist, the ever-present threat of discharge without stated cause, the enlarged workday and the diminished pay check. The only hope of the more intelligent employees was promotion to better jobs; and indeed over the years many of them—through diligence, efficiency, and the ability to keep quiet and stay out of trouble—moved upward on the job ladder.

For their part, Carnegie officials were anxious not to lose their best men. If a department had to be temporarily shut down, foremen were instructed to give them menial repair or maintenance duties—anything to keep them on the payroll. In 1893 the firm purchased the Pittsburgh City Poor Farm near Homestead, erected dwellings, and urged employees to purchase them through low-interest company loans. By 1900 fully a fourth of all Homestead families owned their homes and did not intend to lose them because of protracted unemployment. Tied to the company, they became model employees. The same was true of those who leased houses from the firm. In Munhall, Carnegie dwellings rented for a third less than others, were better built, often provided basic utilities at cost, and when vacated were quickly snapped up by favored employees whose names were at the head of a long waiting list.

More unpleasant was the lot of the unskilled and semi-skilled who were so easily replaceable. Well after the turn of the century Miss Byington found them living on bare subsistence wages in gray, vermin-infested shacks next to outdoor privies. Almost half of these places lacked running water and housed two or more people in each room. Most streets and all alleys were still unpaved. In half a square mile of downtown Homestead and Munhall she counted forty-seven saloons. The men had become accustomed to the twelve-hour day and the double turn each second Sunday. Sometimes, when transferred to a ten-hour schedule, they even requested the previous longer hours which delivered more pay. They were willing to work, and capable of bearing a load of toil which seems incomprehensible today, provided that they could bring home a certain minimum wage. "A man works, comes home, eats and goes to bed, gets up, eats and goes to work," one summed up. Fitch described a trolley ride home after a fourteen-hour night shift: "Nobody was talking. . . . They held their buckets on their laps, or put them on the floor between their legs. 6 or 8 were asleep. The rest sat quiet, with legs and neck loose, with their eyes open, steady, dull, fixed upon nothing at all."

Deaths and injuries continued at the enormous pre-strike level, while the steel masters pinched pennies as usual. In one year in Allegheny County, over half the injured married men received no compensation whatever. Out of thirty-three workers disabled for life, twenty-three were awarded less than a hundred dollars. The Carnegie company was more generous than most. It gave the family of every killed workman five hundred dollars, plus an extra hundred for each child. In that same county 115 elite workers were killed during 1902, and one may guess at the much larger figure of unskilled and semiskilled men who were mortally hurt on the job, since these groups outnumbered the skilled by about four to one. The claims departments of the various companies were less than generous, but as a rule the men or their survivors accepted what was offered. Suing the employer was a waste of time and money. "Under our common law," remarked an attorney who handled injury cases for the Carnegie firm, "the employee has not a chance of recovery in two cases out of a hundred." Discouraged and resentful, the men turned increasingly for protection to mutual insurance plans or private insurance companies, and paid the not-insignificant premiums out of their own pockets. Beggars formerly employed by the mill were a common sight, especially on "pay Friday" night, when Homestead and Munhall came to life in the saloon district. Besieging the Eighth Avenue gate as the men left work, they bore signs such as, "I am injured and blind—my eyes were destroyed by hot steel"; and after a fashion they existed on the donations received.

"I think there will be a labor organization in the mills again," said one employee. "It may not come in our day, but it is bound to come; the men will be driven to it." It

came in 1937, when the Committee for Industrial Organizations—later the Congress of Industrial Organizations
(C.I.O.)—organized the steel industry after a lethal
struggle. Until then, astigmatic to the end, the Amalgamated maintained its policy (with isolated exceptions) of
barring the unskilled, the semiskilled, Negroes, and foremen from membership. What the moribund union thus
hoped to accomplish passeth understanding. Still, it must
be fairly stated that the union was not clairvoyant: it was
not yet absolutely plain that the dividing line between
experienced professionals and untrained amateurs was fast
being erased by mechanization, that a tiny social club of
isolated craftsmen could accomplish nothing against the
world's mightiest trust.

So the immigrants, crowding into the expanding industry, thousands upon additional thousands every year, were
spurned; the union dwindled to a point where it no longer
possessed even nuisance value; and throughout the kingdom of steel the workers retreated into their shells and
accepted their fate. A problem encountered by John Fitch
was that of interviewing the men and women of Homestead. "They are suspicious of one another, of their neigh-
bors, and their friends . . . it is not regarded as safe to
talk about conditions in the steel industry. Concerning the
most patent and generally known facts, intelligent men
display the most marvelous ignorance." An impending pay
reduction was being discussed privately at that time in
every dwelling, but when Fitch asked a workman about it
the atmosphere changed from friendliness to suspicion. "I
don't know anything about it," the man replied suavely. "I
haven't heard of any cut." Fitch talked to a water carrier
about the dangers of millwork. The latter had never heard

about them. When Fitch asked if accidents did not occasionally occur, the man looked at him narrowly and said, "I have never seen anyone hurt."

Paranoid, powerless, overworked, underpaid, reduced in hope and happiness, clinging to their jobs for lack of any practical alternative, poorly housed, insecure, aging rapidly under the stress of millwork: these were the men of Homestead after the war of 1892, "a conflict which does not determine who is right—but who is left." Master of the field, the Carnegie Steel Company was left to consolidate its position and multiply its earnings. Despite the depression of 1893–1897, company profits spiraled. During the seventeen years preceding the strike the company had made $27 million. In the nine years that followed, the figure was $106 million. "Ashamed to tell you profits these days," Mr. Carnegie wrote a friend in 1899. "Prodigious!" And from Scotland he cabled his managers in Pittsburgh: "If you can fill next year at present prices, you may have at least forty millions profit. But it may be fifty. To want more than that seems wicked." Decency, however, prevailed; the 1900 net reached only forty millions.

In recounting the history of the firm, James H. Bridge observed, "It is believed by the Carnegie officials, and with some show of reason, that this magnificent record was to a great extent made possible by the company's victory at Homestead." The slashing of wages, in conjunction with new labor-saving machinery, enabled the firm to roll steel rails in 1897 at the all-time-low cost of twelve dollars per ton. Immediately after the strike, fifteen hundred Carnegie workmen—five hundred from the Homestead mill alone—were discharged. No decrease in output ensued. By 1899, in fact, the tonnage of steel ingots manufactured had reached 2,663,412, compared to 797,286 the year prior to the strike, and this with no appreciable increase in the work force. The era of true automation was dawning.

Inevitably this eroded the value of the skilled steel-worker, while the status of the common laborer—usually Negro or European—remained fairly stable during the decade, a far cry from the magnificent company achievements cited above. In the words of Margaret Byington:

> The analysis of expenditures indicates that the man who earns $9.90 a week, as do a majority of such laborers, and who has a family of normal size to support, can provide for them only a two-room tenement in a crowded court, with no sanitary conveniences; a supply of food below the minimum sufficient for mere physical well-being; insurance that makes provision which is utterly inadequate for the family left without a breadwinner; a meager expenditure for clothes and furniture, and an almost negligible margin for recreation, education and savings. Many can, to be sure, add to their earnings by working seven days a week instead of six; by working twelve hours a day instead of ten; but after all we are talking of standards of life and labor for an American industry, and common sense will scarcely sanction such a week of work. Many . . . take in lodgers, but do it at the cost of decency and health.

But most immigrants flooding the steel labor market were single men, anxious to work for between nine and twelve dollars weekly for a few years, then to return permanently to their homelands with several hundred dollars saved. Such a sum amounted to a fortune in the Balkans. It meant a measure of lifetime security for them and their families, and usually the purchase of a small farm. Understandably, therefore, after the Homestead lockout, immigrants could almost never be induced to strike, even though the rising cost of living nibbled away at their fixed wage. Their disillusionment was often great. Of the great

masses who came during the '90s, about a third returned to
Europe as soon as they could scrape up steerage fare. Those
who stuck it out did so bitterly, and their letters and inter-
views do not make light reading.

"There are different kinds of work, heavy and light, but
a man from our country cannot get the light." "A good
job, save money, work all time, go home, sleep, no spend."
"The man put me in a section where there was terrible
noises, shooting, thundering and lightning. I wanted to
run away but there was a big train in front of me. I looked
up and a big train carrying a big vessel with fire was making toward me. I stood numb, afraid to move, until a man
came to me and led me out of the mill."

One Slav warned a countryman that "if he wants to
come, he is not to complain . . . for in America there are
neither Sundays nor holidays; he must go and work." A
Hungarian churchman complained of the Pittsburgh
works, "Wherever the heat is most insupportable, the
flames most scorching, and smoke and soot most choking,
there we are certain to find our compatriots bent and
wasted with toil." To his wife a Pole wrote, "As long as he
is well then he always works like a mule, but if he becomes
sick then it is a trouble, because . . . during the sickness
the most will be spent." In a single plant, during a span of
twelve years, 3,273 immigrants were killed or injured; their
accident total was twice that of the rest of the workers.

But still they came by the hundreds of thousands, and
there was no keeping them out of non-union iron and steel.
For obvious reasons, the steel masters wanted these cheap,
uncomplaining, hard-working hands. In about five years
almost a third of those who stayed held semiskilled jobs. A
handful moved into well-paid, skilled categories. The pressure of their numbers was irresistible. When needed as

scabs, they and the Negroes could always be counted on, and there was no employee organization to stop them. Gradually a great many original old-timers at Homestead and other Pittsburgh mills moved away into a different life. Immigration, mechanization, the 1892 defeat, the completely open shop, heavy wage cuts across the board except for the day men—all combined to make the average steelworker the most underprivileged member of the United States working class for decades to come.

Some months after the conclusion of hostilities, the Carnegie company, through Knox & Reed, made overtures to William Weihe with a view to ending the legal tangle. An agreement was reached to drop all charges on both sides unconditionally, whereupon the Amalgamated men still in jail were turned free.

All members of the Advisory Committee were blacklisted for life, not only by the Carnegie firm but by every other metal and mining operator in the land. They were barred from steel, iron, iron ore, sheet, tin, coke, and even coal; and there is no record of any of the thirty-five men ever finding a job in these industries or their subdivisions, such as nail, wire, or hoop mills. They scattered to the four winds, and at this writing it would be impossible fully to trace them without interminable investigation.

But a few shreds of fact are extant. "Big Bill" Weihe went to New York where he entered the United States Immigration Service; he died in 1908. William Roberts turned to oratory and local politics. Thomas Crawford went into business with Jack Crawford (no relative) as a booking agent: he also tried politics, but without success.

For a time Hugh O'Donnell traveled as manager of a

concert or vaudeville company. Stubborn, holier-than-thou, a dedicated Republican and yet, somehow, an epitome of the insurrectionary striker, this complex individual managed to alienate everyone on both sides. After the strike he wrote, "Mine has been the sacrifice. Today, in reward for my efforts, I am misunderstood and maligned by the unthinking crowd—a modern Ishmael doomed to wander in the desert of ingratitude." Later he became connected in an editorial capacity with a weekly Chicago journal. There his trail ends. David Lynch, another active member of the committee, became a liquor salesman. Hugh Ross visited his home in Scotland, and for a long time after returning to America was out of work; the nature of his eventual employment is unknown.

Much more has been uncovered about the burgess of Homestead, John McLuckie. When rearrested on one of Knox & Reed's familiar charges late in 1892, he escaped. Pursued by police, he was wounded but managed to get out of Pennsylvania. He lectured for a time, took odd jobs, and drifted toward the southwestern states. His wife died. He crossed over into Mexico. In the spring of 1900, at a ranch in the mountains of Sonora, he was discovered by a friend of Carnegie, Professor John C. Van Dyke of Rutgers College. McLuckie talked freely and confessed that he was flat broke, still unable to get a decent job corresponding to his skills. The professor soon left Sonora and from Tucson, Arizona, wrote Carnegie the whole story. Carnegie replied, "Give McLuckie all the money he wants, but don't mention my name." To Van Dyke's astonishment, McLuckie declined the gift.

The professor was persistent. He recommended McLuckie to one J. A. Naugle, general manager of the Sonora Railway, who hired him as a machinery-repair superintendent. It was an excellent job and he made a success of it. A year later Van Dyke met him again at Guaymas, happy and now wed to a Mexican girl. The professor said, "Mc-Luckie, I want you to know now that the money I offered you was not mine. That was Andrew Carnegie's money. It was his offer, made through me." In surprise McLuckie replied, "Well, that was damned white of Andy, wasn't it?" Since the Carnegie company had effectively ruined him for ten years, the remark may have been sardonic; but to the end of his days Mr. Carnegie preferred to consider it a supreme compliment from a dyed-in-the-wool workingman of the type he professed to love. After three generations no more can be uncovered about McLuckie, but one hopes that he lived happily ever after, south of the border.

A few other threads may be followed to their conclusion. Governor Pattison died, much too young, in Philadelphia in 1904. The stormy life of Emma Goldman can scarcely be recapitulated here. Deported to Russia by the government in 1919 for seditious utterances concerning our participation in World War I, she was allowed to return to the United States only once, briefly, during her lifetime. She died in Canada during May, 1940. The United States Immigration and Naturalization Service permitted her body to be buried in Chicago's Waldheim Cemetery.

Alexander Berkman served thirteen years of his sentence before being released. News of Henry Clay Frick's death on December 2, 1919, reached him the same day. His comment was, "Well, anyhow he left the country before I did." Later that afternoon both he and Emma were placed aboard the "ark" which carried them, along with hundreds of other alleged anarchists and assorted undesirables, to European ports. Sick beyond endurance, he committed suicide with a revolver in France in 1936; and this job, too, he bungled. So poor was his aim that he lingered sixteen hours in agony until death at last arrived.

Mr. Schwab was later handed the helm of the Carnegie grouping and U. S. Steel. There he stayed for only three years and proceeded to his well-known career at Bethlehem Steel, after having been replaced by Judge Elbert H. Gary. Ultraconservative, antiunion, so ignorant of steel manufacture and working conditions that (it was said) he "never saw a blast furnace until his death," Gary resisted mounting public abhorrence toward the twelve-hour day until President Harding brought him around in 1923. So the long stretch and the double turn ended during the reign, paradoxically, of a man cast in Frick's mold.

Bits of this and scraps of that comprise the end of our tale. There are, of course, the interminable hearings of the Senate subcommittee in Pittsburgh and New York chambers; drowsy, paper-shuffling, smoke-filled, cuspidoric affairs attended mostly by down-at-the-heel newsmen who roll their own and smell faintly of the grape. More or less the same witnesses drone their predictable, repetitious testimony, and seldom do the proceedings come to life. One deviation—widely reported and indignantly attacked by devotees of the divine right of property—was the point-blank assertion of William Roberts that the strikers had a moral, economic right to capture the mills and repel the invader:

Now, the men at Homestead were in a peculiar condition. The most of them had started to build their own little homes. Some of them had them about half paid for. They were allowed to enjoy the privilege of belonging to their association, and then to be denied the privilege of belonging to an organization that had done so much for them, as they thought, and, on the other hand, to be forced into accepting a reduction that they didn't think was right, then to be confronted with a gang of loafers and cut-throats from all over the country, coming there, as they thought, to take their jobs, why, they naturally wanted to go down and defend their homes and their property with force, if necessary.

This, the crux of the matter, may be argued endlessly. It touches at the ethos of the entire lockout-strike, smacks on one hand of anarchy, on the other of pragmatic necessity; and it would be best, perhaps, if this narrative gave it a wide berth. The Senate committee, too, preferred to skirt the issue. Its report, published in 1893, *Investigation of Labor Troubles,* merely reprinted the testimony and summarized its findings. The conclusion, however, was surprisingly heated by comparison with the tepid observations of the House investigators. It dealt almost exclusively with Pinkertonism:

As to the character of the men furnished, it is reasonable to suppose that as they are hurriedly assembled to meet an immediate exigency, sometimes responding to newspaper advertisements, they are not of the highest order of morals or intellect.

Every man admitted that the workmen are strongly prejudiced against the so-called Pinkertons, and that their presence at a strike serves to unduly inflame the passions of the strikers, partly from the fact that they are frequently placed among workmen, in the disguise of mechanics, to report alleged conversations to their agencies, which in turn is transmitted to the employers of labor. Your committee is impressed by the belief that this is an utterly vicious system. The laboring man is at the mercy of the detective, who can report whatever he pleases, be it true or false.

The employment of the private armed guards at Homestead was unnecessary. There is no evidence to show the slightest damage to property on the part of the strikers. True, there was apparently an unlawful assemblage which refused to obey the authority of a weak and irresolute sheriff, and committed acts that cannot be defended. . . .

Company spies and camouflaged quasi-armies (such as the Ford Service Department of a later era) weathered the blast, but never again in America did a private detective agency blatantly operate as at Homestead in 1892. This much, if nothing else, was accomplished by the wretched event.

It was not the destiny, perhaps not the desire, of Henry Clay Frick to enjoy happiness as the word is commonly understood, and the remainder of his life cannot be envied except by those who cherish only money. (He left a total estate of $150 million.) After Homestead, he and Carnegie drew further and further apart. In 1895 he resigned his post as manager of the company, sold half of his interest, and returned almost exclusively to directing the Frick Coke Company, his original and basic love. Immediately a battle royal broke out between him and Carnegie concerning the contract price of coke sold to the holding firm. Other disputes followed thick and fast. Carnegie decided to eliminate him; but, to buy him out, an open break was necessary. A pretext was found in the matter of Wiley's Farm.

Frick had secretly bought these four hundred acres adjoining the Braddock works for half a million dollars; he then turned round and sold the land to the Carnegie company for $1,500,000. When Mr. Carnegie noted this transaction at a board meeting, he asked Frick, "What did it cost you?" Frick replied that the price was his personal affair. Carnegie said he would quickly prove that it was not. He rammed through a vote rescinding the purchase and causing Frick to take back his land. The hatred between the two men grew to pathological proportions; their quarrel got almost out of hand, threatened to become a national scandal, and on one occasion reached the physical stage. This happened when Carnegie barged into Frick's office and insisted, upon pain of dire retaliation, that his former lieutenant get out of the firm in exchange for the book value (a low, obsolete figure) of his shares. Frick exploded and flung himself upon the older man. Carnegie fled into the corridor with his assailant in hot pursuit, while employees watched in dismay. But it was not until 1900 that Frick stepped completely out of the picture after a series of ineffable court actions.

He never again spoke to Carnegie. After the breakup, a mutual friend called upon him in his marble Fifth Avenue palace and said, "Mr. Carnegie told me to tell you that he is getting along in years, and that he would like to shake hands with you before he dies and let by-gones be by-gones." The response was, "Tell your friend Carnegie that I will see him in hell where we are both going."

Frick took up golf, played it rather poorly, proving that he was after all human, and amassed a superb art collection. This he willed to the city of New York; he also left $50 million to hospitals and various charitable and educational institutions. To the end he remained active in business and served on the boards of several corporations, including U. S. Steel. A devout Republican (like Hugh O'Donnell), he contributed generously to the party's coffers, his largest single donation being one hundred thousand dollars in 1904 on behalf of Theodore Roosevelt. He died, in 1919, in his sleep as he had lived: quietly, seemingly impassive, and alone, save for an attendant nurse.

All was calm along the Monongahela when Andrew Carnegie returned from Europe in January, 1893. For a day or

two he was roundly criticized and abused by the national
press, nor did a prepared statement, replete with grave
inaccuracies, help his cause: "I did not come to Pittsburgh
to rake up, but to bury, the past, of which I know nothing. . . . Four years ago I retired from active business; no
consideration in the world would induce me to return to
it. . . . I have not the power to instruct anybody connected with the Carnegie Steel Co. Ltd. . . . I do not believe in ruling through the voting power . . . and I
would not if I could . . . I predict that no man who ever
lived in Pittsburgh and managed business here will be better liked or more admired by his employees than my friend
and partner Henry Clay Frick . . . ," and so on. Later that
year he published his book, *Triumphant Democracy*,
which spoke of prosperity without end, the glory of labor,
the sanctity of trade unions, the equal rights of rich and
poor, employer and employee, without "one shred of privilege to be met with anywhere. . . ." In view of the recent
strike and its unhappy consequences for labor, and the fact
that the worst depression in our century-old history was
then raging, the timing of the volume's publication was
unfortunate.

His alleged retirement must be taken with a grain of
salt. Between 1893 and 1898 he caused his mills to be almost entirely rebuilt; he seemed, in the words of one biographer, possessed by "a mania for destruction." Each January he would ask, "Well, what shall we throw away this
year?" The last of the pear-shaped Bessemer volcanoes was
dismantled, and at Homestead the silent, bubbling, bluish
open-hearth converters were enlarged in number until
they covered many new acres of ground eastward in the
Munhall district. The volume of his business, the scope of
his ore holdings, the extension of his rail lines and Great

Lakes steamship fleet, his cost advantages in coke and hidden transportation rebates, his threat to build immense new factories for finished products such as wire and sheet—these factors struck terror to the hearts of other steel masters. How could the little Scotch buccaneer be brought to bay? John Gates and other competitors announced that they would roll their own crude steel, whereupon from Skibo Mr. Carnegie cabled young Schwab to proceed with tremendous new developments at Conneaut on Lake Erie. He quoted Richelieu's advice: "First, all means to conciliate; failing that, all means to crush." "No use going half way across a stream," he warned; we "should aim at finished articles only."

News of his intentions leaked out, perhaps intentionally. Perhaps he was bluffing, but no one knew and no combination could check him. Could he be bought out? The idea was broached to J. Pierpont Morgan, the only man who might have been able to engineer the project. "I would not think of it," Morgan said. "I don't believe I could raise the money." And meanwhile Carnegie and Schwab prepared openly for a price war which could end in only one way. But the year was 1900 and Carnegie was sixty-five—at long last he really did wish to retire. There is no evidence (but little doubt) that he despatched "Smiling Charlie" to address the famous dinner party of December 12 in New York, attended by seventy-five captains of American industry. Was it an accident that Morgan sat directly to Schwab's right? Schwab spoke for an hour. What he advocated was a combination of trusts, a supertrust, which would end anarchic competition and gather unto itself virtually the entire iron and steel industry of the land. Morgan could not get the idea out of his mind. He held further meetings with Schwab, the final one lasting nine hours.

Schwab had all the irresistible answers. It was dawn when Morgan rose to his feet and spoke. "Well, if Andy wants to sell, I'll buy. Go and find his price."

On the following day Andy handed Charlie a slip of paper upon which, in pencil, he had scribbled his terms in cash and exchangeable securities. The total figure came to $492 million. Schwab went to Wall Street and gave the paper to Morgan, who glanced casually at it and said, "I accept." Carnegie's personal share came to almost $300 million and made him the richest man in the world. Estimates of his fortune at this time (1901) vary, but probably it was in the vicinity of half a billion dollars, the equal of two billion dollars in today's coin. Thus was formed the United States Steel Corporation, the world's first billion-dollar company, of which the Carnegie property constituted the overwhelming majority of assets.[2]

Some months later Carnegie and Morgan met on an Atlantic liner. "Do you know, Mr. Morgan," said Carnegie, "I have been thinking it over and I find I made a mistake. I should have asked you another hundred million for those Carnegie properties." Smiling grimly, Morgan replied, "If you had, I should have paid it to you—if only to be rid of you." And Carnegie, according to the *Wall Street Journal*, felt such anguish at these words that he could consume no more marmalade and toast.[3]

---

[2] U. S. Steel was capitalized at $1,321 million against tangible assets of $682 million. About half the securities snapped up by an eager public, therefore, were water. For negotiating the transaction and marketing the various common, preferred, and bond issues, the House of Morgan received $62,500,000. The new company paid four dollars per share on its common stock the first year, and continued to deliver excellent dividends with fair regularity.

[3] In a notable essay, Edmund Wilson (see bibliography) refers to Frick, Carnegie, Gary, Schwab, Morgan, etc., as American giants; yet "they inevitably strike us as comic: for all their immense power, they impress

So the man who had vowed in 1868 to retire in two years drove himself for thirty-three more; and then indeed he commenced giving away his money on a scale never before seen under the sun. He founded the Carnegie Institute in Pittsburgh—$36 million; the Carnegie Institution in Washington—$35 million; the Carnegie Hero Fund—about $13 million; in 1910 the Carnegie Endowment for International Peace—$10 million, quite wasted, one notes with regret; various trusts in the United Kingdom—about $20 million. He caused 2,505 libraries to be erected in both hemispheres. On Dunfermline, his beloved birthplace, he lavished huge gifts of cash, libraries, playing fields and rural development. In 1911 he founded the Carnegie Corporation of New York—the largest of all, $135 million—for "the advancement and diffusion of knowledge and understanding among the people of the United States," as well as Canada and the British colonies.

He too played golf, slaved for a year unsuccessfully to keep America from assaulting our "little brown brother" in the Philippines at the turn of the century, traveled interminably with his wife, and received the freedom of cities in Britain and on the European continent. (Concerning these "freedoms" he chortled, "I have fifty-two and Gladstone has only seventeen.") The administration of his foundations was controlled by a steel hand gloved in velvet. He would say, "Now everybody vote Aye," and policy would be established as he saw fit. His will turned out to be a curious amalgam of sentimentality, indifference, and

---

us, in their great transactions, as rather surprisingly clownish, since—aside from the mere size of their projects—they are seen to have no dignified aims and, except in a debased sense, no honor. Trying continually to cheat one another, whether as rivals or friendly associates, they are the performers of a colossal rogues' comedy."

forgetfulness. Some relatives, friends, and former employees of whom he had been fond were left out altogether. Yet he left pensions for writers, professors, scientists, and statesmen whom he had never met, for two girls who had danced with him during youth, a merchant who had foundered in the sea of commerce, a lad who had held his books while little Andy ran a race seventy years earlier.

He lived through World War I, a forlorn little man in a great mansion on New York's upper Fifth Avenue, his name still one to conjure with. Perplexed, he looked back over the years, the fortune made, the fortune distributed; and he asked his secretary, "How much did you say I had given away, Poynton?" To the reply, "$324,657,399," Mr. Carnegie would ejaculate, "Good Heaven! Where did I ever get all that money?"

The answer could be unkind. Few will deny that his competitive tactics were those of a shark or a leopard and contributed to his success equally with his legitimate business genius. In blood and sweat the men of Homestead— and hundreds of thousands more who had served his empire at the lowest wages he could be induced to pay—also contributed. Inevitably one wonders if this disquieting thought crossed his mind during the final years. He died several months before Henry Clay Frick, in 1919, at Lenox, Massachusetts. A complete inventory of his gifts, foundations, and assorted philanthropies approached $400 million, the residual value of his estate less than one hundred millions.

Also in 1919, 350,000 steelworkers went out on strike in the most serious challenge to management since Homestead. Unorganized and soon disorganized, they were defeated more quickly than their predecessors. Twenty strikers were killed. Back went the losers, over half of them to the eighty-four-hour week. The Amalgamated Association of several thousand key men had helped kill the strike by declining to participate. *Sic transit gloria.*

I suppose that no one enjoyed a greater measure of job security in his day than the healthy artisan who so ably performed his special work. Like the blacksmith—for example. So far as I know, no one ever produced a machine which made a better horseshoe, or could fit it, at lower cost, to Dobbin's hoof. So the blacksmith's job-security was not destroyed by automation. It simply disappeared as the horseshoe was replaced by the pneumatic tire.

> —Roger M. Blough, Chairman,
> United States Steel Corporation

XI *Sequel*

For all practical purposes the steel industry today is a closed shop, manned by 980,000 members of the United Steelworkers of America (AFL-CIO). Production for 1964 was about 120 million tons, almost a hundred times greater than in 1892. This increase has taken place despite the encroaching competition of aluminum and certain plastics. The backbone of the United States is, and probably always will be, constructed of steel. "Steelmakers are activating idle facilities and adding employees to payrolls to keep up with a booming demand," reports *Steel* magazine.

But paradoxically the steelworker's future is gloomy. Few industries have matched steel in its large-scale adoption of automation and cybernetics, and the trend is increasing. To get rid of older, unnecessary workers, the companies pension them off without replacing them. In the auto industry—steel's alter ego—100,000 workers are currently on pension, a method known as "silent firing"; and the same process is taking place in steel, coking, and iron-ore mining. "The fact has to be faced," writes a workingman, James Boggs, that "automation is the greatest revolution that has taken place in human society since men stopped hunting and fishing and started to grow their own food." Nowadays few displaced men have any place to go. "In fact," he continues, "so devastating would be the immediate effects if automation were introduced at one fell swoop that those who would appear to benefit most from it . . . are as afraid of its introduction as the workers threatened with displacement."

The prospect is all the more dangerous to labor because of the speed at which steel can now be manufactured. Sky-high production goals can be reached by less men working less time; and since World War II the industry has never found it necessary to operate at anywhere near capacity.[1] Until recently, Republic Steel allowed substantial facilities at Massillon, Ohio, to remain idle for four years. Open-hearth furnaces 1, 2, 3, and 4 at Homestead have been practically out of action for years, and even furnaces 5 and 6 are worked only sporadically. This state of affairs is commonplace elsewhere in the land. Although steel capacity increased 20 percent since 1955, the work force declined by seventeen thousand hands. U. S. Steel president Leslie B. Worthington declared, "The company is following a policy of more and better steel from fewer plants." Such is the wave of the future, and on what shore it will break, and how and when, is anybody's guess.

Slowly but surely the open-hearth method is being re-

1 In this publication year (1965), U. S. Steel is known to be capable of breaking even at one-third capacity.

placed by oxygen converters. In 1962 at Duquesne, it was reported, 150 tons of steel that formerly took eight hours to produce were turned out in forty minutes by the new system. At the time this was considered a remarkable feat. Yet two years later Jones & Laughlin was making steel at the world's record rate of 491 tons hourly at eight dollars per ton, and more cheaply than by the open-hearth method. Capital spending for new plants and equipment was $1,550 million in the single year 1964. Without doubt, almost all of this mammoth figure went into oxygen converters and "continuous casting" reconversion. By the latter system—definitely as spectacular (or ominous) in its consequences as oxygenation—liquid steel is poured from a furnace, cooled, and shaped all in one continuous flow which bypasses many former steps, saves time, cuts costs, and delivers a better product.

Will these new inventions be the last? On the contrary, an era of faster, more mechanized production seems to be dawning. "In the next 10 years," according to Mr. Worthington, "we'll see more technological advancement in this industry than we've seen in the last 60." The Stora Kaldo process developed in Sweden has significant advantages, as has Germany's new Rotor unit. Republic Steel is working on a way of converting iron directly into steel by an almost magical system which totally eliminates the coke oven, blast furnace, open hearth, and the primary rolling mill. One of the latest innovations, vacuum degassing, removes impurities and cuts costs about eight dollars per ton. Other major refinements are in the offing. They will not replace the open hearth overnight—massive capital assets cannot instantly be scrapped even though the process is obsolescent—but their time will come, and the long-run prognosis for steelworkers is serious.

Since the 1919 upheaval, wildcat strikes and full-scale walkouts have hit steel on innumerable occasions. Mounting automation has been the prime underlying cause, although other issues—wage scales, fringe benefits, working conditions, and so on—have played their part. The biggest of all took place in 1959 when half a million workers, mostly at Bethlehem and U.S. Steel, left their jobs and shut down 85 percent of the nation's production. Finally compromised after four months which wrought havoc in the United States economy, it will not be the last steel struggle in our history.

World Wars I and II and their attendant subsidies from Uncle Sam have vastly swelled the so-called "Homestead District Works" of the United States Steel Corporation. Over the years there has been some expansion in the Munhall area, but generally the movement has been toward west Homestead. McClure Street, for example, which used to end near the river, now stops at Sixth Avenue. At least a hundred acres of that moldy, decrepit section running from the waterfront to Sixth have been swallowed up by the giant mill; gone are any number of shacks, tenements, narrow streets, saloons, rooming houses, alleys, vacant lots, and the happy hustling grounds of whores long departed. Upon their ruins now lies the Company, like a later civilization erecting a new city over the structures and artifacts of the dead.

As a result of this westward growth, the borough of Homestead has shrunk in glory. Its population today is seven thousand, while Munhall has blossomed to twenty thousand. The plant which once hired less than four thousand hands now employs thirty thousand. The median family income of both boroughs is approximately $5,500, not far from the national average. As ever, Homestead is still the greatest single steel-producing unit in the world. From an airplane, miles high, one may perceive its existence by huge yellow block letters painted on a blackish roof: "UNITED STATES STEEL CORPORATION, HOMESTEAD DISTRICT WORKS."

A new bridge spans the Monongahela from Munhall to Rankin (next door to Braddock), and when you stand at its center and survey the mill and the boroughs, especially at dusk, nothing seems to have changed much. There below, just east of the hot metal bridge, you can fix the exact spot where the barges were grounded and *Little Bill* scurried. Docking facilities have been improved, but in the mind's eye you can easily see them stranded at the river's edge just as they were three-quarters of a century ago. The *Little Bill* twists and turns in circles. Thousands of strikers are massed within the mill grounds. They are firing and tossing dynamite at the inboard scow and being shot at in return. The picture is heart-rendingly clear. To add to the illusion of time evaporating, much the same barges and tugs still work the Monongahela; and while you peer, engulfed by memories of things past, they move slowly and smoothly below you. Peacefully they pass the scene where on July 6, 1892, the most dynamic episode in American labor annals was enacted.

Through half-closed eyes you look at the land south of the stream, and it too appears quite unchanged. Here is Eighth Avenue, garish, neon-lit, presently a kaleidoscopic ruin of little stores and taverns. Above it stretches the long Munhall slope, splashed with green shrubbery. Except for plant expansion along the river, the general physical layout of both towns is as it was. There, a few blocks west, is the hot metal span. It still reaches from the Carrie furnaces (they have not been altered) to the heart of the mill, and incessantly cars of molten pig move upon it toward the Homestead converters. Grayish smoke pours from the furnaces. Trolley cars clang along Eighth and the Munhall bridge—noisy little affairs scarcely improved since the year of battle. The similarities between what was and what is are eerie. Everywhere the wraiths of Mr. Frick, Mr. Carnegie, the cowering Pinkertons and wild strikers press upon your brain and tempt you to think that time has stopped.

The old graystone building in downtown Pittsburgh, where the main Carnegie offices were located and where Mr. Frick was assailed, still stands. Frick Park is a few blocks northeast of there. In Pittsburgh proper there is, of course, the Carnegie Institute and Library. The town of Carnegie is located a few miles due west of Homestead. You enter the Carnegie Library in Munhall—a handsome, vine-covered, ivy-laced, old-fashioned structure dedicated personally in 1898 by the great steel master, atop the famous hill in the center of a small park, next to a bandstand —and the first thing that strikes the eye is his colored photograph. The bright blue eyes sparkle and he is smiling his same cheery, rather anxious smile. You cannot escape these men within the smoke of Pittsburgh.

The hypnotic feeling that decades have rolled back is not altered when you walk through the boroughs themselves. Although the Munhall station is now a parking lot, the tragic little Homestead Depot still exists on Amity Street, between Fifth and Sixth. A few clerks work there. It adjoins a tangle of rail lines. But Mr. Frick's wooden fence is a memory, replaced by high strands of barbed wire. The skating rink near Eighth and Ammon is gone. So is the Opera House, or theater, or Hippodrome, somewhat west of the erstwhile rink. The Homestead Local Union

1397, United Steelworkers of America, occupies the second floor of a frame building on McClure near Eighth; its dues-paying members number seven thousand today. You may still gaze upon the imposing mansions (Eleventh Avenue) of former Carnegie managers—large, pleasant, repainted homes now used as rooming houses. Across the river, Braddock is still producing rails and belching smoke.

You will find the hole-in-the-wall tunnel entrance near the main gate on Eighth, where the men used to draw their pay. Once it burrowed under the river all the way to the opposite shore; now, after about thirty feet, it has been sealed off. Everywhere there are overgrown trees, shrubs, and bushes crowding up the hill, just as they did in 1892. The majority of streets and alleys have been repaved, but still you walk upon some dirt and cobblestone paths and discover a few of the old ghastly "squares" between houses. Dogs roam everywhere, some of them in pitiful condition. Most of the Eighth Avenue taverns boast the traditional brass rails, but no stools. The nickel stein of beer now costs ten or fifteen cents. Quite a few of the original rooming houses in this area remain absolutely unchanged. The Stein and Homestead Hotels on Sixth, next to the railroad tracks, for example, consist of the same ancient rooms above taverns. Comment concerning them would be superfluous. It would be advisable for sedentary strangers not to visit these parts after dark.

Pretty girls in Bermuda shorts shop Eighth Avenue—once upon a time such demeanor would have been unheard-of in a mill town like Homestead or Gary or Bethlehem. There is a single movie theater near McClure Street. Up the hill one perceives a thousand television aerials. A taxi gets you across the river and into the metropolis within minutes. In superficial respects all has been modernized and, in a sense, improved. A new and better life goes on.

All in all, however, the classic Baedeker phrase creeps into one's memory: "There is nothing here which need detain the traveler."

Inevitably the main Negro section is near the railroad tracks in Munhall. It is depressing, to put it moderately. As you mount the hill, conditions improve. You find pleasant homes, streets, and lawns. Yet, here and there south of Eighth, you encounter areas nestled in ravines or next to alleys precisely as they once were. Hundreds of frame houses in Homestead and Munhall date back to 1892. They have been repainted a bit, perhaps a little brickwork has been added; but they are truly relics of the past, monuments to the squalor that was Homestead. They are disappearing year after year. Many are mere shells, empty upstairs, with an incongruous tavern occupying the ground floor—this in a so-called residential district. ("Duquesne Beer 10¢ Per Glass.") The second-floor windows are empty, gaping, boarded up. Such rattraps, one by one, are doomed by the Allegheny County Health Department, which posts signs on their front doors: "Order to Vacate Premises." Soon these mementoes will be gone forever. Within innumerable residences the descendant occupants possess (so it is said) Winchester rifles grabbed from the Pinkertons on July 6, 1892.

After C.I.O. unionized steel in the '30s, it erected a gray slab monument about ten feet high on the corner of Eighth Avenue and West Street, a few blocks west of McClure Street. It stands in a grassy, mown area measuring forty by ninety feet, directly in front of a sign reading "$100 Littering Fine." It is kept clean and lightly sandblasted. It shows a brawny, half-naked worker lining a furnace. A wreath of flowers is placed upon this statue every Memorial Day. Most passers-by take no notice of it, and few steelworkers—even those in the union—are aware of its message or memories. But there are some, not necessarily old-timers, who know it well and can recite the inscription verbatim:

> ERECTED BY THE MEMBERS OF THE STEEL WORKERS ORGANIZATION COMMITTEE LOCAL UNIONS IN MEMORY OF THE IRON AND STEEL WORKERS WHO WERE KILLED IN HOMESTEAD, PA., ON JULY 6, 1892, WHILE STRIKING AGAINST THE CARNEGIE STEEL COMPANY IN DEFENSE OF THEIR AMERICAN RIGHTS

A Note on Sources

The following bibliography is incomplete in that some works
and periodicals were used scantily—a phrase here, a single
fact or figure there—and to list them all would be needless.
Each of those named hereafter must be taken with a grain of
salt. Harvey's biography of Frick, for example, is hopelessly
biased in his hero's favor and contains demonstrable inaccuracies. The same is true of Bridge's otherwise admirable
history. Mr. Carnegie's autobiography is self-serving and of
minor value. Stowell and Burgoyne take the strikers' side un-
failingly. Even the disinterested accounts of esteemed historians such as Bemis and David contradict each other flatly
on what should be simple matters of fact. Journals of opinion
such as the *Nation* and the *North American Review* reflect,
of course, their contemporary editorial slant; and so it goes.
I have done what I could to emerge from this labyrinth with
an account which approaches the elusive goddess Truth.

The *Carnegie Papers* in the Library of Congress have been
so microscopically sifted and quoted in prior works that it
seemed useless to examine them again. The Senate and House
hearings were invaluable. In quoting from them I have occasionally compressed or slightly abridged the delivered testimony. This was done to avoid repetitious oral statements by
witnesses; but in no way has their meaning been altered even
slightly.

I found that the New York *Tribune* covered the strike
more fairly and meticulously than any other paper. Various
Pittsburgh dailies furnished interesting details; otherwise they
are not too reliable. Considering the political character of the
Tribune, whose publisher was running for Vice-President on
Mr. Harrison's ticket and had every reason to back the Carnegie interests, its news stories were punctilious and moderate.
The *Tribune* rushed two anonymous correspondents to the
scene of the July 6 battle. One covered the story from
Pittsburgh, the other from Homestead. A month later one
evidently was recalled, leaving the other to work both sides
of the river. Later the *Tribune* relied on local agents who
rewrote Pittsburgh copy, or wired it intact to New York, or
used syndicated material from the Associated Press. One way

or another, this newspaper provided the best running account of the struggle each day from start to finish.

The *Review of Reviews* was, as always in bygone events, exceptionally helpful. I also relied much on Gabriel's classic analysis. I fear that Hendrick admires his man too ardently to be entirely reliable. In reverse the same is true of Winkler.

I would like to think that this reconsideration of the Homestead trauma, which has attempted to compress millions of words of permanent source material and ephemeral reportage into some degree of coherence, will encourage other strike books. To my knowledge, relatively complete narratives dealing with Ludlow, Lawrence, the railroad uprisings in 1877, San Francisco's general strike in the mid-'30s, steel in 1919, and others just as engrossing, have not yet been published. Their accounts are due and payable.

ADAMIC, LOUIS: *Dynamite*. New York: Viking, 1934.

ADDAMS, JANE: *Twenty Years at Hull-House*. New York: Signet, 1961.

ADJUTANT-GENERAL OF PENNSYLVANIA: *Annual Report for the Year 1892*. Harrisburg, Pennsylvania.

ALLEN, FREDERICK L.: *The Lords of Creation*. New York: Harper, 1935.

American Review of Reviews.

AUSTIN, A. *The Labor Story*. New York: Coward-McCann, 1949.

BEARD, CHARLES A. and MARY R.: *The Rise of American Civilization*. New York: Macmillan, 1934.

BEER, THOMAS: *The Mauve Decade*. New York: Garden City, 1926.

BEMIS, EDWARD: "The Homestead Strike," *Journal of Political Economy*, 1893–1894.

BERKMAN, ALEXANDER: *Prison Memoirs of an Anarchist*. New York: Mother Earth Press, 1912.

BIMBA, ANTHONY: *History of the American Working Class*. New York: International Publishers, 1929.

BOGGS, JAMES: "The American Revolution," *Monthly Review*, July–August, 1963.

BOYER, RICHARD O., and MORAIS, HERBERT M.: *Labor's Untold Story*. New York: Cameron & Kahn, 1955.

BRIDGE, JAMES H.: *The Inside Story of the Carnegie Steel Company.* New York: Aldine, 1903.

BRODY, DAVID: *Steelworkers in America.* Cambridge, Mass.: Harvard University Press, 1960.

BURGOYNE, A. G.: *A Complete History of the Struggle of July, 1892, Between the Carnegie Steel Company, Limited, and the Amalgamated Association of Iron and Steel Workers.* Pittsburgh: 1893.

BYINGTON, MARGARET F.: *Homestead: The Households of a Mill Town.* New York: Charities Publication Committee, The Pittsburgh Survey, Russell Sage Foundation, 1910.

CARNEGIE, ANDREW: *Autobiography.* New York: Houghton Mifflin, 1920.

COMMONS, J. R., and ASSOCIATES: *History of Labor in the United States,* Volume II. New York: Macmillan, 1926.

DAVID, HENRY: "Upheaval at Homestead," in *America in Crisis,* ed. Daniel Aaron. New York: Knopf, 1952.

Dictionary of American Biography, 1936.

DOUGLAS, PAUL H.: *Real Wages in the U.S., 1890–1926.* New York: Houghton Mifflin, 1930.

DRINNON, RICHARD: *Rebel in Paradise.* Chicago: University of Chicago Press, 1961.

FISHER, DOUGLAS A.: *The Epic of Steel.* New York: Harper & Row, 1962.

FITCH, J. A.: *The Steel Workers.* New York: Charities Publication Committee, The Pittsburgh Survey, Russell Sage Foundation, 1911.

FONER, PHILIP S.: *History of the Labor Movement in the U.S.* New York: International Publishers, 1955.

Forum, September, 1892.

FRIEDMAN, M.: *The Pinkerton Labor Spy.* New York: Wilshire, 1907.

GABRIEL, RALPH: *Course of American Democratic Thought.* New York: Ronald, 1940.

GARLAND, HAMLIN: "Homestead and Its Perilous Trades," *McClure's Magazine,* June, 1894.

GINGER, RAY: *The Bending Cross.* New Brunswick, N.J.: Rutgers University Press, 1949.

GOLDBERG, HARVEY (ed.): *American Radicals,* Monthly Review, New York, 1957.

GOLDMAN, EMMA: *Living My Life.* New York: Knopf, 1934.

GOLDMAN, ERIC: *Rendezvous with Destiny.* New York: Knopf, 1958.

HACKER, LOUIS M., and KENDRICK, BENJAMIN B.: *The United States Since 1865.* New York: F. S. Crofts, 1932.

Harper's Weekly.

HARVEY, GEORGE: *Henry Clay Frick.* New York: Scribner's, 1928.

HEILBRONER, ROBERT L.: "Epitaph for the Steel Master," *American Heritage,* August, 1960.

HENDRICK, BURTON J.: *Life of Andrew Carnegie.* New York: Doubleday Doran, 1932.

HOLBROOK, STEWART H.: *The Age of the Moguls.* New York: Doubleday, 1953.

House of Representatives Report 2447, 52nd Congress, 2nd Session: *Employment of Pinkerton Detectives.*

HUNTER, ROBERT: *Violence in the Labor Movement.* New York: Macmillan, 1914.

JOSEPHSON, MATTHEW: *The Robber Barons.* New York: Harcourt, 1934.

Journal of the Knights of Labor.

LUNDBERG, FERDINAND: *America's 60 Families.* New York: Vanguard Press, 1937.

MADISON, CHARLES A.: *Critics and Crusaders.* New York: Henry Holt, 1947.

MAY, HENRY F.: *Protestant Churches and Industrial America.* New York: 1949.

MORISON, SAMUEL E., and COMMAGER, HENRY S.: *The Growth of the American Republic,* Volume II. New York: Oxford University Press, 1950.

MYERS, GUSTAVUS: *History of the Great American Fortunes.* New York: Modern Library, 1936.

Nation, July 14, July 21, July 28, August 11, 1892.

New York *Tribune.*

North American Review, September, 1892.

ORTH, S. P.: *The Armies of Labor.* New Haven, Conn.: Yale University Press, 1921.

PERLMAN, SELIG: *History of Trade Unionism in the U.S.* New York: Augustus McKelley, 1950.

Pittsburgh *Commercial Gazette.*

Pittsburgh *Despatch.*

Pittsburgh *Post.*

Pittsburgh *Press.*

Pittsburgh *Times.*

Public Opinion.

REYNOLDS, ROBERT L.: "The Works Are Not Worth One Drop of Human Blood," *American Heritage,* August, 1960.

ROBINSON, JESSE S.: *The Amalgamated Association of Iron, Steel and Tin Workers.* Baltimore: Johns Hopkins Press, 1920.

ROE, WELLINGTON: *Juggernaut.* New York: Lippincott, 1948.

ROWAN, RICHARD W.: *The Pinkertons.* Boston: Little, Brown, 1931.

Senate Report 1280, 52nd Congress, 2nd Session: *Investigation of Labor Troubles.*

STOWELL, M. R.: *Fort Frick.* 1893

SULLIVAN, MARK: *Our Times,* Volume I. New York: Scribner's, 1926.

WILSON, EDMUND: "American Heroes: Fremont and Frick," in *The Shores of Light.* New York: Farrar, Straus & Young, 1952.

WINKLER, J. K.: *Incredible Carnegie.* New York: Vanguard Press, 1931.

WRIGHT, CARROLL D.: "The Amalgamated Association of Iron and Steel Workers," *Quarterly Journal of Economics,* July, 1893.

YELLEN, SAMUEL: *American Labor Struggles.* New York: Harcourt, Brace, 1936.

References

Sources plainly identified in the text of this book are not included in the following list. All others—with a few exceptions, such as the first note—refer to the Bibliography.

PAGE   Chapter I: The Famed Decade

1   Baer quote. *The American Past,* by Roger Butterfield (New York: Simon & Schuster, 1957), p. 320.

1   "During the whole." Morison, p. 214.

2   "One might search." Hacker, p. 71.

2   "If a Martian visitor." Beard, p. 589.

2   The 1893–1897 economic collapse. Morison, p. 234.

2   Twelve hundred strikes. Hacker, p. 234.

3   "There are three great crops." Boyer, p. 109.

3   Average workday and insecurity. Gabriel, p. 189.

3–4   Average pay of skilled and unskilled. Morison, p. 161.

4   The 1892 dollar (footnote). Los Angeles *Times,* September 22, 1963.

4   Women's pay in San Francisco. Boyer, p. 79.

4   Christmas day in Hull House. Addams, p. 148.

4   "assisted by incredibly small children." Addams, p. 149.

4   The Minnesota legislature. Boyer, p. 79.

4–5   "Combination of capital." Morison, p. 153.

5   Negro lynchings. 1953 *Encyclopaedia Britannica,* vol. 14, p. 526.

271

5   The unbroken belt of states. Morison, p. 102.
5   "I never saw over a $20 bill." Eric Goldman, p. 37.
6   "In God we trusted." Boyer, p. 109.
6   "The good Lord gave me my money." Gabriel, p. 149.
6   "To secure wealth is an honorable ambition." Gabriel, p. 149.
6   Marshall Field's people. Eric Goldman, p. 35.
6   "Now the poorest laborer." David, p. 132.
6–7   "By the proper use of wealth." Gabriel, p. 148.
7   "theft . . . to deprive us." Gabriel, p. 147.
7   "First, to set an example." Gabriel, p. 151.
7–8   "Avenues greater in number." Gabriel, p. 152.
8–9   The plutocracy and the less triumphant. Beard, chap. XXV, "The Gilded Age."
10   Advertising quotes. *Harper's Weekly,* July 2, 1892.
10   "flamboyant lines and meaningless details." Hacker, p. 239.
10   Carnegie on competition. Gabriel, p. 150.
11   The trusts. Hacker, pp. 278 ff.
11   Fate of 5,000 small establishments. Eric Goldman, p. 34.
12   The Populists. Hacker, pp. 305 ff.
12   "the imbecility of the system." Boyer, p. 83.
12–13   "a castle in the air." Gabriel, p. 210.
13   "The Red Scare." Boyer, p. 69.
13   "The unemployed, if they bore foreign names." Harry Barnard, quoted by Boyer, p. 70.
13–14   The Knights of Labor. Roe, pp. 24 ff.
14   "tired of pulling the chestnuts." Hacker, p. 229.
14–15   Terence V. Powderly. Orth, p. 85.
15   "Mr. Powderly, do you concede the right." Foner, p. 159.
15   "I will talk at no picnics." Boyer, p. 87.
15   "Just think of it!" Boyer, p. 89.
15   "Mr. Powderly seems to me." Foner, p. 159; quote dated May 7, 1888.
16   "More!" *The Great Quotations,* by George Seldes (New York: Lyle Stuart, 1960), p. 285.
16   "We have no ultimate ends." Austin, p. 105.
16   "a fair day's wage." Austin, p. 109.
16–17   "At no time in my life." Morison, p. 158.
17–18   The immigration threat. Bimba, p. 140.
17–18   Ellis Island and the immigrant quote. *Reader's Digest,* May, 1963.
18   "frequently herded from steerage." Boyer, p. 67.

18-19   Deficiencies of wrought iron. Brody, p. 8.

19   Bessemer steel rails. Fisher, p. 123.

19   "Two pounds of iron stone." Morison, p. 133.

20   Michigan surveying expeditions. Morison, p. 130.

20   The Mesabi range. Fisher, p. 133.

20-21   Advantages of Bessemer conversion. Fisher, p. 127.

21   Homestead's 16 open hearths. Stowell, p. 20.

21   Total U.S. open hearth production. Fisher, p. 126.

21-22   Frick's youth. Harvey, p. 12.

21   Frick in 1892. Hendrick, pp. 288-290.

22-23   Frick and the 1873 panic. Josephson, p. 261.

22   The Coke King sets the price. Josephson, p. 263.

22   A millionaire at 30. Hendrick, p. 295; Josephson, p. 263; Bridge, p. 172.

23   "We found that we could not get on without a supply." Carnegie, p. 222.

23   "We must attach this young man." Hendrick, p. 287.

23   "Surely, Andrew, that will be a fine thing." Harvey, p. 75.

23   "Carnegie and Frick made an extraordinary team." Hacker, p. 192.

23   Carnegie company's coal and coke holdings. Bridge, p. 173.

24   Frick's minority in coke firm. Harvey, p. 79.

24   Frick named Carnegie's general manager. Harvey, p. 93.

24   Profits and tonnage upon Frick's entry. Bridge, p. 170.

25   "The fields of Connellsville." Josephson, p. 264.

25   How Frick dealt with strikes. Yellen, p. 73.

25   His hatred of unions and union officials. Hendrick, pp. 376-379.

25-26   The 1890 coal strike. Harvey, p. 131.

26   "The Frick Company was fully prepared." Harvey, p. 91.

27   "Thou shalt not take." Bridge, p. 187.

Chapter II: Homestead

28   Carnegie quote. *Forum* article cited by Bemis, p. 371.

28   "cursing feebly." *The Savage Years,* by Brian Connell (New York: Harper & Brothers, 1959), p. 59.

28   Hamilton and the Whiskey Insurgents. *The Forum,* September, 1892.

28-29   John McClure and Amity Homestead. Bridge, p. 150.

29   Assistant roller John McLuckie. Burgoyne, p. 130.

29   The Monongahela and the borough. Byington, pp. 23 ff.

30–31   The borough (continued) and Garland's quote. Bridge, p. 194.

31–32   Wages and savings. Bemis, p. 372.

32   Iron puddlers and work shifts. Fitch, p. 38.

32   "Tell me, how can a man get any pleasure." Fitch, p. 15.

33   Alcohol as a stimulant. Fitch, p. 227.

33   Saturday night and payday. Fitch, p. 228.

33   East Europeans and their hovels. Byington, p. 112.

33–34   Churches in Homestead. Byington, p. 6.

34   "Let the preachers go into the mills." Fitch, p. 17.

34   Holy Trinity Church case. *The Nation*, July 13, 1963, p. 25.

34, 37   Death and injury statistics. Fitch, p. 64.

34–38   Working conditions. Fitch, pp. 22 ff.

35–36   "The men, I dare say." Brody, p. 33.

36   "You can't help it . . . you become more and more a machine." Bridge, p. 197.

36   "Everywhere in the enormous sheds." Quoted by Bridge, p. 196.

36   128-degree temperatures and "gorilla men." Brody, p. 33.

37   Hot jobs, crane men, pressure work. Fitch, pp. 51 ff.

37   Accidents in the pressure divisions. Byington, p. 92.

37–38   Company recompense for accidents. Brody, p. 91.

38   Employee insurance policies. Byington, p. 96.

38   The Amalgamated treasury. Bemis, p. 370.

38–39   Wages of technicians. Fitch, p. 156.

39   "in Prince Albert coats wearing top hats." Roe, p. 44.

39    $100 monthly the average wage. House Report, p. XLI.

39   "Whether you work by the piece." *The Great Quotations* (above), p. 54.

40   Local Amalgamated membership reaches 752. Fitch, p. 98.

40   Amalgamated organization and policies. Hendrick, pp. 382–388.

40–41   "The Giant Puddler." Wright, p. 54.

41   "The Association never objects to improvements." Brody, p. 51.

41   Slashes in the 1889 scale. Brody, p. 52.

41–42   Union officials, demands and complaints. Bridge, p. 202.

42   Rarity of Amalgamated strikes. Wright, p. 97.

42–44   The mill and adjacent areas. Burgoyne, pp. 3 ff.

44   Specialized production at Homestead. Carnegie, p. 220.

44   Boiler plate, armor, value of the Homestead plant. Bemis, p. 369; Stowell, p. 20; House Report, p. 134.

44-45 The Duquesne plant and its capture. Bridge, p. 176.

45 "the leading mills in the United States." Carnegie, p. 176.

45-47 Other personal Carnegie holdings. Burgoyne, p. 10.

47 "twenty-five dollars monthly." Carnegie, p. 32.

Chapter III: Mr. Carnegie

48 Carnegie's birth. Bridge, p. 13.

48 His father, William. Carnegie, p. 12.

48 Family sails for the U.S. Carnegie, p. 25.

49 Carnegie's background in Dunfermline. Carnegie, p. 10.

49 His religious views. Carnegie, pp. 50, 278.

49-50 Arrival in New York and early jobs. Carnegie, pp. 28 ff.

50 The Ohio Telegraph Company messenger. Bridge, p. 14; Hendrick, chap. 3.

50-52 Carnegie's promotions and advancements: Josephson, p. 43; Heilbroner, p. 8; Hendrick, chap. 5.

50-51 "Our public lands for almost unlimited extent." Josephson, p. 42.

51-51 His investments in various firms, oil land, iron works, etc. Heilbroner, p. 8; Carnegie, p. 80; Josephson, p. 44; Heilbroner, p. 9; Hendrick, p. 120; Bridge, pp. 20 ff.

52 "Whatever I engage in I must push inordinately." Josephson, p. 254.

52-53 Keystone bridges and Pittsburgh locomotives. Carnegie, p. 114.

52 "Thirty three and an income of $50,000." Hendrick, p. 147.

52-53 "To continue much longer." Boyer, p. 29.

53 The Edgar Thomson mill at Braddock. Hendrick, chap. 11.

53 His interest in the Mesabi range, and the *Iron Age* quote. Fisher, p. 34.

53 "the little Scotch pirate." Winkler, p. 14.

54 "I get no sweet dividend." Brody, p. 4.

54 The 40 millionaires. Winkler, p. 5.

54 "I have enough trouble." Carnegie, p. 203.

55 "Bubbling with enthusiasm." Josephson, p. 104.

55 Production at Edgar Thomson in 1879. Bridge, p. 91.

55 "Pioneering don't pay." Holbrook, p. 78.

55 "The day of Iron has passed." Josephson, p. 108.

55-56 "Puppy dog number three." Bridge, p. 113.

56 Cablegrams following above. Josephson, pp. 256-257.

56 "simply stealing." Josephson, p. 258.

56 "When was there ever such a business!" Josephson, p. 256.

56 The cruelest taskmaster in U.S. industrial history. Winkler, p. 3.

56–57 "Mr. Carnegie, they tell me at the office." Winkler, p. 168.

57 Commencement of rail production at Homestead, and the decisive walkout. Bridge, pp. 152, 158.

58 Carnegie acquires the mill. Bridge, pp. 151 ff.

58 "Wise man. Shake, pard." Winkler, p. 167.

58 Establishment of the Hartman works at Beaver Falls. Bridge, p. 185.

58–59 Capture of the Duquesne operation. Bridge, pp. 175 ff.

59 End of the battle for supremacy in U.S. iron and steel. Yellen, p. 72.

60 "Presently he would descend from his rail-perch." Bridge, p. 114.

60–61 The Carnegie company as the 1890s approached. Brody, pp. 3–5.

61 U.S. production compared to England's. Holbrook, p. 80.

61 Tariff on English and German rails. Morison, p. 134.

61 Costs, prices, demand for ferrous products. Bridge, pp. 99–102.

61 The McKinley Tariff and its surpluses. Hacker, p. 94.

62 1867 lockout of iron puddlers. Bridge, p. 31.

62 1875 and 1884 labor problems at Edgar Thomson and Beaver Falls. Bridge, p. 185.

62–63 Difficulties at Braddock in 1885 and 1887. David, p. 142.

62 "The right of the workingmen to combine." Yellen, p. 74.

63 The next-to-last strike at Edgar Thomson. Bridge, p. 189.

63 "it gives one a poor opinion of the American workman." Yellen, p. 74.

63 Carnegie's views on arbitration and conciliation. Hendrick, pp. 371–373.

63–64 The 1887 coke strike. Bridge, p. 191.

64 Frick crushes the 1890 coke strike. Bridge, p. 191.

64 "that the ties of brotherhood may still bind." *The Great Quotations* (above), p. 143.

64 Carnegie's statement that he had never hired a strike-breaker. David, p. 142.

65 "upon the sacredness of property civilization itself depends." *The Great Quotations* (above), p. 143.

65 "If I returned to work tomorrow" and four following quotes. Carnegie, pp. 253, 232, 241, 249, 251.

66 "Carnegie never wanted to know the profits." Brody, p. 3.

66 His famous sliding scale. David, p. 143.
66–67 His tactics during the 1889 strike. Bridge, p. 200.
67 "both sides are victors." Bridge, p. 201.
67 Compromise of the strike and Carnegie's reaction. David, p. 144.
67–68 Selling price of 4 by 4's in July, 1889. Fitch, p. 122.
68 "head and shoulders higher than ever." Bridge, p. 201.
68 Billet prices prior to 1892. Fitch, p. 122.
69 Typical Pinkerton classified ad. Friedman, p. 7.
69–70 The Pinkerton agency and its role in labor disputes. *Encyclopaedia Britannica;* Senate Report, p. X; Burgoyne, pp. 43–44; Boyer, p. 50.
70 Output of the 32-inch mill. David, p. 135.
71 Billets sag to $23.75 early 1892. Fitch, p. 122.
71 Baseball, songs of the day, Bryan. Sullivan, pp. 1–4.
71–72 Pennsylvania's Governor Pattison. Data concerning him and other politicians mentioned elsewhere were largely derived from the 1936 *Dictionary of American Biography.*

Chapter IV: The Issue Joined

73 Gallinger and Bruce exchange. Senate Report, pp. 190–193.
73 Negotiations begin in January. David, p. 145; Senate Report, p. 205.
74–76 Further figures and facts at this meeting. Bridge, p. 208; Senate Report, p. 205.
76–77 Officials refer to the South Chicago rail mill. Bridge, p. 207.
77 Improvements since 1889 in the 119-inch mill. Bridge, p. 208.
78 Rebuttal by union negotiators. Bemis, p. 379.
78 The organized men dispute company claims. Yellen, p. 79.
79 "Mr. McLuckie stated that we had purchased." House Report, p. 163.
80 "You can tell your people we are willing." Senate Report, p. 205.
80 Amalgamated gains nationally since 1889. Brody, pp. 54–55.
80 "These Works having been consolidated." Bridge, p. 204.
81 "Should this be determined upon." Bridge, p. 205.
81 Abnormal production in May, 1892. Brody, p. 54.
81 1959 steel walkout (footnote). *The Haunted Fifties,* by I. F. Stone (New York: Random House, 1963), p. 293.
81 "the magnitude of our business." Harvey, p. 109.
81–82 Quotes by Roberts and Potter. Senate Report, pp. 206–207.

82 "The scales have had the most careful consideration." Harvey, p. 109.

82 "the Amalgamated placed a tax on improvements." Brody, p. 54.

82 "As I understand matters at Homestead." Bridge, p. 205.

83 Carnegie cables of June 17 and 28. Bridge, p. 206.

83 "The mills have never been able to turn out." Harvey, p. 177.

83 "We were persuaded to vote the Republican ticket." Burgoyne, p. 25.

83 Carnegie concerning Homestead (footnote). Carnegie, pp. 229–230.

83–84 Cleveland's platform, wage cuts elsewhere, Republican appeals to Frick. Burgoyne, pp. 28–29.

84 Frick writes Robert Pinkerton, June 20. Yellen, p. 83.

84 Knox and McCleary concerning deputizing the Pinkertons. David, p. 148.

84–85 Erection of the fence around the mill. Stowell, p. 29.

85 "There stands today with great pretense." Foner, p. 207.

85 The June 23 conference. Burgoyne, p. 31; Bemis, pp. 376, 380.

86 "We will want 300 guards." Harvey, p. 114.

87 Final company and union moves during late June. Harvey, p. 111; House Report, p. XXXIV; Burgoyne, pp. 13, 32–39.

89 The 33rd Street mill and structural contracts. Stowell, p. 30.

89 Shutdowns on June 28. Stowell, p. 30.

89 "Frick had patently tried to force the workmen." Yellen, p. 81.

89–90 Non-union employees vote to strike. Burgoyne, pp. 36–37.

90 "The Committee has, after mature deliberation." Bridge, p. 210.

91 "Hereafter the Homestead steel works." Burgoyne, p. 39.

92 "All Discussion of the Wage Question." Bridge, p. 211.

92 The *Edna* and other defensive tactics. Bridge, p. 211; Hendrick, p. 392.

93 Carnegie advertisements for steelworkers. Foner, p. 209.

94 The Advisory Committee curbs drinking and enforces the law. Pittsburgh *Commercial Gazette,* July 3 and 4, 1892.

95 Carnegie unable to be reached "on the Continent." Winkler, p. 200.

95–96 Deputy Cluley's reception in Homestead. House Report, pp. 66–67.

97–98 Potter's attempt to secure 260 skilled workers. Yellen, p. 83.

98 Independence Day and July 5. New York *Tribune*, July 4 and 5, 1892.

Chapter V: Invasion

100 Gallinger and Pinkerton exchange. Senate Report, pp. 251, 264.

101 "The element of danger which is usually found." Senate Report, p. 71.

102 The Pinkertons reach the barges. Yellen, p. 85; Harvey, p. 116.

102–103 The barges and their reconstruction. Burgoyne, p. 53.

103 Arms loaded inside the barges. Rowan, p. 307.

103 Heinde and Nordrum. Senate Report, p. 251, 143, 79.

104 "This will introduce Col. Joseph H. Gray." Harvey, p. 117.

104 Rodgers and the Tide Coal Company. Pittsburgh *Commercial Gazette*, July 6, 1892.

104–107 Barges en route to Homestead. Stowell, p. 31; House Report, p. 135; Burgoyne, p. 53; Bimba, p. 213.

107 "If you are sheriff of this county." Senate Report, p. 150.

108 "We are coming up that hill anyway." Senate Report, p. 70.

108 "It's no use returning the fire." Senate Report, p. 150.

110 "Don't let the black sheep land!" Stowell, p. 40.

110 The battle on the shoreline begins. Stowell, p. 42; Foner, p. 210; Holbrook, p. 84; Senate Report, pp. 150, 182.

113 The conversation between O'Donnell and Nordrum. Senate Report, p. 150; Stowell, pp. 46 ff.

114 "Situation at Homestead is very grave." House Report, p. 57. (Further wires back and forth between the sheriff and the governor, cited in this chapter, are also in the House Report subsequent to p. 57.)

117 The Pinkertons see the fiery raft. Burgoyne, p. 68.

117 "If you surrender you will be shot down." Senate Report, p. 71.

118 Rutter and Morris mortally wounded. Burgoyne, p. 67.

118 "What in the name of God." House Report, p. 135.

118 Rockets fired into natural gas. Harvey, p. 121.

119 O'Donnell throughout the morning of July 6. Stowell, p. 51.

119 Mary Jones and Silas Wain. Burgoyne, p. 70.

121   The "mob" possessed by "fiendish delight." Senate Report,
      p. 182.

121   Steering "by dead—or at least dazed—reckoning." Rowan,
      p. 309.

121–122   Further casualties and deliberations. Burgoyne, pp. 72 ff.

122   O'Donnell's peace plea fails. Stowell, pp. 52 ff.

122–123   The Pinkertons hold out apathetically. Pittsburgh Com-
      mercial Gazette, July 6, 1892.

123   "We have positive assurance." New York Tribune, July 7,
      1892.

123   "Burn the boats—kill the Pinkertons." Bridge, p. 219.

123   Speeches by Garland and McEvoy. Burgoyne, p. 80.

124   Anarchists and other outsiders arrive. Burgoyne, p. 82.

124   O'Donnell's harangue and its response. Stowell, p. 60.

125   "This is enough of the killing." Pittsburgh Commercial
      Gazette, July 6, 1892.

Chapter VI: The Militia

127–130   Pinkertons run the gantlet. Stowell, pp. 61 ff; Senate
      Report, pp. 72, 79; Holbrook, p. 85; Rowan, p. 311.

130   "The information received up to this time." New York
      Tribune, July 7, 1892. "I believe it would be suicide."
      Same issue.

131   "It is not the duty of the soldiers . . . the strike of the
      metal workers at the Homestead Mills." Both quotes by
      Governor Pattison from the New York Tribune, July 8,
      1892.

131   "Why, the Sheriff of Allegheny." Yellen, p. 89.

131–132   McCleary is rebuffed again. New York Tribune, July 9,
      1892.

132   Advisory Committee members go to Harrisburg. Yellen,
      p. 90.

133   Funeral of Morris, Wain and Fareis, and Rev. McIlyar
      quote. Burgoyne, p. 93; Stowell, pp. 84 ff.

133   "Our little home was almost paid for." Stowell, p. 89.

133–134   Funeral of Streigle, Sotak and Weldon. Stowell, p. 96.

134   "Father Was Killed by the Pinkerton Men." Holbrook,
      p. 86.

134   "We held off until the last moment." Pittsburgh Com-
      mercial Gazette, July 6, 1892.

134-135   Rumors, telegrams, etc., through July 9. New York *Tribune,* July 7, 8, 9, 10, 1892.

135   O'Donnell willing to drop all wage demands. Harvey, p. 128.

135   Frick's reply for publication. Harvey, pp. 128 ff.

136   House and Senate committees appointed. Hunter, p. 294.

137   Gompers: "I am a conservative man." New York *Tribune,* July 7, 1892.

137   "it is doubtful if, save in the presence." *American Journal of Politics,* p. 277.

137   Quotations from the *Review of Reviews* dated August, October and November, 1892, respectively.

138   Concerning Sen. Voorhees, "Pinkertonism," newspapermen in Homestead, Mr. Hardie, the interview of Carnegie near Loch Kinloch. Burgoyne, pp. 99-107.

139   Mr. Carnegie nicknamed "Baron Carnage-y." Yellen, p. 88.

139   DeLeon: "These troubles at Homestead." Yellen, p. 88.

139-142   Berkman and Goldman in Worcester and New York. Emma Goldman, pp. 84 ff; Drinnon, pp. 42 ff.

142   "Mob law is absolute." Harvey, p. 124.

142   "Strikers Prepared to Dynamite Any Incoming Train." Pittsburgh *Commercial Gazette,* July 9, 1892.

143   The finest militia in the land. Burgoyne, p. 110; Stowell, pp. 101-116; *Harper's Weekly,* September 3, 1892.

144   "Thick clouds of smoke overcast the sky." Berkman, p. 22.

145   Other speeches quoted by Berkman in Homestead. Berkman, pp. 25 ff.

145   "And the fine ladies on horseback." Berkman, p. 32.

145   "The situation at Homestead has not improved." Harvey, p. 130.

146   "Have ordered Maj. Gen. George R. Snowden." Harvey, p. 131.

146   "This man Pattison is acting quietly." Burgoyne, p. 112.

146   Tunes suggested for the brass band. Burgoyne, p. 113.

146   "No. 23 was wrecked above this place." Burgoyne, p. 117.

147   "TROOPS FOR HOMESTEAD," O'Donnell's interview, a load off McCleary's mind, death of O'Day, Snowden's statement. New York *Tribune,* July 11, 12, 13, 1892.

147-148   Headlines that swamped the Pittsburgh region. Pittsburgh *Commercial Gazette,* July 11, 1892.

148   "The law is very explicit on this point." Harvey, p. 131.

148–149 "If Governor Pattison was right." "The speeches were terribly noisy." New York *Tribune,* July 12, 1892.

149 Strikers greet Gen. Snowden. *Harper's Weekly,* July 23, 1892.

150 "On the part of the Amalgamated Association." Yellen, p. 92.

150 Following exchange between O'Donnell and the general. New York *Tribune,* July 13, 1892.

150–151 Troops detrain and take up positions. *Harper's Weekly,* July 23, 1892.

151 Snowden sets up headquarters and is interviewed. Stowell, pp. 128–130.

151 "That was the secret of Sheridan's success." Stowell, p. 170.

151 "General, is it intended to use your troops." Stowell, p. 131.

152 Snowden forbids fraternization. New York *Tribune,* July 14, 1892.

152 All other Carnegie plants go out on strike. Harvey, p. 133.

152 "There have been published numerous statements." Harvey, p. 135.

Chapter VII: Berkman and Frick

153 Taylor, McLuckie, Boatner exchange. House Report, p. 93.

153–154 Emma's attempt to become a prostitute. Emma Goldman, pp. 91 ff.

155 Berkman meets Frick in mid-July. Harvey, p. 137.

156 "When the Pinkertons fire upon the people." House Report, p. 222.

157 "I hardly think that is a fair question." House Report, p. 29.

157 "Well, that is all. He has evaded this question." New York *Tribune,* July 14, 1892.

158 "a band of cutthroats, thieves." *Economic Journal,* p. 315.

158 "I am sure the crowd near the water." Burgoyne, p. 129.

158 "From the experience we have had with arbitration." House Report, p. 82.

158–159 Boatner, Bynum, Oates, Roberts exchange. House Report, pp. 106 ff.

159–160 Boatner, McQuade exchange. House Report, pp. 189 ff.

160 Testimony of Gray, Kennedy and Frick. Stowell, pp. 149–167.

160   Frick's *non-sequitur* concerning higher productivity. Burgoyne, p. 127.

161   "But in the negotiations we do not think." House Report, p. XI.

161   "I dissent from the conclusion of the majority." House Report, p. LXII.

161–162   Oates' quote concerning Frick, arbitration, Pinkertons, the McKinley tariff, etc. *The North American Review,* September, 1892.

163   Street disinfected with lime. Annual Report of the Pennsylvania Adjutant-General, letter dated November 30, 1892.

163–164   The bivouac area, mail delivery, etc. Burgoyne, p. 144; *Harper's Weekly,* July 23, 1892; New York *Tribune,* July 16, 1892.

164   "Pennsylvanians can hardly appreciate the actual communism." Foner, p. 212.

165   The nervous young man with posters. Yellen, p. 93.

166   Strikebreakers trickle in, Snowden foiled at the Frick Hotel, McCleary a changed man, etc. Burgoyne, pp. 123–138.

167   "It is, of course, possible that we or some of us." Stowell, p. 198.

167   "did of their malice aforethought feloniously." Burgoyne, p. 142.

168   "I had a good rest in jail." New York *Tribune,* July 21, 1892.

168   Arrival of Governor Pattison. Stowell, p. 202.

168   Renovation of mill ground interiors. Foner, p. 212.

169–170   Conditions in town, patrolling, expectoration, flare-ups, etc., during mid-July. New York *Tribune,* various issues.

170–175   The Berkman-Frick episode. *Harper's Weekly,* August 6, 1892; Berkman, chap. 3; other secondary sources.

173   "Don't shoot, leave him to the law." Harvey, p. 138.

173   "Lynch him! Shoot him!" *Harper's Weekly,* August 6, 1892.

173–175   Immediate aftermath of the assault. Berkman, Harvey, various portions following above page references.

175   Berkman in prison, New York headlines, and Emma. Emma Goldman, pp. 97 ff.

176   "Too glad of your escape to think of anything." Hendrick, p. 402.

176   Frick wrathful and uncompromising. Bemis, p. 386.

176–177   Following four letters and cables from Carnegie and Frick. Hendrick, pp. 402–413.

Chapter VIII: Private Iams

178   *Post-Dispatch* quote. Bridge, p. 233.

180–181   "the arch-sneak of this age," other reactions to Carnegie, and comments from England. Winkler, pp. 213–214.

181   Navy Secretary Herbert (footnote). Winkler, p. 227.

181–182   Iams' offense and punishment. Stowell, pp. 219–222, and other secondary sources such as Burgoyne, pp. 153 ff.

183   "His conduct was that of aiding, abetting." David, p. 152.

183   "I have my own opinion as to the character." New York *Tribune*, July 30, 1892.

183   "shooting, not torture." *Harper's Weekly*, August 13, 1892.

183–184   Subsequent reactions and quotes concerning Iams' punishment. New York *Tribune*, July 26, 27, 1892.

184   Col. Norman Smith's quote. Burgoyne, p. 164.

184–185   Berkman in jail before trial. Drinnon, pp. 53 ff.

185   Police Chief O'Mara and Pittsburgh anarchists. Foner, p. 214.

185   "Who Furnished the Lazy and Poverty-Stricken." New York *Tribune*, July 26, 1892.

186   "falling loosely over her forehead." Drinnon, p. 55.

186   "Too bad you didn't kill him." Berkman, p. 54.

186   "I hate him as much as I hate Frick." New York *Tribune*, July 27, 1892.

187   "I did not expect justice." New York *Tribune*, September 20, 1892.

188   "that the bullet from Berkman's pistol." Bemis, p. 386.

188   Potter, Crawford, the decision to fight it out. Burgoyne, p. 166.

188–189   Concerning skilled specialists, Potter's interview, the boycott plan, etc. New York *Tribune*, August 9–13, 1892.

189   Gompers: "I don't know why." Burgoyne, p. 168.

190   Milwaukee *Sentinel* quote. July 30, 1892.

190   Further quotes in this paragraph. David, p. 153.

190   "It just keeps us going to get bondsmen." Foner, pp. 215–216.

191   Last slab of armor plate for the *Monterey*. Burgoyne, p. 191.

192–193 Curtis in *The North American Review,* September, 1892, p. 366.

193 "The 240 men who have been reduced." Yellen, p. 95.

193–194 Newman-Coyne affair and other acts of violence. Burgoyne, pp. 186–187.

194 Fyock, Homer, Milliken disturbances. New York *Tribune,* September 28, 1892.

194 McCleary and phrase "would be an idiot." Burgoyne, p. 210.

194 Death of George Rutter. Burgoyne, p. 145.

195 Stoning of Potter. Bridge, p. 241.

195–196 Warrants by McLuckie, continuing violence, the luckless switchmen, August 1 quote by Frick. New York *Tribune,* August 3 to September 1, 1892.

196 Chauncey Depew: "the Homestead strike." Bridge, p. 247.

197 "The mills of the gods grind slowly." Bridge, p. 247.

197 "I am a Republican and a Protectionist." New York *Tribune,* November 8, 1892.

198–199 Quotation from Mr. Godkin's *Nation.* Yellen, p. 88.

199 "morally responsible for Berkman's performance." *The Nation,* July 28, 1892.

199 "The right of any man to labor." Yellen, p. 89.

199–200 All quotes in following paragraph. May, pp. 105–107.

200 "With for a church the biggest mill." Winkler, p. 215.

Chapter IX: Treason!

202 Chauncey Black quote. September, 1892.

203–204 Letter from O'Donnell to Reid. Bemis, p. 384.

204 "We have telegram from Tribune Reid," and "after due consideration." Bridge, p. 231.

205 Temperatures up to 150 degrees. Stowell, p. 246.

205 Removals "at such a lively rate." New York *Tribune,* August 10, 1892.

205 Forced feeding under the Brooks law. Bemis, p. 392.

205–206 The Stocher incident and quote. Stowell, p. 232.

206 Further petty incidents, production curve, etc., in the following two paragraphs. Stowell, pp. 236–251.

207–208 Hugh Dempsey and the poisoning episode. Bridge, pp. 242 ff, and other secondary sources.

208 "The leading witnesses against Dempsey." January 21, 1893.

208   Gallagher recants and blames the Pinkertons. Stowell, pp. 292 ff.

208   "There is no desire to interfere," and "The firmness with which these strikers hold on." Harvey, p. 176.

209   167 true bills, and informations made by McLuckie. Foner, p. 214.

210   Sworn evidence against Clifford, and Ewing's quote. Burgoyne, p. 194.

211   Treason under the 1860 Crimes Act. Burgoyne, p. 200.

211-212   Developments and quotations concerning this charge. Stowell, pp. 257-259.

212   Prior statute passed by Pennsylvania Assembly. Foner, p. 214.

212   Gibbons in the *Chicago Law Journal*. *Review of Reviews,* December, 1892.

212   Paxson consents to instruct the jury. Burgoyne, p. 203.

212-213   Reactions in Homestead to the charge. New York *Tribune,* October 1, 2, 1892.

213   "A mere mob, collected upon the impulse." Bemis, p. 388.

213   "The employer cannot compel." Burgoyne, p. 205.

213-214   "Chief Justice Paxson's charge, which, in some respects." Senate Report, p. XV.

214   "a mass of stale, medieval verbiage." David, p. 169.

215   Concerning Mr. Morrison's horseless carriage. Sullivan, p. 5.

215-216   October 17 hirings, and further quotes and poems in this section. Burgoyne, pp. 213-216.

216-217   "Homestead Day" in Chicago. Burgoyne, p. 220.

217   4,000 on strike relief, and Crawford's quote. Foner, p. 215.

218   "BULLETS FLY AT HOMESTEAD," racism, increased violence. New York *Tribune,* November 14, 1892.

219   "It seems to me that you would enjoy." Harvey, p. 170.

219   "I am at a little loss to know." Bridge, p. 245.

219-220   Schwab replaces Potter. Bridge, pp. 245 ff.

221   "I am very sorry for President Harrison," and subsequent quotes in next two paragraphs. Harvey, pp. 157 ff.

222   Suicide of a desperate striker. Bridge, p. 249.

223   "Great battles are rarely ever fought." Stowell, p. 286.

223   The blacklist, and rehiring of 1300 strikers. Burgoyne, p. 230.

223-224   Total strikers, profits, wage losses. New York *Tribune,* November 21, 1892.

224 Davis and Dempsey quotes. New York *Tribune,* November 21, 1892.

225 Pinkerton license revoked in Denver. David, p. 154.

225 Pennsylvania legislature and Pinkertonism. Burgoyne, p. 239.

225 "Strike officially declared off yesterday." Winkler, p. 218.

225 "Life worth living again!" Winkler, p. 219.

225 "so that we swallowed the dose as we went along." Harvey, p. 177.

226 "Think I'm about ten years older." Winkler, p. 219.

226 Thanksgiving Day in Homestead and Munhall. Burgoyne, pp. 231–234.

227 New York *Tribune* estimate of casualties. November 21, 1892.

Chapter X: Fruits of Victory

229 Mechanization and Schwab's opinions. Brody, p. 58.

230 Exit of the Amalgamated from the steel industry. David, p. 170.

230 The Amalgamated in sheet and tinplate. Brody, pp. 60 ff.

230 "Fight them to a finish with hard gloves." Brody, p. 51.

230 Carnegie company bars all union members. Foner, p. 217.

230–231 1896 and 1899 comeback attempts. Brody, pp. 56 ff.

231 Shaffer challenges U.S. Steel, Roe, p. 47.

230–231 Collapse of the 1901 strike, and further failures. Brody, p. 68 ff.

232 Espionage, work conditions, etc., after 1892. Brody, pp. 83–84.

232 No more decisions "by an agreement." Brody, p. 78.

233 Wage figures by Fitch, p. 153.

233 O'Donnell's wage figures (from Bemis), p. 388.

234 Second wage listing by Fitch (1892–1907), p. 156.

235 Byington's wage analysis by ethnic groups, p. 38.

235–236 Comparable pay in west Pennsylvania mines. Yellen, p. 100.

236 Beatrice Webb quoted by the *Nation,* September 7, 1963, from *Beatrice Webb's American Diary, 1898* (University of Wisconsin Press).

236 Reed and other strikers turn anti-union. Brody, p. 84.

236–237 Dwellings erected on the City Poor Farm. Brody, p. 87.

237–238 Byington reports other conditions in the boroughs, pp. 1 ff.

237 "A man works, comes home, eats." Brody, p. 94.

238   Deaths and injuries continue unabated: the statistics. Brody, p. 92.

238   "I am injured and blind." Byington, p. 37.

238–239   "I think there will be a labor organization." Fitch, p. 19.

239   "They are suspicious of one another," and following quotes. Fitch, pp. 214–215.

240   "a conflict which does not determine who is right." *Roget's Thesaurus*, (New York: Crowell, 1962), p. 522.

240   Carnegie company profits, 1893–1897. Austin, p. 134.

240   "Ashamed to tell you profits these days." Hendrick, vol. 2, p. 1.

240   "It is believed by the Carnegie officials." Bridge, pp. 295 ff.

241   "The analysis of expenditures indicates." Byington, p. 180.

242   "There are different kinds of work," and following quotes by immigrants. Brody, pp. 99 ff.

243   Last years of "Big Bill" Weihe. Fitch, p. 107.

243–246   Later story of Roberts, Crawford and other strikers. Burgoyne, p. 297.

244   "Mine has been the sacrifice." Bemis, p. 387.

244   The odyssey of John McLuckie. Carnegie, pp. 236–237.

245   "Well, anyhow he left the country before I did." Harvey, p. 145.

246   "he never saw a blast furnace until his death": Quoted in *The Liberal Hour*, by John K. Galbraith (Cambridge: Houghton Mifflin, 1960), p. 95.

246   "Now, the men at Homestead were in a peculiar condition." Bemis, p. 382.

247   "As to the character of the men furnished." Senate Report, p. X.

248   Frick's $150 million estate. Hendrick, vol. 2, p. 113.

248   The matter of Wiley's farm. Josephson, p. 419.

249   "Mr. Carnegie told me to tell you." Winkler, p. 7.

249   Further details on Frick's final years. *Encyclopaedia Britannica*.

250   "I did not come to Pittsburgh to rake up." Bridge, p. 251.

250   Concerning Carnegie's *Triumphant Democracy*. Beard, p. 209.

250–251   His alleged retirement between 1893 and 1898. Hendrick, vol. 2, p. 35 ff.

251–252   Prelude to the great iron and steel merger. Allen, pp. 16 ff.

252   "Well, if Andy wants to sell, I'll buy." Hendrick, vol. 2, p. 136.

252 Formation of United States Steel Corp., the Morgan quote, capitalization of the firm (footnote). Josephson, pp. 425 ff.

252 "Do you know, Mr. Morgan." Myers, p. 600.

253 The Carnegie philanthropies. *Encyclopaedia Britannica.*

253–254 Carnegie's freedom of cities, administration of foundations, fortune distributed, final years. Heilbroner, p. 111.

Chapter XI: Sequel

256 Blough quote. *The New Yorker,* May 23, 1964, p. 133.

256 1964 production. *U.S. News and World Report,* June 22, 1964.

256 1892 production relative to 1964. Bridge, p. 297.

256 "Steelmakers are activating idle facilities." Quoted in the Los Angeles *Times,* August 24, 1964.

256–257 100,000 auto workers on pension. Boggs, p. 30.

257 "Automation is the greatest revolution." Boggs, p. 38.

257 20% steel capacity increase since 1955. Los Angeles *Times,* June 15, 1964.

257 "The company is following a policy." *Greater Pittsburgh,* October, 1962.

258 1962 record production at Duquesne. *Greater Pittsburgh,* October, 1962.

258 Jones & Laughlin output, and subsequent technical data. *U.S. News and World Report,* June 22, 1964.

258 Stora Kaldo and other refinements. Fisher, pp. 309 ff.

259 1959 steel strike. *The World Almanac,* 1960 ed., pp. 47, 113.

259–260 Present population and median incomes in Homestead and Munhall. From various Pittsburgh Chamber of Commerce bulletins.

260–264 The word-sketch of the boroughs was derived from a personal visit. See Foner, p. 210, for the monument's inscription.

Index

Picture Credits

I   top left—Culver Pictures
top right—Carnegie Library
bottom left—from A. G. Burgoyne, *A Complete History of the Struggle of 1892* . . . , Pittsburgh
bottom right—*Harper's Weekly*

III   left—*McClure's Magazine*
right—Carnegie Library

V   top—Carnegie Library
bottom—from A. G. Burgoyne, *A Complete History of the Struggle of 1892* . . . , Pittsburgh

VI   top left—from James H. Bridge, *The Inside Story of the Carnegie Steel Company,* Aldine
top right—from A. G. Burgoyne, *A Complete History of the Struggle of 1892* . . . , Pittsburgh
bottom left—*Harper's Weekly*
bottom right—from M. R. Stowell, *Fort Frick*

VII   top—*Harper's Weekly*
bottom left—*Harper's Weekly*
bottom right—*Harper's Weekly*

VIII   top—from A. G. Burgoyne, *A Complete History of the Struggle of 1892* . . . , Pittsburgh
bottom left—from M. R. Stowell, *Fort Frick*

Format by Mort Perry
Set in Linotype Baskerville
Composed, printed and bound by American Book–Stratford Press
HARPER & ROW, PUBLISHERS, INCORPORATED

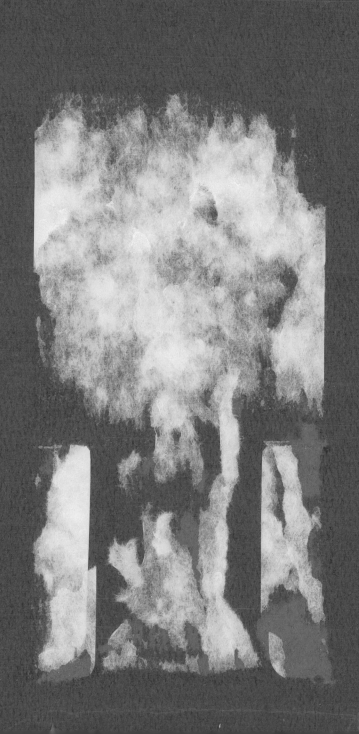